BUTCHER ON THE BLOCK

BEEF HAMMER
(PAGE 238)

BUTCHER ON THE BLOCK

**Everyday Recipes, Stories, and Inspirations
from Your Local Butcher and Beyond**

MATT MOORE

HARVEST

An Imprint of WILLIAM MORROW

HarperCollins books may be purchased for educational, business, or sales promotional use. For information, please email the Special Markets Department at SPsales@harpercollins.com.

FIRST EDITION

Designed by Tai Blanche
Parts 1 and 2 photographs © Andrea Behrends
Maison Maillard photos © Mimi Giboin
Part 3 photographs © Helene DuJardin
Family photographs © Matt Moore
Content spread photo © Marian Weyo/Shutterstock
Photo borders © Sanches11/Shutterstock

Library of Congress Cataloging-in-Publication Data has been applied for.
ISBN 978-0-358-67030-8

23 24 25 26 27 TC 10 9 8 7 6 5 4 3 2 1

For my Giddy,

Abraham Samuel Dennis,

and our loving family

CONTENTS

ACKNOWLEDGMENTS

I'm continuously astonished by the love of family, friends, and you, the loyal readers and enthusiasts who support and provide for me a platform to share. Thank you. To my loving family, especially to my wife, Callie, and girls, Vivienne and Everly. Your unconditional support and sacrifice are never lost on me. It is all about family, and I'm honored to have the opportunity to continue to share stories and experiences that matter. To my extended family, thank you for taking the time to recount history and revisit memories from those who have shaped us. To my agent, Stacey Glick, the journey just keeps getting better. Wow, book number five! Thank you for always championing and guiding me in my work. To Andrea Behrends, it's always a pleasure to experience these places, people, and life with you. This particular book season also offered an opportunity for me to witness you become a mother, from shooting street food six months pregnant, to our time spent with baby Bear and your husband, Christian, on the road and beyond. What a ride. To my editor, Sarah Kwak, and the entire Harvest team, thank you for believing in me, in this work, and sharing my philosophy that promoting great food and people never goes out of style. And, of course, to the butchers who so lovingly provided me with the fabric and soul necessary for this work. I'm forever grateful.

INTRODUCTION

This is not a book about butchering, per se. Rather, it is about the butcher. This particular work cuts even deeper than just the trade—it is personal. After all, the art of butchering runs in my blood.

As my mother was told, my grandfather Abraham Samuel Dennis was in his early twenties in the fall of 1941 and stationed at Keesler Field, in Biloxi, Mississippi, serving as a mess sergeant in the United States Army Air Forces. Rumors of orders came to deploy my grandfather's unit to a base little known to most Americans, in Honolulu, Hawaii. Its name was Pearl Harbor.

Though the war raged in Europe, the Pacific theater was still very much an afterthought to most Americans—especially to those living stateside. At the time, Pearl Harbor would have served as a dream-worthy outpost, filled with all things étranger: palm trees, Rip Curls, hula skirts, and pig roasts. To this point, Abraham, or "Abie" as he was known, had rarely traveled outside the family confines in Southern Georgia.

In the weeks leading up to deployment, my grandfather and his comrades were ordered to remain in Mississippi. A few months later, on December 7, 1941, history was changed forever. It is a day that lives in infamy—the awakening of the sleeping giant of the American war machine. As the war progressed, my grandfather eventually went on to serve time at Pearl Harbor, yet while most of his action remained behind front lines, he largely remained stoic and reticent in regard to his time in the service. Abe's younger brother, my great-uncle, David, however, was not only more outspoken, he could command an audience with his stories better than anyone I've ever known. Even as he reached his later and final years, his brilliant mind ensured that names, dates, and details were never forsaken, not to mention some slight stretching of the yarn.

My favorite story of his comes from his time in New Guinea, also serving in the Army Air Forces. Lucky Strikes and news from home provided a bit of respite from life in the foxholes, dodging the daily sorties from the Japanese Zeroes. One day, an airmail package arrived—light blue thirty-two-ounce mason jars stuffed with newspapers and with lids pressure sealed. As David relayed, my great-grandmother Sophie had sent fried chicken across the Pacific, and David and his friends made fast work gnawing down on our family pride. My cousin Sam (David's son) and I often laugh over bourbons poured neat about the veracity of such a story, but when you've had our family's fried chicken, it can make you believe in the impossible.

When both Abe and David returned as heroes from their time in service, life went much back to "normal," assuming family responsibilities while running the Dennis Food Store in Valdosta, Georgia. Both Abe and David built upon the business of their parents, my grandfather primarily

serving as the in-house butcher while David took on an array of responsibilities, including a hobby shop within the store. My grandfather took much pride in his work, expanding the traditional butcher shop offerings with specialty cuts, dry-aging techniques, and meat sourced only from Kansas City—a city known for providing the best quality in those days. With his dedication to quality and experience, the store gained a reputation for having the best meats and steaks in town. Along with their sister, Mary, they carried on the business until they eventually retired. When they sold the store, a new crop of large chain grocery stores was changing the entire landscape of food consumerism as we know it.

As it turns out, the art of butchering doesn't just run in my own blood, but in my wife Callie's as well. Conrad Margowski, her great-uncle, served as a fatherlike figure to Callie, and for many years before his passing, I was honored to spend quality time with him, drinking cold Red Dog beers and talking about his passion of woodworking. Raised in La Salle, Illinois, and serving time in the Marines as a supply sergeant during the Korean War, Conrad spent his years in the military at Camp Pendleton, California, meeting his wife, Billye.

Upon returning to La Salle after his time in the service, Conrad started his butchering career training in-house at the local A&P grocery chain. In those days, butchering in the larger chains looked very much like a smaller shop today, with sawdust-laden floors and primal cuts still being broken down by local hands. When the A&P chain shuttered its doors, Conrad finalized his career as the head butcher at Sullivan's, a small, locally owned grocery chain in Princeton, Illinois, for nearly two decades, until retirement. His art, elaborate woodwork of train sets, birdhouses, and other creations, still exists at present, but his chivalrous legacy and dedication to family are perhaps the surviving traits I most remember.

This book is personal. As a storyteller, I've long regaled accounts from my own family history, including my grandfather's career as a butcher. But truth be told, I've known little about the background and trade beyond just the title. I went on a journey of discovery, to learn, share, and honor not only my own family but also the grand tradition of butchering that permeates all cultures and cuisines.

We often say that life is a game of give and take. However, above all, my travels and this book

highlight what the butcher gives. The art of giving was not only fostered in my own family's service to their country but in their daily routines cultivated by the trade. "Gimme a quarter pound, plus a little more of this," customers will request. "Can you cut it this way, maybe shave off a little of that?" ask others. "I need a special order, cut and tied and ready in an hour," one demands. And of course, my favorite, "How do *you* cook this?" As always, the butcher gives, providing constantly in order to serve others.

Gleaning upon the traits of those uncovered, I find myself also in a place to give. As I have done in all of my books, I welcome you to join me on the road, or up in the blue skies in my ole Piper Cherokee, to track down the people, stories, and recipes that foster the art of giving: butchering. By starting our journey at the butcher, we will uncover an array of recipes and techniques, from raw to deep-fried to smoked and grilled, that encompass cuisines and styles from all over the globe. You might even be surprised to learn that butchering has expanded beyond just the traditional fare to include varying styles of preparations, even vegetables too!

I invite you to devour these pages with the same enthusiasm in which they have been written. And whether you have familial ties or not, my hope is that this work will serve as a conduit to create your own friendships, insight, and trust that can come only from knowing your very own butcher on the block.

So, sharpen your knives, folks—let's get to work.

Happy Retirement Conrad Margowski

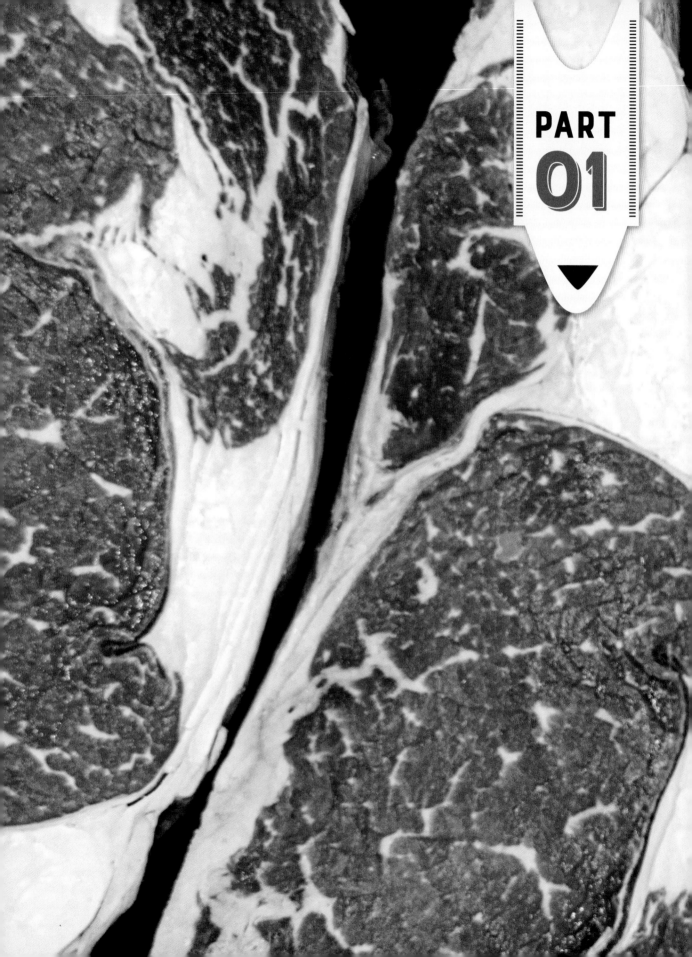

BUTCHERING PRIMER

"I like to call myself a 'live to eater.' My entire life revolves around food," says James Peisker, who wields a sharp boning knife in one hand and a cup of black coffee in the other. As a butcher, business owner, and COO of Porter Road Butcher in Nashville, Tennessee, James and cofounder Chris Carter have spent the past decade building an empire while also fulfilling their mission of fueling a better tomorrow through properly raised meats.

"I own a meat company, and even I tell people to eat less meat," says James. But there's one caveat James shares: "People should eat better meat."

I called on James to showcase some of the basic skills and techniques that one might use to further their skills in butchering common items at home. Admittedly my request could come off as somewhat counterintuitive: Porter Road Butcher and butchers across the country make their living by serving their customers, creating custom cuts or orders on demand. But James was happy to oblige my ask by spending a day showcasing his skills and philosophy. "The fun part of my job is educating people—to enjoy food and cooking."

While the following pages will serve as a basic primer on the trade, I walk away with a much stronger sense that James has taught me more than just technique and best practices. He's opened my eyes to the potential of a better future of how we responsibly raise, source, and consume meat to benefit not only ourselves but also our livestock and the environment.

After meeting each other working as chefs at the Hermitage Hotel, James and Chris had an instant connection. They decided to ditch their jobs and enter the world of entrepreneurship by starting their own catering company. But within a few months of their gig, something continued to hold them back. "I was trying to create the perfect meal," says James, "and that's when I realized the meat needed to be better."

Sticking to their mission, the two founded Porter Road Butcher in 2011 and never looked back. But the journey always leads back to the source. "We felt that it was time to relabel 'farm-raised' to something more authentic—'raised the *right* way,'" says James. "You can hit a lot of marketing and packaging buzz words, but still not raise correctly." Beyond their retail location, James and Chris took their practice seriously by working with farmers in Tennessee, Kentucky, and Pennsylvania to source and raise their products. From there, they created their own slaughtering and processing facility to control every aspect of the journey.

"Our goal is to decentralize the meat industry," says James, "to give the power back to the farmers. Farmers want to do things the right way, but a better system is needed to reward their work." In other words, additional expenses. "I often tell people not to question why things are a bit more expensive, rather why other things are so inexpensive," says James. It's a delicate balance to manage running a mission-oriented business against giant conglomerates, but the booming success of Porter Road Butcher's retail, wholesale, and online business proves that respect is earned, and success favors hard work.

After we finish our day I too return home in search of that perfect meal. It starts with the hand-cut tenderloin James generously contributed. It is perfection.

Now it's on me to not screw it up!

A PRIMER ON BUTCHERING AT HOME

For all intents and purposes, the focus of this work is on the stories, traits, and recipes from a wide array of talented butchers with origins across the globe. Additionally recipe concepts celebrate cuts and ingredients that can be procured at your local butcher, or involve some sort of at-home butchering technique while promoting broad styles of cuisine.

Of course, there are many common areas in which home cooks can become familiar and enhance their repertoire and practice at home. You will glean other tidbits of tips and techniques in the chapters that follow. This primer is for those looking to introduce themselves to or explore basic at-home techniques of butchering.

Beyond the traditional array of texts and books devoted to this subject, I also encourage and promote those seeking more refined knowledge to take advantage of technology— videos, podcasts, applications, online education, as well as virtual events. These are now widely available to take your butchering to the next level.

But in my humble opinion, whatever your method of self-study, it is also best polished off with creating a relationship with your own local butcher, as the trend of sharing knowledge within this trade is contagious.

On that note, a defining characteristic that I uncovered throughout my travels is that most butchers learn the art of butchering just as much through trial and error as they do through apprenticeship. And while the trade has thousands of years of refinement, it continues to evolve. Practicing and learning these techniques, whether basic or in-depth, can provide a lifetime of enjoyment and self-improvement, not to mention an opportunity to pass on knowledge and passion to those that follow.

THE ENVIRONMENT

Unlike in the old days, modern butcher shops do not typically contain sawdust-laden floors with mineral-scented, funky air. Primarily you will find a well-lit, well-designed shop that's squeaky clean. As James Peisker says, it all changed after *The Jungle*, Upton Sinclair's novel that exposed the meat processing industry of the past, ushering in new standards and regulations that are still practiced today. If you plan to handle raw meats and other items at home, you should follow the practice embraced by professionals.

At home, the countertop is typically the most stable and best surface for butchering. It should be cleaned and sanitized regularly. Ideally the countertop is also at a comfortable height. Leveraging the steady counter for cutting and chopping is vital, but using gravity to rest certain items on the counter, while pulling or tearing other items that hang from the surface, can also be useful when working with larger portions. If you are working in a tighter kitchen, be aware of any other items that might be around the butchering area that should be moved prior to working, like a fruit bowl, as you want to eliminate the chance of unintentionally contaminating other surfaces or items. If countertop space is an issue, any sturdy, sanitized surface can be used, such as a table or dedicated butcher block.

Having access to a nearby trash can will allow you to easily discard items without touching other surfaces. Of course, keeping your hands and other items clean is of vital importance, so a sink in which to wash your hands and tools with warm water and antimicrobial soap throughout the process is ideal. When you have finished your work, it's important to properly clean and sanitize the surfaces and any tools used during the practice.

Also, be mindful of your clothing. Since sometimes the practice can be messy, it's best to wear a washable apron or clothing.

Like most things in life, preparation is key here. I like to create a mental game plan of my process in advance so that I'm not running back and forth, potentially contaminating other surfaces, like the handles of my refrigerator and cabinet pulls. If you are storing larger quantities, be sure to have plenty of ice and storage options on hand, and clear out room in your refrigerator and freezer prior to starting your routine.

The more thought out your process, the better your results and the easier your cleanup.

THE TOOLS

I pressed James on what items are necessary for butchering at home, and I got a sense he's somewhat of a minimalist. "Find a sharp knife that you are comfortable with—that's all you really need," he says. For James, that sharp knife really means two boning knives: one that is stiff and another that is semi-flexible. The stiff knife can be used for jobs that require more heavy-duty work, such as cutting through joints, small bones, and cartilage, whereas the semi-flexible boning knife has a bit of give to it, something that comes in handy when filleting a fish or trimming away silver skin from a tenderloin. So while a sharp knife is James's primary tool for the trade, I do gather a few more items that are helpful for the at-home butcher, which can be sourced at most kitchen supply stores or online outlets.

Knives
- Stiff and semi-flexible boning knives, breaking knives, paring knives, heavy-weight cleaver.

Honing/Sharpening Steel
- Used to hone the blade of a sharpened knife.

Sharpening Tool or Machine to Sharpen Knives at Home
- Note: Several kitchen-supply or retail locations as well as mail-order companies now conveniently offer this service.

Boning Hooks
- Used to secure meats on a cutting board when butchering.

Gambrels
- Used to suspend or hang cuts of meat.

Cut-Resistant Mesh Gloves

Kitchen Apron

Kitchen Shears

Butcher Paper

Butcher's Twine

Masking Tape
- Used to secure wrapped butcher paper, if desired.

Sharpie Marker
- Keep handy to denote contents and dates of wrapped items.

Cutting Boards
- Ideally have one plastic board solely dedicated for use with poultry.

Storage Vessels
- Baking sheets, wire racks, sealable containers, and ziplock bags.

Clean Towels

Hand Soap and Dish Soap

Nontoxic and Antimicrobial Cleaners
- If you prefer to avoid harsh chemicals, you can create your own cleaning solution to use on countertops, cabinets, cutting boards, and other surfaces. Simply combine 1 cup of white distilled vinegar with 1 cup of distilled water. A few drops of lemon and/or orange essential oils can be added to enhance the cleaning power and provide a clean scent. Note: Due to the acidity of the vinegar, it's best to avoid using this on softer stone surfaces such as granite or marble.

First Aid Kit

DRY-AGING AT HOME

For James, the dry-aging process is a key component to the flavor of the meat. But this dedication to a better product comes at a sacrifice. Most of the items Porter Road Butcher sells, especially beef, are dry-aged at least fifteen days, meaning that a certain percentage of the meat (weight) is lost to the dry-aging process. In addition, another portion of the aged meat must be trimmed prior to selling or packaging, thus the process of dry-aging directly impacts the total yield for use or sale. Most larger meat producers are aware of this loss and use a "wet age" method to age the meat immediately after slaughter without exposing the meat to air. While this method prevents the majority of weight loss, it sacrifices the rich flavor of the dry-aging process.

The art of aging can take years to master, which is why most folks tend to rely on their butcher or meat supplier to manage this process as part of their offering. Don't be afraid to ask your butcher about their aging process—some will even custom age cuts for you if you ask! You might also find that you have a specific butcher or shop you prefer due to its expertise in aging meats.

For those wanting to take matters into their own hands, nowadays you can further the dry-aging process safely at home by using dry-aging bags that are specifically designed to allow the meat to age and breathe within your home refrigerator. Notice I said that these bags are specifically designed for this process—do not try to use a standard plastic bag or other container. While you are able to age meats at home without the use of these bags, I find them to be an affordable and efficient means to produce consistent, safe results. Be sure to follow specific manufacturer instructions related to dry-aging products at home.

If you plan to experiment with dry-aging at home, it's best to start with the largest cut possible. In other words, if you pick up a few trimmed fillets from your local butcher, dry-aging them further, or individually, is going to cost you a premium by the time the meat ages (loss of mass) as well as the additional trimming that is necessary prior to cooking. So you should always consider aging larger portions, such as rib roasts and whole tenderloins, or primal cuts.

COMMON BUTCHERING TECHNIQUES

WHOLE CHICKEN

In my mind, breaking down a whole chicken is a necessary skill for the avid home cook. Yet whenever I find myself perusing my local grocery store, I can almost spot the fear in people's eyes when it comes to breaking down a whole bird. First and foremost, buying the entire chicken is typically at least 20 to 30 percent cheaper than purchasing a single cut. You get the best of all worlds: a nice selection of white and dark meat to feed the family, while also putting that backbone or other trimmings in the freezer for a stock to elevate the rest of your meals (see page 320). That said, not all chickens are created equal.

James Peisker is a big believer in sourcing hormone-free birds that have had plenty of territory to roam. You can taste the results—the meat is a touch darker in color, more flavorful, and super tender. As mentioned previously, it's a good practice to always dedicate a plastic board solely to working with poultry. The following method is just one way (James's way) of breaking down a chicken, which can be emulated for turkey as well as game birds. That said, there are many different techniques that you can utilize to get a similar result.

1. With the breast up and butt end of the bird facing you, pull the legs of the chicken to loosen and, using a stiff boning knife, slice through the skin to expose the legs.

2. Turn the chicken over and, using your hands, pop the thigh bones out of the sockets by pulling the legs to the backbone.

3. Shove your thumb into the oyster, the small circular piece of dark meat on the back of the thigh, and invert the legs, slicing each thigh away from the back—there should be little resistance when following the natural break of the thigh bone.

4. Separate the legs from the thighs, using your knife to follow the thin line of fat as a guide to the joint.

5. Rotate the chicken, placing the neck portion on the board, and use the knife to follow the natural seam to remove the backbone from the breastplate, using a bit of force to cut through the rib bones.

6. Using the point of the knife, stab into the middle of the breastplate, and slice the breastplate to cleanly separate the two breasts.

7. Pop the wing out of the socket from one of the breasts, and slice the wing at the joint away from the breast. Repeat with the remaining wing and breast.

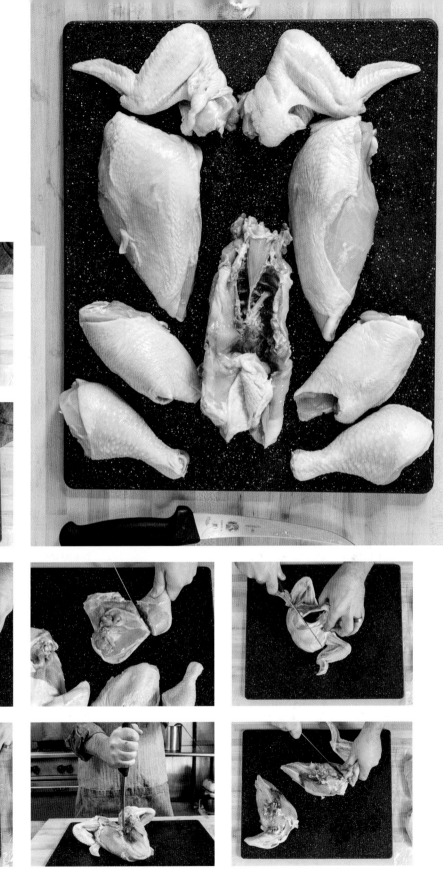

WHOLE BEEF TENDERLOIN

As with breaking down a chicken, this simple technique allows you to purchase whole tenderloins, carving them into a large roast to feed a crowd, or slicing into individual steaks. Often during the holiday season, you will find steep discounts on whole tenderloins, and breaking them down at home is a realistic and affordable way to put those discounts to good use. A whole tenderloin consists of the head, center (or chateaubriand), and tail, and it's typically composed of two chains of meat. Don't fret if you are already confused—the biggest advice I can relay here is to use your hands. Follow the natural lines of the meat and you'll be just fine.

1. Using your hands, pull away the excess fat, or suet, from the meat. Most of the fat will pull easily and naturally from the tenderloin, but as necessary, a knife can be used to trim away any stubborn portions that do not simply peel away.

2. Slide your hands down the tenderloin, with your thumb in the center, to find the seam between the two chains of the meat. One of the chains will be roughly 30 percent smaller in size than the other, typically with more fat. Trim the smaller chain away from the tenderloin (this piece of meat can be ground for burgers, or pounded thin for fajita or other stew meat).

3. Working with the larger chain, carefully use your knife to trim away the silver skin and any additional excess fat from the meat. The key to removing the silver skin without having any waste is to pull on the silver skin back and forth, allowing the knife to gently cut it away.

4. Looking at the smaller tail portion, determine the point at which the tail could be folded under the tenderloin to create a consistent thickness throughout.

5. At that point, use your knife to cut the tail of the tenderloin roughly 75 percent through the meat and fold the tail underneath the tenderloin to have an even, consistent piece of meat.

6. To single tie the roast, use butcher's twine to go underneath the tenderloin, and wrap the twine onto itself two times to hold it in place. Tie a standard knot firmly to secure the twine. Continue in this method until the entire tenderloin is evenly tied. This method is most useful if you desire to cut the loin into individual steaks, secured by the twine.

7. If cooking the entire tenderloin, you can use a continuous knot method by once again going underneath the tenderloin to tie a secure knot for the first hold. Wrap the twine around your hands to create a circle, and slide that circle down and around the tenderloin, pull on the line to tighten, and once again create a new circle in your hand and slide that circle down and around the tenderloin, repeating the method until the tenderloin is firmly tied, and finishing the tying with a final knot at the end.

8. Trim into individual steaks or leave whole, as desired.

WHOLE FISH

Whole fish can be procured at fishmongers or butcher shops, but most often, to preserve freshness, the fish has been gutted prior to sale. When determining the freshness of a fish, James Peisker of Porter Road Butcher shares that it's important to use all of your senses. The eyes of the fish should be very clear and round in shape, not sunken in or glossy. The fish should feel clean and wet, without any slime, and pushing into the flesh, it should not indent, but quickly re-form. The gills should be bright red and the fish should smell like the sea.

The following technique shows how to break down a whole flat fish, such as red snapper, into fillets. Since the skin is discarded, scaling the fish for this breakdown is not necessary. If desired, you can scale the fish by using the back side (opposite of the sharp edge) of your knife to "brush" and remove the scales, working from the tail to the head portion to remove.

1. Use kitchen shears to remove the fins from the fish—this includes the top dorsal fins, pectoral fins from the sides, tail fin, ventral or pelvic fins, as well as the anal fins on the bottom.

2. Starting from the head, feel for the backbone at the top of the fish. Using a semiflexible boning knife, carefully cut into the fish, stopping at the backbone, and drag the knife from head to tail to remove the fillet from the backbone.

3. Using the knife, cut along the collar (right behind the gills), from the top to the bottom of the fish.

4. Hold the belly, and use the knife to cut down the back, away from the bones, about halfway down the fish. Use gentle pressure to allow the knife to cut through the rib bones to remove the fillet.

5. Repeat steps 2 through 4 for the remaining side of the fish.

6. Carefully cut away the rib cage and belly from both fillets.

7. To remove the skin, lay the fillets flesh side up. Working from the tail, use the knife to cut into the meat, stopping just at the skin. Turn the knife to be slightly parallel to the skin, and pull on the skin to allow the knife to gently cut away the flesh. Pulling the skin and not forcing the knife through the meat will reduce the amount of wasted flesh on the skin.

8. Run your hands down the middle portion of the fish to feel for any pin bones to remove.

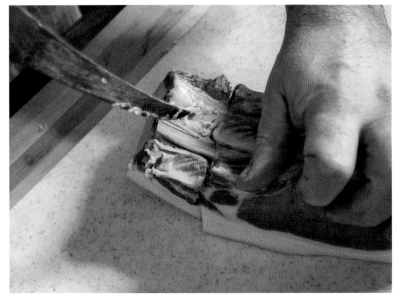

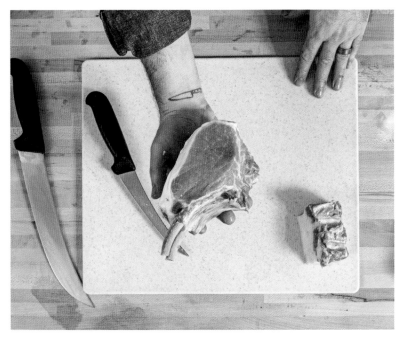

FRENCHED DOUBLE-CUT PORK CHOP

Any day of the week, I'll take a perfectly cooked pork chop over a steak. And while you might be less familiar with purchasing this particular bone-in cut that comes from the pork loin, you might be more familiar with nearly the exact same cut of beef known as a standing rib roast. But

purposely I've asked James to break down this particular hunk of pig, as it is a great purchase for a backyard grill-out. To add even more technique and presentation, the chops are cut into thick double-cut portions, with the bones "frenched" (cleaned) for good measure.

1. Remove the small feather bones by slicing away from the backbone.

2. To separate into a double-cut chop, count two rib bones and slice between the ribs, often at a slight angle to follow the natural curvature of the ribs. If desired, single-cut chops can also be created by portioning at every bone.

3. To french the bones, cut away the connective tissue and scrap from all four sides of the bones.

4. Using your hands, peel away the cut scrap to cleanly reveal the bones. A cloth towel can also be used to assist in cleaning the bones.

5. Trim the excess exterior fat on the side of the chop to ⅛- to ¼-inch thickness, or as desired.

THE RIHM FAMILY, RIHM FOODS

Cambridge City, IN

"I suppose I started cutting meat by the time I was, well, about *this* tall." Though Jerry Rihm stands at more than six feet, he commands a much larger presence, something more akin to that of a wise, broad oak tree. I watch as he motions, with one hand floating below his hip and a melted scotch teetering slightly in his other hand. Though Jerry doesn't give me an exact age, I can only surmise that he has been "cutting meat" before most folks learned to read.

I arrived in Cambridge City, Indiana, on the advice of a good friend and filmmaker, Clay Hassler. For years Clay has constantly opined to me that his uncle Jerry is a character among characters. With time, Clay's earnest stories of the camaraderie, family, and food became too convincing not to pass, so I fired up the Piper,

embracing a hairy crosswind at Mettel Field outside of Cambridge City.

When we drive up to the redbrick farmhouse with a barn in the back, several dogs and horses bark and whinny, and I sense immediately that I'm welcomed. We meet Clay's aunt and Jerry's wife, Angie, and rather quickly I ease into a gentle back-and-forth with her as she generously shares old paper clippings and photos and recounts stories of family history. "People will say the Rihm family is all about work," says Angie. Frankly I would say that's just part of the story.

Jerry serves as part of the fourth generation in a butcher bloodline that first started stateside with his great-grandfather George, who emigrated from Germany through the Erie Canal and began his business in the late 1880s in Piqua, Ohio. His grandfather George Jr. eventually settled into what is now home, Cambridge City, in 1928, after purchasing the Lee Meat Market. As I'm catching up with Angie, Jerry soon makes his way home from the processing plant, greeting me at his back door with a mason jar full of peach moonshine. A shot or two later, I'm not sure I'll ever want to leave.

But my stomach begins to rumble, and Clay informs me that it's time to depart to meet Joseph, Jerry's son, who is carrying on the fifth generation of family pride. On our drive over, I get a sense that if you ever get lost in the collective towns of Cambridge City or Dublin, which make up a part of Indiana's Wayne County, one simply needs to make a few right turns. One of the many Rihm Foods signs will lead you either to a family home, the retail store, or the processing plant. Pulling up to Joseph's place, I quickly get to admiring his

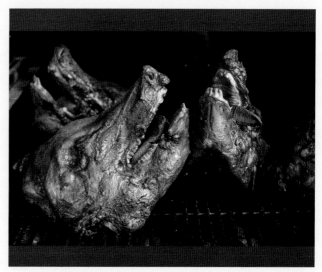

multiple grill and smoker setup that's spread out on his front porch. Joseph raises the lid on one smoker to reveal a slew of smoking hogs' heads.

As the hours pass, people pull on and off Highway 40, the main road fronting the property, dropping in on Joseph's porch uninvited to sample a feast of fried sweetbreads, hog's head tacos, county fair pork burgers, steak tips, and a meat and cheese plate that is entirely made up of Rihm family goodness. I get a sense that these kinds of strangers are no strangers at all; rather, these types of gatherings are quite common, as it's a chance for the family and others to partake and relish in the fruits of their labor.

Just prior to eating, Joseph motions to an ATV, asking if I want to go for a ride up to the plant. Grabbing a few cold "travelers" for the trip, we meander through the hills and trees, spotting morel mushrooms along the way, cutting across property lines, until we arrive at his daily place of work, six days a week. "I sometimes go this route to the plant, back and forth every day, it's peaceful," says Joseph. I get a sense that much responsibility in taking over the family business has been laid upon this man's shoulders. While it's clear that Joseph has grown up rather fast, his younger brother, Gus, in the ATV behind us, seems to be just coming around to the fact that his life could also yield a privileged responsibility. But duties must be earned, not inherited.

I learn about this mantra from Angie, as she shares that the Rihm family business has not been passed down—it has been acquired by each generation. "Each family member has to buy in, literally," Angie relays about the economics of inheritance. Jerry eventually bought into the business from his father, Walter, going so far to solely acquire it from his brothers, Jim and Don. I sense that there's much integrity in this arrangement, ensuring that each new generation takes the responsibility of work and investment seriously, while also preserving the family relationships.

After my ride, I get back and focus on more important matters—eating. The house-ground pork burger combines both pork and smoky jowl bacon, and with two hands and an open heart, I plow through this meaty masterpiece as soon as it makes its way off the grill. The smoky flavor of the pork patties combined with the crunch of fresh vegetables and sweet barbecue sauce makes me wonder why pork burgers haven't taken over the country. Satisfied with my main course, I scarf down a smoky and gelatinous hog's head taco in one hand, polishing off a cold Busch Light in the other.

Working somewhat backward from mains to appetizers, I also peruse my way through the meat and cheese platter, favoring the venison smoked sausage, which Jerry tells me folks drive all the way from West Virginia to keep in annual

supply. But my favorite dish is also the simplest. Like most good butchers, Jerry wastes nothing of an animal—it is sacred. When customers ask for their steak ends to be removed from rib eyes or strips prior to sale, Jerry takes the time to carve out the delicate pearl of meat found just in the tail. These are the butcher's cuts, made better after a soak in Worcestershire, and eaten raw. This one bite stops me in my tracks—tender, smoky, and simply delicious. I realize *this* is what I've come all this way for. Well, also the moonshine.

Trying to glean some further secrets from Jerry, I ask him about the difficulty of the butchering trade altogether. Though it's the physical work that takes its toll, he tells me nonchalantly that when it comes to cutting meat, eventually you learn that all "protein is protein," and common butchering techniques and methods can be leveraged for a wide array of animals. A sharp knife and a willingness to learn can expedite the craft for a lot of home cooks. Yet over his lifetime, Jerry has seen the industry change greatly.

In the old days, the food store and meat counter served as a gathering place in Cambridge City—a central destination for folks to purchase

and pick up what they needed for weeks at a time. "That's when people cooked," says Jerry with a smile. With the advent of restaurants and familiarity of outsourced meals, the store and trade itself began to lose step to more commercial operations. Instead of fighting the trend, Jerry embraced it altogether, firing up his own catering business, eventually cooking for up to five thousand people a weekend at Tom Raper's famous RV rallies outside of Richmond, Indiana. When I ask what it was like to pull off such a catering feat, Jerry tells me, "If you want a dog and pony show, don't call me. I make sure the food is good, it's served hot, and there's plenty of it." Gotta love Uncle Jerry.

When you live long enough, the pendulum always swings. Recently the latest generations are rediscovering the quality and sanctity of animals by calling on the Rihms to custom process their own livestock and game, bringing the entire operation full circle. I get a glimpse of the experience as we tour the plant, first built in 1972 and now facing expansion due to demand. From the cutting room floor to the packing room, I see a ton of pride as Jerry surveys the new layout,

knowing both Joseph and perhaps Gus will carry the torch for the next generation.

After a long evening of eating and drinking, Jerry invites us back the next morning to sit at the table over hot coffee, homemade sourdough pancakes, and his family's hot sausage patties and jowl bacon. It's becoming clear that our time spent together will soon come to an end, and admittedly I'm not ready to leave. But nothing gold can stay, and as I'm packing up to go, Jerry brings me an ice pack so full of meat that I'm worried it will throw off the weight and balance of the plane. It's a risk worth taking, I suppose.

As we say our goodbyes, Jerry returns right back to the kitchen, picking up the dishes, washing them, and cleaning up after the meal he provided. Clay looks at him, smiles, and says, "You don't have to do that, Uncle Jerry—you are always the one serving us."

"Well, what else can you do?" says Jerry. ■

WHOLE HOG'S HEAD TACOS

This dish proves the point that tacos make everything great, and though it might sound unexpected to smoke a whole hog's head at first, I can promise that this dish is absolutely divine. As a custom meat supplier, the Rihm family ensures that nothing good goes to waste, which is the genesis behind this recipe. The head itself contains plenty of great meat, especially in the cheek areas, and it just needs some low and slow love to allow things to break down and pull off the bone in the same way you would a pork shoulder or ribs. Joseph Rihm tells me he created this dish for a wedding party, of all things, and it's been a family favorite ever since. You can request hogs' heads from any butcher or supplier, and of course for those less adventurous, sub the head meat for a few pounds of traditional pulled or chopped pork.

Serves 6 to 8	Hands on: 45 minutes	Total: 10 hours

TACOS

- ☐ 1 whole hog's head, rinsed and patted dry
- ☐ ½ cup yellow mustard
- ☐ 2½ tablespoons Creole seasoning
- ☐ 15 corn tortillas

PICO DE GALLO

- ☐ 8 roma tomatoes, cores removed, seeded, and diced into ¼-inch cubes
- ☐ ½ green bell pepper, diced into ¼-inch cubes
- ☐ ¼ red onion, finely minced
- ☐ ¼ cup finely chopped fresh cilantro leaves
- ☐ 2 tablespoons minced jarred jalapeños
- ☐ 1 teaspoon kosher salt
- ☐ 1 lime, juiced

1 Using your hands, coat the hog's head with an even layer of yellow mustard. Next, rub the Creole seasoning into the meat, ensuring the mixture is well seasoned into every nook and crevice.

2 Open the bottom vent of a charcoal grill completely. Pour a large pile of charcoal onto the bottom grate on one side of the grill. Light a charcoal chimney starter filled halfway with additional charcoal. When the coals are covered with gray ash, pour them onto the pile of existing charcoal. Adjust the vents, nearly closing them, as needed to maintain an internal temperature of 200° to 225°F. Coat the top grate with oil; place on the grill. (If using a gas grill or smoker, preheat to low [200° to 225°F] on one side.)

3 Add the hog's head and smoke over indirect heat about 8 hours, or until internal temperature taken from the cheek or jowl reaches 205°F. Remove from the heat, tent with foil, and allow to cool for 1 hour.

4 Meanwhile, make the pico de gallo. In a medium bowl, combine the tomatoes, bell pepper, onion, cilantro, jalapeños, salt, and lime juice and keep cool until ready to serve.

5 Using two forks, or your hands with insulated gloves, begin to pull the meat from the head—it should pull clean from the bone and shred into bite-sized pieces. Continue in this manner until no more meat remains, yielding a few pounds of pulled meat in total.

6 Gently warm the corn tortillas over the grill, fill each with pork, and top with pico de gallo. Serve.

RIHM'S MEAT and CHEESE PLATE

A major part of the Rihm operation lies in their smoking and curing business, something they were careful to remind me of time and time again. It is its own unique trade beyond just butchering. In the months of November and December, the plant shuts down to focus entirely on processing venison from hunters across the heartland. Their snack sticks and summer sausages have become things of legend, and appropriately this meat and cheese plate is rounded out by some of the many items they carry at the retail store or ship throughout the country. Of course, you can use this dish as your own inspiration to source local or similar ingredients, or pick up items from Rihm's directly by ordering online.

Serves 6 to 8	Hands on: 15 minutes	Total: 15 minutes

- ☐ ½ pound German bologna, sliced into bite-sized pieces
- ☐ ½ pound venison and pork summer sausage, sliced into bite-sized pieces
- ☐ ½ pound braunschweiger, sliced into bite-sized pieces
- ☐ ½ pound sweet beef bologna, sliced into bite-sized pieces
- ☐ 8 ounces Colby cheese, sliced into bite-sized pieces
- ☐ Assorted crackers
- ☐ Assorted sliced pickles

Artfully arrange the meats, cheese, crackers, and pickles on a large serving platter. Serve.

COUNTY FAIR BURGER

One of Indiana's best kept secrets is one of the simplest—the pork burger. Frankly I'm not sure why subbing out beef patties for pork hasn't caught more national attention, but one bite of this delicious, juicy burger will convince any burger purist. The Rihm family makes their patties in-house, combining ground pork and their famous jowl bacon to produce a meaty, moist, and smoky base to this classic. I pressed both Joseph and Jerry as to why it's earned the county fair moniker, and both tell me that you eat them at the county fair. I can't argue with that! You can dress up this burger as you wish, and it's most often served with either mustard or barbecue sauce—no mayo or ketchup, please.

Serves 3	Hands on: 15 minutes	Total: 45 minutes

- ☐ 1 pound ground pork sausage
- ☐ 1 pound hickory smoked bacon, finely diced
- ☐ Kosher salt and fresh-cracked black pepper

- ☐ 6 slices American cheese
- ☐ 3 large Hawaiian hamburger buns
- ☐ Barbecue sauce, to serve
- ☐ 6 slices cooked bacon

- ☐ Optional toppings: thick slices sweet yellow onion, thick slices tomatoes, hamburger pickles, iceberg lettuce

1 Using your hands, combine the sausage and bacon and mix gently until evenly incorporated. Gently create 6 patties, about ¼ pound each, with your hands, and transfer to a baking sheet. Season each patty liberally on both sides with salt and pepper.

2 Open the bottom vent of a charcoal grill completely. Light a charcoal chimney starter filled with charcoal. When the coals are covered with gray ash, pour them onto the bottom grate of the grill, and then push to one side of the grill. Adjust the vents as needed to maintain an internal temperature of 400° to 450°F. Coat the top grate with oil; place on the grill. (If using a gas grill, preheat to medium high [400° to 450°F] on one side.)

3 Add the burgers over direct heat, and grill for 6 to 8 minutes, keeping the grill covered as needed to avoid flare-ups. Flip the burgers and cook an additional 3 minutes over direct heat. Transfer to indirect heat and continue to cook until the internal temperature reaches 165°F, 4 to 6 more minutes.

4 Place a slice of cheese over each patty, cover the grill, and cook for 45 to 60 seconds, until the cheese is just melted. Remove the patties from the grill and transfer to a clean plate. Quickly toast the buns by grilling them, cut sides down, over direct heat for 1 to 1½ minutes, until slightly charred.

5 Assemble the burgers by spreading a generous portion of barbecue sauce on the tops and bottoms of the toasted buns. Arrange 2 patties on each bottom bun, and top with 2 slices of bacon. Continue to add more toppings per your preference and finish with the tops of the buns. Serve.

◀

WHOLE HOG'S HEAD TACOS (PAGE 21)

▼

MATT AT THE RIHM FAMILY HOME

FRIED SWEETBREADS

This dish exudes richness with every tender bite and helps utilize as much of the animal as possible. Sweetbreads are actually the thymus gland (or sometimes pancreas), which is found just behind the neck of the cow. For those who are less experimental in the world of offal, sweetbreads should be your starting point. My favorite part is the fact that you almost can't overcook these—so fear not as you experiment and learn to love this cut. I always recommend that you ask your butcher to ensure the membranes have been thoroughly cleaned and removed so that you can immediately get cooking. If you can only source them with this portion still attached, I recommend simmering the sweetbreads in water for a few minutes. When they are cool, you can easily clean and remove the membranes before moving on to the recipe.

This recipe calls for my preferred method of preparation, frying the pieces in butter to create a crispy exterior, while the inside remains meaty and almost creamy in texture. I fry the sweetbreads in cast iron over an outdoor grill setup, though you can always fry these in the same style pan on a standard stove top.

Serves 4	Hands on: 15 minutes	Total: 45 minutes

- ☐ Four 6- to 8-ounce portions of sweetbreads, membranes removed and rinsed clean
- ☐ 2 cups all-purpose flour

- ☐ 2 tablespoons kosher salt, plus more as needed
- ☐ 1½ tablespoons fresh-cracked black pepper, plus more as needed

- ☐ 4 tablespoons unsalted butter
- ☐ 1 cup pilsner-style beer
- ☐ 1 lemon, cut into wedges, to serve

1 Drain the sweetbreads and pat dry. In a separate bowl, combine the flour, salt, and pepper and mix until the flour is evenly seasoned. Dredge the sweetbread portions in the flour to coat on all sides and place on a baking sheet until ready to fry.

2 Open the bottom vent of a charcoal grill completely. Pour a large pile of charcoal onto the bottom grate on one side of the grill. Light a charcoal chimney starter filled halfway with additional charcoal. When the coals are covered with gray ash, pour them onto the pile of existing charcoal. Adjust the vents, as needed to maintain an internal temperature of 350° to 375°F. Coat the top grate with oil; place on the grill. (If using a gas grill or smoker, preheat to medium [350° to 375°F] on one side, or if using the stovetop, preheat to medium.)

3 Place a large cast-iron skillet over direct heat and add the butter. When the butter begins to foam, add the sweetbreads one at a time, working in batches as needed to not overcrowd. Shallow-fry the sweetbreads for 6 to 8 minutes per side. They should be browned and crispy.

4 Next, add the beer, tent the skillet with foil to help the sweetbreads steam, and cover the grill. Continue to cook the sweetbreads an additional 8 to 10 minutes, until firm when pressed with your index finger, flipping at least once during the process.

5 Remove the sweetbreads and slice on the bias into 1-inch-thick slices. Serve with the lemon wedges on the side.

STEAK TIPS 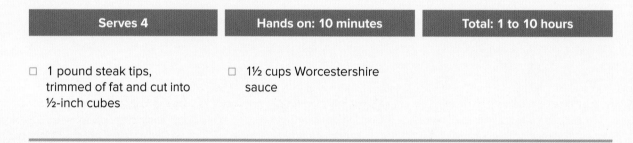 WORCESTERSHIRE

I almost left the Rihms without this recipe, as I had asked Jerry about one of his most favorite snacks, and he conveyed to me that the following dish wasn't planned for the evening menu. But Jerry, who is ever the consummate host, drove up to the plant at the end of the day and spent some time cutting up steak tips and ends so that he could share this delight. When buying meat, customers often want more bang for the buck, demanding that the fattier tail pieces be removed so as not to add additional weight and cost. These pieces contain plenty of good fat for grinding into burgers, but there's usually a little knuckle of good meat that often is overlooked—though not by a skilled butcher. Jerry takes the extra time to carve these out and then soaks them in Worcestershire and serves them as raw, bite-sized snacks. Considering most at-home cooks do not have a whole slew of steak ends laying around, you can simply dice up a piece of strip or sirloin to get the same effect. Here's your new two-ingredient snack of wonder.

Serves 4	Hands on: 10 minutes	Total: 1 to 10 hours

- ☐ 1 pound steak tips, trimmed of fat and cut into ½-inch cubes
- ☐ 1½ cups Worcestershire sauce

In a shallow bowl, combine the steak and Worcestershire sauce. Cover the bowl and place in the refrigerator and allow the steak to marinate in the sauce for at least 1 hour, or up to 10 hours. Remove from the bowl, drain and discard the excess marinade, and transfer the meat to a serving dish. Serve.

SIMON CHEUNG AND ERIC CHEUNG, HING LUNG COMPANY

San Francisco, CA

It's 10:30 a.m. in one of San Francisco's most bustling neighborhoods—Chinatown. As the morning fog lifts from the bay, outside of Hing Lung Company, the oldest Cantonese-style BBQ shop in California, a line snarls down Stockton Street and up Broadway. Though most of the other Cantonese BBQ joints have already put out their siu yuk, or roasted pig, brothers and co-owners Simon Cheung and Eric Cheung are just pulling a nearly seventy-five-pound whole hog

out of one of their vertical ovens. "All of those other places are about volume, bro," says Simon, "but here, we care about quality."

Hing Lung Company is a pint-sized butcher shop in a neighborhood filled with diverse food markets, trading companies, and family-owned restaurants. When the line finally calms, I peruse the storefront as men cut meat on a whizzing band saw and place the freshly cut pieces into refrigerated cases for sale. The siu yuk, chopped by hand at the steady pace of a metronome, has sold out within minutes, and the shards of pork belly and char siu hanging alongside roasted ducks and soy-poached chickens are already being replenished from the back of the house. But before one can find their way to the back, one must admire the monument sitting over the entry threshold honoring Guan Yu, the Chinese god of protection. "That's been up there since we were kids, man," says Simon. "For our culture, business is war."

As I step through the door and enter the back room, a baptism by fire begins to take its hold. The temperature rises easily by ten degrees, and at my left, two wok stations are under flame, as duck fat is being heated, rendered, and bathed over roasted ducks, ensuring perfectly crispy skin when the customer orders it either whole or chopped in half by hand. Toward the back, giant stainless-steel vessels are at work containing hanging pieces of meat awash in fire. On my right side, orders are flying in as iPads buzz by the minute with new takeout orders—it's a modern surprise in a room that is steeped in history.

Standing in the depth of the room and wearing bulky rubber boots and all black à la Johnny Cash is the "big guy," as I refer to him most of the afternoon, the oldest brother, Eric. When I ask Eric about his favorite part of the job, he curtly responds, "Roasting the meat." Ever jovial, Simon laughs, saying, "He is the quiet one," but as I start asking Eric about the practice he's perfected, his gentle, teacher-like mentality begins to come to life. "That's how it is in Chinese culture, man. If you are the oldest, you have to lead by example, be a good sibling to your brothers and sisters. If they do something wrong, somehow *you* get in trouble for it," laughs Eric. It's the first bit of levity I've gleaned from him thus far.

But trust is earned, and I can respect that. So I begin to find some common ground as I ask about how he's perfected his roasting technique. His personality comes alive.

Though Eric is built like a linebacker, the vertical ovens he's working, or "the twins," as he and Simon call them, are an impressive display. "These ovens come from Hong Kong," Eric shares as he uses his foot to control the gas heat that's shooting up from the bottom, closing the swinging doors to maintain both heat and pressure. The best way I can describe these ovens is they're like a Texas-style barrel smoker upended vertically. Instead of having items traditionally rest on a grate, everything is skewered and hung, ensuring the heat evenly reaches each and every crevice of the meat. Though Simon's arms are covered in ink, Eric has darkened scars up and down his arms from the singeing heat of the convective panels. I'm reminded again that business is war, and these are battle scars to prove it.

I'm absolutely fascinated by the Cantonese-style approach of barbecue. Instead of the traditional low-and-slow mantra embraced by most pitmasters of the American South, this style calls for roasting whole pigs at over 600°F. With sweat furling from his brow, Eric says that "eighty percent of the success is in the prep." He scuffs off small pieces of char from the skin of the pig using light strokes of steel wool, as if he's almost painting the animal.

Simon shares that he can debone the entire pig, with the exception of the ribs, in less than five minutes flat. "It's important to have everything at the same thickness, with even consistency," Eric shares. After all, this entire hog is cooked and ready in less than ninety minutes. When I do finally get my chance at sampling, I'm astounded by the crisp sheet of skin as it crackles and crunches on top of the juicy, savory meat. As I chew, the crunch of the skin and the tender meat homogenously combine. I gulp it down and quickly grab a few other bites right off the cutting board, like an anxious kid who can't wait for dinner. I've eaten a lot of barbecue in my lifetime, but nothing quite like this.

Eric shares with me that he borrows an American technique by using wood to impart some smoke on the meat, though he'll only tell me it's a "fruit wood." Like any great master, some secrets are too good to share. To pick up the sweetness, nearly every meat that comes out of the smoker is washed in orange blossom honey. "We go through gallons of this stuff every day, man," Eric tells me as he's dipping whole chicken wings, some of the largest I've ever seen, into a huge vat of honey. The sweetness is an invitation, if you will, to enjoy every creation, but the textures of the crispy skin and savory balance of the lightly smoked, perfectly cooked meat is what will keep you up at night, dreaming of its perfection.

During their childhood, the two brothers emigrated with their family from Hong Kong to San Francisco with their father, Wing Cheung, finding work at Hing Lung, eventually taking over the shop as its owners. Both did stints working at the shop in their teens, but set out to carve their own paths—Eric selling cell phones and pagers at the advent of the tech boom, while Simon attended culinary school. Eventually their journey brought them back to the shop, where they learned the butchering and roasting trade from sifus, masters or teachers, at the shop.

The truth of the matter is that garnering business within this district is won on customer loyalty and tradition. Sure, there are the tech kids and tourists who read the reviews and come to witness greatness, but the success of Hing Lung is still firmly rooted in the classics and local clientele. As customers come into the shop, I can

almost feel the pressure that Simon and Eric are under. Many of the elder Chinese are as demanding as ever, requiring consistency with traditions, many of which stretch back thousands of years. For both Eric and Simon, though they respect culture and tradition, I sense that they are also ambitiously defiant, keeping one foot in the past and stepping forward at the same time.

Take, for example, the soy-poached chicken that's served with the house-made ginger sauce. This particular chicken is relished in traditional culture, and though it never touches the fire, it's poached in a savory and aromatic brine that turns out a juicy, salubrious bird. Making a classic dish with new techniques further cements the fact that Hing Lung Company is firing on all cylinders with each one of their creations, new and old.

Eric's sign stating "goduckyourself" is a stark, almost tongue-in-cheek contrast to the culture and other traditional shops. It's a mentality he's working to spread wide and far. "Chinatown is like my college, where I do my research and development," he says. "My father worked hard to provide us with this place, but man, we are second generation—we speak English," Eric tells me. I further press the American dream when he tells me that he wants to build a #goduckyourself empire, something along the lines of a chain phenomenon à la Panda Express.

While my day with Eric and Simon must come to a close—they remind me that they have work to do, hanging their second siu yuk for the dinner rush—I do not feel that our day was spent in haste. These brothers have reminded me of the most ancient principles.

Tradition takes time. Tradition is important. And while the past and prevalent culture at Hing Lung is being certainly honored by both Simon and Eric, its future, and perhaps destiny, has never looked brighter. ■

GRILLED HONEY BBQ CHICKEN WINGS
with GINGER SAUCE

Like everything in Eric Cheung's oven at Hing Lung Company, the wings are hung vertically, ensuring that they do not get too much direct heat while also cooking evenly to perfection. You can emulate this technique on a grill by cooking over indirect heat, or you can also source some metal skewers to mirror the hanging effect. Instead of separating the wingette and drumette, Eric leaves these two pieces together, meaning you get the best of both worlds with each wing. You'll notice a slightly red hue to the meat, which largely comes from the preserved bean curd in the brine. You can pick up this ingredient at any Chinese or specialty grocer, or online. The ginger sauce is more of a spread and is served with nearly everything at the shop. The ginger and scallions are very prominent, held together by just a bit of oil. It's a refreshing, zingy, and savory sauce that complements the sweet and smoky meat—which is also good eaten simply on its own.

Serves 4	Hands on: 1 hour	Total: 25 hours

- ☐ 2½ pounds whole chicken wings
- ☐ ½ tablespoon kosher salt
- ☐ ½ tablespoon sugar

- ☐ ½ tablespoon five-spice powder
- ☐ 1 tablespoon hoisin sauce
- ☐ 2 tablespoons preserved bean curd

- ☐ 1 cup orange blossom honey
- ☐ Ginger Sauce (recipe follows), to serve

1 In a large mixing bowl, add the wings, salt, sugar, five-spice powder, hoisin sauce, and bean curd, cover with water, and stir until well combined. Cover the bowl and place it in the refrigerator for 24 hours.

2 Open the bottom vent of a charcoal grill completely. Light a charcoal chimney starter filled with charcoal. When the coals are covered with gray ash, pour them onto the bottom grate of the grill, and then push to one side of the grill. Adjust the vents as needed to maintain an internal temperature of 350° to 375°F. Coat the top grate with oil; place on the grill. (If using a gas grill, preheat to medium [350° to 375°F] on one side.)

3 Remove the wings from the brine, discard the brine, and pat the wings dry. Place the wings on the grill over indirect heat, cover, and cook, undisturbed, for 25 minutes. Flip the wings, cover the grill, and cook for an additional 25 to 30 minutes, until the internal temperature reaches approximately 160°F. Move the wings over direct heat and cook, uncovered, for 2 to 3 minutes on each side to firm up the skin, being careful not to burn it. Remove the wings from the grill and brush with the honey. Serve with ginger sauce.

GINGER SAUCE

- ☐ ¼ cup peanut oil
- ☐ 1 cup freshly grated peeled ginger
- ☐ ½ cup thinly sliced scallions
- ☐ 1 teaspoon kosher salt

Heat a small nonstick skillet over medium heat and add the oil. When the oil begins to shimmer, add the ginger and lightly cook for 1½ minutes, being careful not to burn it. Reduce the heat to low, add the scallions, and continue to stir until the scallions have just cooked down, about 2 minutes. Add the salt, stir to combine, and turn off the heat. Allow the ingredients to cool to room temperature. Transfer the sauce to a mason jar. Serve or keep in the refrigerator for up to 1 week.

GRILLED HONEY BBQ RIBS

While many believe the only way to create prophetic ribs is with low heat and lots of time, I'm a big proponent that great ribs can also be cooked relatively hot and fast. And so it goes with this particular style, using St. Louis–cut ribs that Eric Cheung scores generously across the meat to ensure it has even more chance to absorb the flavor of the brine and smoke. Be sure to always remove the thin membrane that covers the bone. Simply use a paring knife to get under the membrane and a paper towel to grab hold and pull it from the rack.

These ribs aren't in the fall-off-the-bone camp—instead, they are bite-off-the-bone heavenly, with just enough sweetness from the honey to balance out the meaty, rich pork. Like all of the meats prepared at Hing Lung, these ribs are hung and cooked vertically, which can be performed in a barrel-style setup, or also indirectly on a grill. This method is a nice change of pace if you are looking to branch out from the standard dry-rub, smoked-rib routine.

Serves 4	Hands on: 1 hour 30 minutes	Total: 25 hours

- ☐ 2 whole racks St. Louis–cut ribs, membranes removed
- ☐ 1 tablespoon kosher salt
- ☐ 1 tablespoon sugar

- ☐ 1 tablespoon five-spice powder
- ☐ 2 tablespoons hoisin sauce
- ☐ 3 tablespoons preserved bean curd

- ☐ 1 cup orange blossom honey
- ☐ Ginger Sauce (page 35), to serve

1 Using a sharp knife, diagonally score the meaty sides of the ribs in 1-inch increments. Repeat the scoring procedure in the opposite diagonal direction to create a crosshatch pattern. Place the scored ribs in a large baking dish and add the salt, sugar, five-spice powder, hoisin sauce, and bean curd. Cover with water and stir until well combined. Cover the dish and place in the refrigerator for 24 hours.

2 Open the bottom vent of a charcoal grill completely. Light a charcoal chimney starter filled with charcoal. When the coals are covered with gray ash, pour them onto the bottom grate of the grill, and then push to one side of the grill. Adjust the vents as needed to maintain an internal temperature of 350° to 400°F. Coat the top grate with oil; place on the grill. (If using a gas grill, preheat to medium [350° to 400°F] on one side.)

3 Remove the ribs from the brine, discard the brine, and pat the ribs dry. Place the ribs, meaty sides down, on the grill over direct heat. Cover the grill and cook until the ribs are lightly browned and charred, about 15 minutes, turning once halfway through the process. Move the ribs to indirect heat. Cover the grill and cook at least 55 minutes, or until a thermometer inserted into the thickest portion of the ribs registers 180°F. Remove the ribs from the grill and brush with the honey. Serve the ribs with ginger sauce.

CHAR SIU FRIED RICE

Though Eric and Simon focus their efforts primarily on roasting meats, they also have a busy to-go service where they incorporate their delicious primary cuts into traditional favorites. Case in point, this BBQ fried rice that Simon whips up in less than ten minutes flat. He adorns the dish with sliced char siu, which is derived from the pork collar, bones removed, that's been brined and roasted like the rest of the signature meats you find at Hing Lung Company. You can always use the fried rice recipe below as a base, and then add some char siu (or cook your own) or sub in other proteins, such as chicken, duck, or even smoked tofu. This is a hefty, comforting dish that cooks up quickly, and the leftovers are even better the second time around.

Serves 4	Hands on: 15 minutes	Total: 15 minutes

- ☐ 3 tablespoons vegetable oil
- ☐ ½ cup sliced yellow onion
- ☐ ½ cup chopped carrots
- ☐ ½ cup frozen green peas
- ☐ 3 cloves garlic, minced
- ☐ 6 large eggs
- ☐ 8 cups cooked jasmine rice, chilled overnight
- ☐ 2 tablespoons light soy sauce
- ☐ 1 tablespoon dark soy sauce
- ☐ 1 teaspoon white pepper
- ☐ 1 pound char siu, sliced thin

1 Heat a wok or large stainless-steel skillet over high heat. Add 2 tablespoons of the oil, followed by the onion and carrots. Cook them for 1 to 1½ minutes, stirring and flipping constantly until the onion is just translucent. Add the peas and garlic, and cook for an additional 1 minute. Transfer the vegetables to a plate.

2 In a small bowl, beat 2 of the eggs. Place the wok or skillet back over high heat and add the beaten eggs. Scramble the eggs quickly, about 1 minute, until they are still moist but firm. Transfer the eggs to a plate.

3 Add the rice to the wok, stirring and tossing to quickly heat and lightly fry. Next, add the soy sauces and pepper, and stir to mix and incorporate. Add the vegetables and scrambled eggs and continue to stir and mix the ingredients until evenly distributed and warmed through, 1 to 2 minutes.

4 Remove the pan from the heat and divide the fried rice among four plates. Top each evenly with the char siu.

5 Return the wok or skillet to high heat and add the remaining 1 tablespoon of oil. Gently break each of the remaining 4 eggs onto the surface. Fry for 2 minutes for sunny-side-up eggs, or longer, if preferred. Place an egg on top of each plate of fried rice. Serve.

SOY-POACHED CHICKEN

While most of everything at Hing Lung Company meets fire, this dish is poached in an aromatic, soy-based broth until it's deliciously tender and full of flavor. In the back of the shop, several large pots are constantly at a slow simmer cooking up these birds, while up front they are being cut up and sold to the masses. After a few bites, I was convinced this is one of my new Sunday go-to meals, the kind where you cook it up for a dinner that evening and save the leftovers for the week ahead. While the soy adds plenty of savory, there's also a sweet flavor from the sugar and aromatics that balances everything out. And while the skin itself is not roasted, it still comes out almost silky, as Eric says. I believed it after I devoured nearly an entire thigh while he was talking. Once again, the ginger sauce is a great condiment to serve on the side of this deliciously simple dish.

Serves 4	Hands on: 20 minutes	Total: 2 hours

- ☐ 4 cups chicken stock
- ☐ 1 cup light soy sauce
- ☐ 4 star anise pods
- ☐ 2 sticks cinnamon
- ☐ 2 bay leaves

- ☐ ¼ cup sugar
- ☐ 3 to 4 slices peeled ginger
- ☐ 2 pieces dried white licorice
- ☐ 1 whole free-range chicken, about 4 pounds

- ☐ 1 cup orange blossom honey
- ☐ Ginger Sauce (page 35), to serve

1 In a large, 6-quart dutch oven, combine the stock, soy sauce, anise, cinnamon, bay leaves, sugar, ginger, and licorice. Bring the mixture to a slow boil over medium heat. Carefully add the chicken and reduce the heat to medium low. Note: If the stock does not completely cover the chicken, add additional water until the chicken is covered by 1 inch of liquid, using a plate to place over the chicken to keep it submerged.

2 Return the stock to a very slow simmer, a few burps and bubbles, or if using a thermometer, a target temperature of 190°F. Cook the chicken for 45 minutes. Turn off the heat and allow the chicken to sit in the liquid for an additional 30 minutes.

3 Remove the chicken from the pot and cool for 15 minutes. Brush with the honey. Cut the chicken into 6 pieces, removing the backbone. Separate the drumsticks from the thighs and debone the thighs and breasts prior to serving. Serve the chicken with ginger sauce.

GOOD DUCK'ING NOODLES

Ducks hanging from the window are the iconic sight that one would expect from any tour through Chinatown. Eric and Simon joke with me that their roasted ducks have almost a cult-like following, hence their motto, #goduckyourself. But most of the other shops around town do not go through the extra processes to roast their ducks a touch darker, followed by a wash in extra duck fat to ensure the skin is extra dark and crispy, as done at Hing Lung Company. While you can pick up a half or whole duck to go, another secret is this dish, which incorporates chopped duck meat into a savory and sweet stir-fried noodle dish that's highly addictive.

Of course, if you can't access your own locally sourced roasted duck, you can always sub in seared chicken, pork, or even thin strips of steak for good measure. The same goes for the lo mein noodles—in a pinch I will use a good-quality spaghetti instead. But enough with the substitutions already. This dish is as fun to eat as it is to tell people what it is called.

Serves 4	Hands on: 15 minutes	Total: 25 minutes

- ☐ 2 tablespoons vegetable oil
- ☐ ¼ green bell pepper, sliced into thin strips
- ☐ ¼ red bell pepper, sliced into thin strips
- ☐ ¼ yellow onion, sliced into thin strips

- ☐ 1 stalk celery, cut in half and sliced into thin strips lengthwise
- ☐ 1 pound Chinese roast duck, chopped into bite-sized pieces
- ☐ 1 pound lo mein noodles, cooked and drained

- ☐ 2 tablespoons light soy sauce
- ☐ 1 tablespoon dark soy sauce
- ☐ 1 tablespoon sugar
- ☐ 1 teaspoon kosher salt
- ☐ 1 teaspoon white pepper

1 Heat a wok or large stainless-steel skillet over high heat. Add the oil, followed by the bell peppers, onion, and celery. Fry the vegetables in the oil, stirring or flipping constantly, until the vegetables are just tender, 1 to 2 minutes. Remove the vegetables to a plate.

2 Add the duck to the pan and stir for 45 to 60 seconds to heat. Next, add the noodles, tossing and stirring with the duck to combine. One at a time, add the soy sauces, sugar, salt, and white pepper, and continue to stir and fry the dish, tossing constantly for 45 seconds to incorporate. Return the cooked vegetables to the pan, toss and stir to combine, and cook until completely incorporated and hot, about 2 minutes. Transfer the noodles to bowls and serve.

AMAURY NOIRCLÈRE AND CHRISTOPHE GAULTIER, MAISON MAILLARD

Antibes, France

For Amaury Noirclère and Christophe Gaultier, the morning commute is a short one. Departing their respective families in adjacent apartments, the two business partners simply walk down a single flight of stairs to commence their day at ground level in Maison Maillard, a sun-drenched butcher shop just steps away from the Mediterranean Sea in Antibes, France. While the jaunt to work might be quick, the journey of getting here has been a marathon.

My day with Amaury and Christophe starts by savoring a quick café and scanning the array of hand-carved meats in their cold lockers while Christophe begins breaking down a whole quarter of lamb. Yielding a large cleaver on a well-worn cutting block, Christophe avoids technology like saws or machines, preferring a more hands-on approach, with brute strength and a sharp knife. He is efficient and deft in all of his work—it looks as though he's been doing this for a lifetime.

"We met in New York City," Amaury tells me when I ask about the foundation of his and Christophe's butcher brotherhood. As IT engineers, the two fostered a friendship and a dream while working long hours and making the best of a career that lacked personal fulfillment.

When I ask which of the two had the great idea of giving up a steady gig and good money to earn a living the hard way, Amaury rebukes my theory when he tells me it was a third party—alcohol. So it was these imbibed conversations combined with rich fortitude that led to Amaury and Christophe quitting their jobs and entering, green with ambition, into the cutthroat world of butchery.

But in France, earning the proper certifications and qualifications in any career can often be an antiquated process, filled with delays and bureaucracy. Since the two already possessed professional degrees, an additional year was spent in school to earn the right accreditations to further an apprenticeship, one that Christophe found working under Andriy Maximov at Meat Couture in the small town of Brest, in French Brittany. "When I called to ask for the job, Andriy asked if I could be there tomorrow," Christophe laughs, astonished at the opportunity but also realistic that moving his life across the country would take a beat. Nevertheless, Christophe eventually found his way to Brest, crediting his time in that role as a foundational building block toward starting his new career. "Typically, most butchers here in France start working at the age of fifteen, spending ten years working two to three hours a day to master their craft," says Christophe. "To catch up, I worked ten hours a day for three years."

In the meantime, Amaury led the search to find the perfect location for their dream, finally settling on a government building that, like the education system, required the right permitting and persistence to finally attain ownership.

When training and red tape finally released their grasp, the two were still a year or so from opening, as they took on the responsibility of construction and building that was required to turn their former office space into a storefront. At this point, I'm enjoying a glass of a spicy and lively Rhône wine, laughing admirably with both

Amaury and Christophe over a cigarette—I indulge only when in France!—knowing that both had *no* clue what they were getting themselves into. Blame it on the alcohol, or blame it on naivete, but with much passion and persistence, the two had no choice other than to press on.

About that time, the phone starts ringing, forcing us all back inside as customers are calling in special cuts and orders to pick up for the week. While the two might have had a background in IT engineering, they have completely shunned technology for a stained and tattered paper ledger of weekly orders and obligations. It seems that some customers don't even pay on each visit, perhaps settling their tabs based on mutual trust

and store credit when the timing is right. "It's easier this way," says Christophe with a jovial smile.

Meanwhile, Amaury is in the back of the house, plating up his plat du jour, a pork shoulder stew studded with local olives and sage to serve to the lunch crowd. Sensing my hunger, he serves me a small portion to keep it somewhat at bay. The pork is fall-apart tender, enveloped in a gravy that gets a further punch from the salty, acidic olives.

The more time I spend with these two, the more I start to gain a sense of a true partnership, where each friend contributes their expertise in equally beneficial ways. While Christophe might tackle the primary obligations of cutting the meat, Amaury takes the lead in the kitchen, cooking up not only the plat du jour and other daily offerings

but also creating a stock of items à emporter (to go), from weekly terrines to his famous pâté en croûte to lasagnas and other specialties.

After working their way through the lunch rush, the two suggest that we all take a pause from our "labor" to enjoy a bite to eat. I welcome the hospitality, taking a chance to sit at a small table, soaking in the sunshine with a crisp glass of local rosé. Amaury joins me with a few plates, making the most of the hand-trimmed and sliced beef from Christophe to mix together a French classic, beef tartare, prepared tableside with Amaury's own personality and distinctive ingredients. With ratatouille and potatoes dauphinoise as supporting characters, I settle into the meal one might expect only at an haute cuisine restaurant, certainly not from the local butcher. The dish turns out to be one of those that I seek regularly but rarely find. Time, place, and the universe coincide in this moment to produce the kind of meal, and experience, that will last forever in my memory.

Beyond the delectable food, wine, and joie de vivre, perhaps what I admire most about the French is their fixation on preserving traditions. Take Sundays, for example, which are still very much sacred, maintained in nearly every setting as a day of rest. Additionally the quotidian

practice to faire les courses, or make the rounds by shopping at the local boulangerie, boucherie, and weekly farmers markets, is still a romantic and charming routine for most. However, times are changing. Nowadays many larger supermarchés can be found on the outskirts of the city center, altering the daily habits of the French and its people. Many of these markets are also now open on Sundays and holidays, driving a more capitalistic culture focused less on quality than quantity.

So as a foreigner looking in, I'm even more cognizant of the sacrifice that both Amaury and Christophe have made in the marathon toward finding success. I admire not only their pivot toward taking on a life of entrepreneurship, a move much more difficult in France than America, but also their dedication toward preserving an art that is so formidably linked to the French society. Perhaps even better, in the same way that both Amaury and Christophe learned from others, they are now passing on their knowledge—not only of the craft but also running a business—to foster apprenticeships with the younger generation. Amaury and Christophe have established a place of both work and home, but I would go further to

say that they have laid the path toward their legacy. It is time well spent, and a life well lived.

As the afternoon sun sets on this seaside town, we pick at the leftovers scattered across the table, including a blue-rare steak of delight and a terrine of veal and pork served alongside hand-torn homemade bread. Of course an array of goods, including foie gras, local cheeses, and other accoutrements that one can procure in the paradise that is Maison Maillard, find themselves within our grazing distance.

Time seems suspended, but I am aware that I must catch a flight back to Paris, and eventually back home to Nashville. Excited at the prospect of rejoining my family, I still feel a sense of melancholy knowing that I must depart this moment, this time. Reluctant to leave, I procrastinate.

Although I'm painfully full, I decide to ask the two, somewhat jokingly, what else they might have to eat.

Amaury laughs, telling me, "You can eat anything you want . . . besides the butchers." ∎

PORK SHOULDER STEW
ⓦ SAGE ⓐ OLIVES

Ragoût de Épaule de Cochon à la Sauge et aux Olives

The honorable plat du jour, or daily meal, often cooked with what's on hand, is a true mechanism of running a butcher shop. This is common practice for many butcher shops in France. A daily specialty is made for those customers looking to perform double duty by picking up some meat to cook for the week and taking advantage of a butcher's specialty dish. On the day of my visit, Amaury Noirclère fashioned chunks of pork shoulder into a hearty stew studded with local Cailletier olives and served over pasta. Even though it's a humble dish, I was astonished by Amaury's dedication to perfection, from the preparation of the dish to its final, beautiful plating. "You should never have anything you cannot eat on a plate," says Amaury. As for me? I ate everything.

Serves 6	Hands on: 1 hour	Total: 5 hours

STEW
- ☐ 2½ pounds pork shoulder, or country-style ribs, cut into 2-inch cubes
- ☐ 1 tablespoon kosher salt
- ☐ 1½ tablespoons vegetable oil
- ☐ 3 cups white wine
- ☐ One 15-ounce can tomato puree
- ☐ 1 bunch fresh sage, tied together using butcher's twine

- ☐ 3 cloves garlic, minced
- ☐ ¼ cup all-purpose flour
- ☐ 4 tablespoons unsalted butter
- ☐ 1 cup Cailletier olives, or kalamata olives, pitted

PASTA
- ☐ 1 pound uncooked penne pasta
- ☐ 4 tablespoons unsalted butter
- ☐ 1 clove garlic, minced

- ☐ 2 leaves fresh sage, torn

GARNISH
- ☐ 6 sprigs fresh thyme
- ☐ 2 tablespoons thinly sliced mini leeks, or scallions
- ☐ 12 Cailletier olives, or kalamata olives, pitted
- ☐ 2 tablespoons thinly sliced poivrons salade, or miniature bell peppers

1 Heat a large dutch oven over medium-high heat. Pat the pork pieces dry and season liberally with the salt on all sides. Add the vegetable oil to the dutch oven. Add the pork pieces, being careful not to overcrowd and working in batches as necessary, and sear on each side for 2 to 3 minutes to create a dark crust on each piece.

2 In a separate skillet, add the wine and reduce by half over medium-high heat, about 15 minutes. Meanwhile, preheat the oven to 250°F.

3 Add all the pork pieces back into the dutch oven and pour the reduced wine over the seared pork. Add just enough water to cover the pork, followed by the tomato puree, bunch of sage, and garlic. Cover and return to a slow simmer. When the mixture reaches a slow simmer, place the dutch oven into the preheated oven and cook, undisturbed, for 4 hours.

4 Remove the pork and sage bunch from the stew mixture and set the meat aside, discarding the sage. Return the dutch oven to the stove top and bring to a slow boil over

medium-high heat, reducing the liquid by ½ inch or so, about 20 minutes. Meanwhile, combine the flour and butter in a separate sauté pan over medium heat and whisk together, stirring often until a slightly brown roux forms, about 3 minutes. With the stew mixture simmering, whisk the stew vigorously while adding the roux slowly. Allow the stew mixture to come back to a simmer, then reduce the heat to low. Add the pork back into the pot along with the olives and keep warm.

5 Meanwhile, cook the pasta al dente according to the package instructions. In a large skillet over medium heat, add the butter and cook until it gently foams. Add the garlic and sage leaves and cook for 1 minute. Drain the pasta and add it into the skillet with the garlic and sage butter, tossing to coat the pasta evenly.

6 Plate the dish with a generous portion of the pork stew alongside the pasta. Garnish each plate evenly with the thyme, leeks, additional olives, and thinly sliced peppers. Serve.

MAISON MAILLARD STEAK TARTARE

Tartare de Boeuf de la Maison Maillard

A dish celebrated at nearly every French bistro or fine dining establishment, a proper steak tartare relies primarily on quality ingredients and expert preparation. The foundation of this dish is, of course, the steak. While most chefs and restaurateurs utilize the ultimately tender cut of filet mignon, Christophe prefers using a cut known as plat de tranche grasse, a flavorful, readily tender cut that lends a bit more body and "smack" as the base of the dish, but you can substitute sirloin steak in a pinch. Removing all fat and silver skin, Christophe slices the cut several times across the grain to reach his desired consistency. After that, the perfectly prepped steak is sent to the back of the house, where Amaury prepares the dish with a sans-egg twist, also shunning traditional parsley for the brighter, slightly more acidic cilantro, which adds his own spin to this beloved dish. The key is to source the best quality beef possible, taking care to ensure your surfaces and utensils are sanitized, and to prepare this à la minute, consuming the dish just as it's completed.

Serves 2	Hands on: 20 minutes	Total: 20 minutes

- ☐ ½ pound plat de tranche grasse, or substitute sirloin steak, silver skin and fat completely removed
- ☐ 1 tablespoon finely minced shallot
- ☐ 1 teaspoon minced fresh cilantro
- ☐ 1 teaspoon lemon zest

- ☐ 6 small cornichon pickles, finely minced
- ☐ 1 teaspoon finely minced capers
- ☐ ½ tablespoon dijon mustard
- ☐ ½ tablespoon ketchup, such as Heinz
- ☐ 2 dashes Worcestershire sauce

- ☐ 2 turns fresh-cracked black pepper
- ☐ 1 pinch kosher salt
- ☐ 1 dash Tabasco hot sauce
- ☐ ⅓ cup extra-virgin olive oil

1 On a steady and clean cutting board, very thinly (about ⅛-inch thick) slice the steak against the grain. Rotate the sliced pieces 180 degrees and stack the slices on top of one another. Slice the steak again very finely, creating thin strips. Once again, rotate the strips 180 degrees and slice the strips very thinly to create very small cubes of steak.

2 Place the steak along with the shallot, cilantro, lemon zest, pickles, and capers on a plate.

3 Meanwhile, in a medium mixing bowl, add the mustard, ketchup, Worcestershire, pepper, salt, and hot sauce. Using a fork or whisk, mix together the ingredients, slowly streaming in the olive oil to create a quick emulsion.

4 Add the steak and ingredients from the plate into the bowl with the emulsion and loosely toss the mixture together using two spoons.

5 Carefully transfer the mixture to a serving plate, forming it into whatever shape you prefer, and serve immediately.

VEAL ⓐⓝⓓ PORK TERRINE ⓦⓘⓣⓗ PISTACHIOS

Terrine de Veau aux Pistaches

Within seconds of tossing down this terrine, I told both Amaury Noirclère and Christophe Gaultier in my best Franglaise and Southern twang that "this is the best darn meatloaf I've ever had." The translation or drawl on my part might have been a bit slow to comprehend, but we all quickly connected with a laugh, heads nodding up and down as we consumed this chilled, savory concoction with some fruity, spicy Côtes du Rhône and foie gras. Indeed, Amaury had his sights set on teaching me how he makes his beloved pâté en croûte, but when he informed me it takes a hundred times to master the dish, I opted for the simpler yet still-outstanding terrine. To my surprise, the dish really is similar in formation to that of a traditional meatloaf, combining the best of pork and veal together for a light yet satisfying texture. My only complaint? Amaury is adamant that this dish must be fully cooled to room temperature, then chilled for two to three days to best allow the flavors to meld together. Though I'm an immediate satisfaction kind of guy, I do appreciate the French discipline. Fortunately for me, Amaury had already prepared this dish days prior to my arrival, ensuring that I could devour it right away. Give this a whirl for your next charcuterie platter or picnic, or better yet as the primary character in your late-night sandwich entourage.

Serves 6 to 8	Hands on: 1 hour	Total: 4½ days

- ☐ 6 cups water
- ☐ 3 large eggs
- ☐ ¾ cup heavy cream
- ☐ 1 tablespoon kosher salt
- ☐ ½ teaspoon white pepper
- ☐ 1 pound ground veal
- ☐ 1 pound ground pork
- ☐ ¼ cup finely diced shallots
- ☐ ½ cup finely grated Parmigiano-Reggiano cheese
- ☐ ¼ cup shelled pistachios

1 Preheat the oven to 275°F.

2 In a medium saucepan, bring the water to a slow boil.

3 In a large mixing bowl, whisk together the eggs, cream, salt, and pepper until evenly combined and slightly foamy. Add the veal, pork, shallots, and cheese and mix with your hands until combined, being careful not to overwork the mixture. Add the pistachios and mix thoroughly just one time to make sure they are evenly distributed throughout the mixture.

4 Grease a 9 x 13-inch baking dish and pour in the meat mixture. Use the back of a spoon soaked in ice water to evenly spread out the mixture and ensure there are no air pockets,

as well as a smooth top layer. Rest the baking dish inside a larger baking dish with sides at least 2 inches high. Carefully pour the boiling water into the larger baking dish until it reaches approximately 1 inch up the sides of the 9 x 13-inch dish. This creates a bain-marie, which will make for a gentler cooking process.

5 Transfer both dishes to the oven and bake 1½ hours, or until the internal temperature of the terrine reaches 160°F. Remove the baking dishes from the oven and set aside to cool. When the dish with the terrine is cool to the touch, cover it with plastic wrap and place it in the fridge. Allow to chill for 2 to 3 days prior to serving. Serve cold or at room temperature. The terrine will keep, covered, for up to 5 additional days in the refrigerator.

STRIP STEAK TAGLIATA STYLE

Faux-Filet en Tagliata

My job is to always find "the good stuff." Whether it's the content of the stories or the actual recipes themselves, I always feel a certain responsibility to pull back the curtain, showcasing the best of each person and locale. In the case of this dish, I didn't have to work too hard to uncover the good stuff, as both Amaury and Christophe at Maison Maillard fluttered with excitement when they described the technique and style of this creation. While the faux-filet can sometimes have different interpretations, as in a "false filet," or otherwise known as a contre-filet ("against the filet," in reference to a porterhouse), I prefer to utilize the strip, or shell, cut to serve as the standout in this dish.

Frankly this is more of a technique than it is a recipe, and while I'm being honest, we owe the Italians the credit here. The idea is to sear the steaks as quickly as possible in a high-temperature fat or oil, slice them blood-rare, then serve them on a warm platter so they gently cook just to temperature. I learned about this dish halfway around the globe while working with and learning from two of the kindest people as they shared their passion for celebrating all the goodness and community that great food can bring. Whether you serve this dish and technique as an appetizer or a main course, I hope it helps to stop time and place and provides that right bit of respite, as it did for me.

Serves 2 to 4	Hands on: 20 minutes	Total: 20 minutes

- ☐ 4 tablespoons veal fat, or high-temperature cooking oil, such as grapeseed oil
- ☐ Two 10-ounce New York strip steaks, ends removed and trimmed of all fat
- ☐ ¼ cup extra-virgin olive oil
- ☐ 1½ tablespoons fleur de sel, divided

1 Preheat the oven to 300°F. When the oven reaches the desired temperature, place an oven-safe serving platter in the oven to warm.

2 Meanwhile, heat a cast-iron skillet over medium-high heat and add the fat. When the fat begins to smoke, add the steaks and cook, undisturbed, for 1½ minutes. Flip the steaks and cook for an additional 1½ minutes. To finish, cook the steaks on each of their larger sides for 1 minute each. Remove the steaks from the pan, and let the steaks rest for 5 minutes.

3 After resting the steaks, return the same pan back to the stove top over high heat. When the fat begins to smoke again, add the steaks back to the pan and flash-cook for 15 seconds per side. Remove the pan from the heat and transfer the steaks to a cutting board. Carefully remove the warmed serving platter from the oven.

4 Drizzle 2 tablespoons of the olive oil and scatter half of the salt over the platter. Slice the steaks against the grain into ¼-inch-thick pieces and carefully arrange them on the heated platter, making sure each piece is in contact with the platter and not overcrowded. Finish the dish by drizzling the remaining 2 tablespoons of oil over the steaks and season with remaining salt. Serve.

TOMMIE KELLY, KROGER

Nashville, TN

"Daddy, there's your brother," says my daughter Vivienne. As I'm perusing the array of cellophane-packed meats, brightened rather vividly by the fluorescent lights, it takes a minute for my focus to dualize, only to realize that apparently my daughter is aware of a sibling I do not have.

When I press Vivienne to explain, she tells me that my "brother," Mr. Tommie, is just down the way, stocking the lunch case. I suppose in the mind of a five-year-old, when two men greet each other by "hey, brother," it can cause some confusion. But frankly, looking at each other, both Tommie and I are quick to realize we are not, indeed, biological siblings.

Vivienne laughs, in the best melodic rhythm a child can offer, saying, "Daddy, he's not your brother—he *is* your cooking brother." Tommie and I both bust out a glorious laugh, the kind that two girl-dads, Tommie with three girls and me with two, can share in the moment.

While I have access to an array of local butcher shops and specialty markets in Nashville, the truth remains—we become creatures of convenience. A quick bike ride, or a jaunt with the car seats, often takes me to the Kroger store less than a mile from my home in East Nashville to procure the weekly groceries and kids' lunches, or simply to give my wife a break by taking my two daughters on a grocery store "adventure."

While I might have an array of sourcing options, the reality is much different for others.

Throughout our country, finding conveniences such as a large grocery center can sometimes be few and far between—it's the "food desert" crisis that strikes both rural and urban America. So you could say that while I proudly support independent entrepreneurship, I'm also a realist. While your "local supermarket" might not be locally owned, it shouldn't distract from the real fact that great people serve these businesses and its constituents every day. As Paul once said about the church, it's not about the physical building, or the ownership, for that matter. Rather, it's about the people.

I get a sense that a solid portion of faith dominates the day-to-day workings for Mr. Tommie. And while we have known each other rather casually for years, my first question beckons. "What is your last name?" I'm a bit embarrassed to ask, given how long we've operated without the formality. Tommie smiles, unoffended, and pleasantly informs me. His proper name is Tommie Kelly. The attribution and spelling of his first name comes from his grandmother.

In high school, Tommie enjoyed playing sports, including baseball and football. To challenge the latter, I suggest we get down in a three-point stance, my attempt at showing photographer Andrea Behrends these two old dads still got it. We get down in the stance, as muscle memory is like riding a bike, but getting out of said stance isn't as easy as when we were both seventeen years old.

It was at that young age that Tommie entered into his next phase of life, taking a night job working at a Kroger store on Gallatin Pike. Noticing his talent and work ethic, the meat department manager Ms. Alecia Shores asked Tommie if he'd like to make more money, and he's been cutting meat ever since.

"You ain't a true butcher until you get nicked at least once," Tommie laughs as he shows me a proud scar on the top of his thumb. Through trial and error, and with Ms. Shore's mentorship, Tommie worked his way up the ranks to eventually settle into his own kind of rhythm. When I press Tommie on what skills are necessary for the job—beyond a good knife and a sturdy cutting surface, he smiles and tells me that "practice makes perfect." Personally I take advantage of this practice, often being that guy who asks for custom cuts from behind the counter, and Tommie is always happy to oblige.

A few years into his tenure, an assistant manager, Bobby Ferguson, suggested that Tommie apply for a continuing education program offered by Kroger to further his career. Over the next year and a half, Tommie spent his weeks at the University of Kentucky, obtaining a certification in agriculture science, learning the ins and outs of slaughtering, processing, and cutting.

But all work and no play makes for a dull knife. In the years that followed, Tommie was wrapping up a choir rehearsal at church when a brown outfit caught his attention. "We had known each other casually for a bit, but when I saw her that day, that's when I hooked her," he says, flashing a confident smile. Alecia fostered the flirtation, and knowing Tommie's penchant for the trade, asked if he could suggest a meal for her to whip up for Sunday lunch. "Pork tenderloin," Tommie told her, not expecting her to turn the table and invite him over to share.

When I ask how it went, Tommie laughs again, saying the lunch went "very well"—leading to marriage and a family of three lovely girls. Funny how good food creates a spark. By the way, I ask for the tenderloin recipe, but I don't get it.

While Tommie lives an hour's drive from his assigned store, he's spent the last few decades enduring the commute because he loves the people. That goes for both the shoppers and his

believe that this store—the environment, the people—have become Tommie's own version of his church. "I love the people. Most come into the store to chat about life, the good and the bad. I love hearing about other folks," he says. I myself have found a friend in my procurement of not just goods but a champion in the routines of life. This is Tommie's own unique version of ministry, and it goes beyond just cutting meat and leading others. I, myself, am a devoted proponent that a good butcher is faithful, trusted, and well revered. As the Bible says, love is patient, it is kind.

But for Mr. Tommie, he takes this idea a step further—perhaps even deeper. Steadfast reliance and trust can take a lifetime to silently master, but thoughtfulness and generosity are the day-to-day recognizable actions of living a life of purpose. It's these that take the most persistence to maintain.

Scarred, nicked, or not, Tommie's hands go beyond the physical, keeping us all in good hands. ■

crew, most of whom have been with him the entire time, as his example-driven leadership lays the foundation for his team to follow.

While we spend our day together, it strikes me how much one can learn about someone by just changing up the routine, spending time outside of the everyday boundaries of life. Standing over a charcoal fire, we toss an array of different meats over the coals, swapping stories and life lessons all the same. We probably learn more about each other in just a few quality hours than we have in my decade of regular stops into the store. I firmly

THIN-SLICED CHICKEN BREASTS with HONEY BBQ SAUCE

My local Kroger butcher Tommie iterates to me time and time again that he's a simple kind of cook. That's fair, as I believe simplicity always trumps complicated. But I keep telling Tommie not to sell himself short. This dish is an example where a bit of technique and a simple "spin," using a few basic ingredients for a sauce, creates a hearty main that can be a go-to dish anytime. Thinly slicing the breasts ensures that they will cook quickly and evenly. The sauce comes together easily and is slathered on the chicken in the final moments of cooking, with the remainder served on the side for dipping.

Serves 4	Hands on: 20 minutes	Total: 30 minutes

- ☐ 4 boneless, skinless chicken breasts, thinly sliced into ¼-inch-thick portions
- ☐ ¼ cup vegetable oil
- ☐ 1 tablespoon garlic powder

- ☐ 1½ tablespoons kosher salt
- ☐ 1 tablespoon fresh-cracked black pepper
- ☐ One 10-ounce bottle Heinz 57 Sauce

- ☐ 2 tablespoons honey
- ☐ Chopped fresh parsley, as garnish

1 Open the bottom vent of a charcoal grill completely. Light a charcoal chimney starter filled with charcoal. When the coals are covered with gray ash, pour them onto the bottom grate of the grill, and then push to one side of the grill. Adjust the vents as needed to maintain an internal temperature of 350° to 375°F. Coat the top grate with oil; place on the grill. (If using a gas grill, preheat to medium [350° to 375°F] on one side.)

2 Arrange the chicken on a baking sheet, drizzle with the oil, and toss to coat. Season both sides of the chicken with the garlic powder, salt, and pepper.

3 Combine the 57 Sauce and honey in a small saucepan and place the pan over direct heat on the grill. When the mixture begins to simmer, stir the sauce, and move to indirect heat to reduce and slightly thicken, stirring on occasion, 2 to 3 minutes.

4 Place the chicken slices over direct heat and grill for 4 minutes. Rotate the slices 45 degrees and cook for an additional 2 minutes. Flip the chicken and cook for an additional 2 to 3 minutes, until the internal temperature reaches 160°F.

5 Using a brush, generously slather the sauce over the top of the chicken, cover the grill, and cook for 1 minute. Remove the chicken breasts to a serving platter and place the additional sauce in a shallow bowl. Garnish the chicken with parsley. Serve with the sauce alongside.

SMOKED PORK STEAKS

Everybody loves a pork steak, says Tommie, my local Kroger butcher. Oftentimes, I give Tommie advance notice to order up more of these when I want to entertain, as the thinly sliced pork shoulder provides a great meaty and tender option that is affordable and delicious to serve a crowd. Once again, the ingredient list might be short, but the technique of slowly grilling these steaks will ensure that the meat pulls right off the bone and remains meaty and juicy. You can serve these as is, laden with smoke and char, or brush them with your favorite BBQ sauce or mustard. I typically round this meal out with a potato salad and baked beans. Leftovers go well, bone removed, on a sandwich of white bread, onions, and pickles.

Serves 4	Hands on: 20 minutes	Total: 60 minutes

- ☐ 4 pork blade steaks, about ½ inch thick
- ☐ ½ tablespoon kosher salt

- ☐ ½ tablespoon fresh-cracked black pepper

- ☐ Barbecue sauce or mustard, to serve (optional)

1 Open the bottom vent of a charcoal grill completely. Pour a large pile of charcoal onto the bottom grate on one side of the grill. Light a charcoal chimney starter filled halfway with additional charcoal. When the coals are covered with gray ash, pour them onto the pile of existing charcoal. Adjust the vents, nearly closing them, as needed to maintain an internal temperature of 225° to 250°F. Coat the top grate with oil; place on the grill. (If using a gas grill or smoker, preheat to low [225° to 250°F] on one side.)

2 Arrange the pork steaks on a baking sheet, and season both sides of the pork with the salt and pepper.

3 Place the steaks on the grill over direct heat, cover, and cook, undisturbed, for 20 minutes. Flip the steaks and continue to cook for 25 to 30 minutes, until the internal temperature reaches 160°F. Brush with barbecue sauce or mustard, if desired. Serve.

GRILLED CHICKEN WINGS

While there might be a thousand different ways to cook up a chicken wing, my preference is to always have them bite-off-the-bone tender with crispy skin. I usually source whole chicken wings, using my cleaver to find the joint between the wingette/flat and drumette and slice them into separate portions. From there, I will also remove the tip from the wingette/flat and store it in the freezer with my other trimmings to use for stock (see page 320). Though wings are traditionally fried, I typically smoke my wings for tenderness and follow that by grilling them over direct heat to crisp up the skin. What I like about Tommie's method, however, is that the twenty-four-hour marinade in the Italian dressing does most of the "tender" work for me—meaning I can skip the extra hour or so of smoking the wings and just put them over a medium fire, turning regularly to prevent burning, until the chicken is cooked through with that crispy skin. Not only does the marinade add its zingy flavor, it also ensures that the chicken remains moist and tender. You could, of course, toss these in a sauce of your liking, but I prefer to serve them as is, rounded out with some carrot and celery sticks and blue cheese or ranch dressing.

Serves 4–6	Hands on: 1 hour	Total: 25 hours

- ☐ 48 chicken wings, ideally an even mix of wingettes/flats and drumettes
- ☐ 2 cups Italian salad dressing

- ☐ 2 tablespoons kosher salt
- ☐ Carrot and celery sticks, to serve

- ☐ House Blue Cheese (page 284), or store-bought blue cheese or ranch dressing, to serve

1 Place the chicken wings into a large plastic zip container, add the Italian dressing, close, and toss to ensure the dressing is evenly distributed. Place the wings in the refrigerator for 24 hours.

2 Open the bottom vent of a charcoal grill completely. Light a charcoal chimney starter filled with charcoal. When the coals are covered with gray ash, pour them onto the bottom grate of the grill, and then push to one side of the grill. Adjust the vents as needed to maintain an internal temperature of 350° to 375°F. Coat the top grate with oil; place on the grill. (If using a gas grill, preheat to medium [350° to 375°F] on one side.)

3 Remove the wings from the dressing, discard the dressing, rinse the wings, and pat dry. Arrange the wings on a baking sheet and season both sides with the kosher salt.

4 Place the wings on the grill over indirect heat and cook for 10 to 15 minutes. Flip the wings and place over direct heat. Grill for 6 to 8 minutes per side, being careful not to burn. Continue to cook, shifting the wings from direct heat (to crisp the skin) to indirect heat as needed to prevent from burning, for 35 to 45 minutes, or until the wings are crispy and internal temperature reaches 165°F.

5 Remove the wings from the grill and arrange on a large platter with the carrot and celery sticks and blue cheese or ranch dressing. Serve.

PLANKED SALMON (with)
SMOKED HIBACHI SEASONING

One of the things Tommie, my local Kroger butcher, likes best is working in front of the service counter, stocking the meats and lunch items, as it gives him a great chance to be on the floor, serving his customers. But that doesn't mean he doesn't know his way around the back of the counter. With such an array of goods in the store, many items are preseasoned for shoppers' convenience, and this salmon recipe is a happy accident. The sweet and smoky hibachi seasoning blend wasn't always used on the salmon, but once Tommie gave it a spin at home, it became an instant hit, eventually finding its way onto the salmon for sale in the seafood case. You can purchase the seasoning at most stores, or online, to use as a catchall blend on steaks, chicken, pork, and seafood. Planking, or resting and cooking the salmon on a cedar plank, adds just a touch more smoky flavor, allowing the salmon to cook gently and remain moist and tender. If you don't have planks handy, you can simply place the salmon, skin sides down, over indirect heat on the grill.

Serves 4	Hands on: 20 minutes	Total: 45 minutes

- ☐ Four 6- to 8-ounce center-cut salmon fillets, skin on and patted dry
- ☐ 3 tablespoons hibachi seasoning, such as Simply Asia brand

- ☐ 2 cedar grilling planks, each large enough to hold 2 salmon fillets, soaked for 30 minutes in water

- ☐ 1 lemon, sliced
- ☐ Finely chopped fresh chives, as garnish

1 Open the bottom vent of a charcoal grill completely. Pour a large pile of charcoal onto the bottom grate on one side of the grill. Light a charcoal chimney starter filled halfway with additional charcoal. When the coals are covered with gray ash, pour them onto the pile of existing charcoal. Adjust the vents, nearly closing them, as needed to maintain an internal temperature of 225° to 250°F. Coat the top grate with oil; place on the grill. (If using a gas grill or smoker, preheat to low [225° to 250°F] on one side.)

2 Dredge the salmon fillets in the seasoning, ensuring the top and sides are well coated.

Place 2 salmon fillets, skin sides down, on a cedar plank, and arrange half of the lemon slices around the salmon. Repeat with the remaining salmon and lemon on the second plank.

3 Place the salmon planks on the grill over indirect heat, cover the grill, and cook, rotating the planks on occasion, for 35 to 40 minutes, until the internal temperature of the center of the fillets reaches 140°F for medium.

4 Remove the cedar planks from the grill and transfer the fillets and lemon slices to plates. Garnish with chives. Serve.

GRILLED RIB EYE STEAKS with GARLIC BUTTER

This is the moment we've been waiting for—thick-cut, beefy rib eye steaks grilled to medium-rare perfection and slathered with a house-made garlic butter. Let me tell you something: You cook this steak and serve it to a stranger and you'll have a friend for life. I like to make extra quantities of the garlicky butter. That way, I have plenty around for not just this recipe but to spread on bread, add to pastas, or serve with other grilled proteins throughout the week. Be sure to request a thick-cut steak from your butcher, about 1½ inches, as that thickness allows you to develop a strong sear on both sides without worrying about overcooking the center of the meat. Over a hot fire, this recipe comes together rather quickly, so don't forget the most important part: allowing five to ten minutes for the steaks to rest after they come off the fire. That cools the steaks down enough so that the butter is just melting as you serve it to your guests.

Serves 4	Hands on: 35 minutes	Total: 3 hours

GARLIC BUTTER
- ☐ 8 tablespoons unsalted butter, softened
- ☐ 2 cloves garlic, finely minced
- ☐ 2 tablespoons finely minced fresh parsley
- ☐ 1 teaspoon lemon juice

- ☐ 1 pinch kosher salt

STEAKS
- ☐ Four 12-ounce thick-cut rib eye steaks, about 1½ inches thick
- ☐ 1½ tablespoons kosher salt

- ☐ 2 tablespoons vegetable oil
- ☐ 1 tablespoon flaky sea salt
- ☐ Chopped fresh parsley, as garnish
- ☐ Toasted bread slices, to serve

1 A few hours prior to grilling, make the garlic butter. Combine the butter, garlic, parsley, lemon juice, and salt in a small bowl and use a fork to mash the mixture together. Cover the bowl and place it in the refrigerator.

2 One hour before grilling, place the steaks on a baking sheet. Dry brine the steaks by seasoning each side with some of the kosher salt. Allow the steaks to rest at room temperature for 1 hour.

3 Open the bottom vent of a charcoal grill completely. Light a charcoal chimney starter filled with charcoal. When the coals are covered with gray ash, pour them onto the bottom grate of the grill, and then push to one side of the grill. Adjust the vents as needed to maintain an internal temperature of 500° to 550°F. Coat the top grate with oil; place on the grill. (If using a gas grill, preheat to high [500° to 550°F] on one side.)

4 Rinse the steaks with cold running water and pat dry. Drizzle them with the oil on both sides and add the steaks to the grill over direct heat. Grill the steaks, uncovered, for 2 minutes. Rotate the steaks 30 degrees and cook for an additional 2 minutes. Rotate the steaks 30 degrees again and cook for 2 more minutes. Flip the steaks and cook over indirect heat for another 3 to 5 minutes, until the internal temperature reaches 130°F for medium rare. Remove the steaks from the grill and let rest for 5 to 10 minutes.

5 Serve the steaks with a generous sprinkle of the sea salt over the top and a dollop of garlic butter. Garnish the steaks with fresh chopped parsley and serve with toasted bread on the side.

JARED AUERBACH, RED'S BEST

Boston, MA

"Man, I'm serious. I grew up with no connection to this industry. No parents, no grandparents, nobody I knew had any ties to fishing. Heck, even none of my friends had boats," says Jared Auerbach, founder of Red's Best in Boston, Massachusetts. Sitting in his bright corner office atop the famous Boston Fish Pier, I'm astonished to learn that Mr. Auerbach lacks any of the family DNA that one might think is required to start a fishing empire. But what Jared might lack in generational ties, he's made up for with an insatiable ability to connect with people.

"I'll show you," Jared reiterates to me nearly every couple of minutes, making our way down a stairwell. His Xtratuf fishing boots ping the metal stairs as we pass a sign that reads to all employees that hard work and respect are required at Red's Best. When we reach the ground floor of the pier, a buzzing operation of trucks, equipment, and employees visually zigzags the warehouse, and the clean scent of the sea permeates the entire facility. "These are the people that make everything happen," Jared says. "I care about these people."

Within a few minutes of meeting Jared, I quickly realize that he makes friends with everybody. Growing up in Newton, a small suburb just outside of Boston, Jared was raised in a family of well-educated parents—his father a neurologist and his mother with a PhD. "Since I was a little kid, I always loved the idea of being able to harvest my own food," he says. That habit was fostered on Crystal Lake, a "great pond" tucked away in the trees of a residential landscape, where Jared first learned how to fish.

"I'll never forget this one day—heck, my mom still tells the story," shares Jared. "I came home from a day at Crystal Lake, beaming with pride with a sunfish still on the end of my line, telling my mom that I had provided the family dinner."

Before Jared left for college at University of Colorado Boulder, a family friend gifted him a book, *Into the Wild* by Jon Krakauer, which ignited his heart's desire to explore the vast expanse of Alaska. The summer after graduation provided the right time to pursue the Alaskan dream, and as I learn in my time with him, Jared never shies away from being uncomfortable. "I knew nobody, man. So I called, emailed, networked, and contacted as many people as I could. I did whatever it took to find my way to Alaska." The persistence paid off when a friend of a friend shared a potential opening on a fifty-eight-foot purse seiner stationed out of Gig Harbor, Washington. "I called the captain, and without any promises of work, I drove to Washington with the mindset that I would do anything for the experience."

Upon arrival, the captain of the *Sea Gem* offered to put Jared to work. Jared spent his first few days sanding the deck of the boat. "It's the kind of story you would expect written into a movie," says Jared, "but within a few weeks of doing odds and ends, I proved that I was ready to go to sea." It took three days going eight miles per hour to make the trek from Washington to Petersburg, Alaska. Over the next few months, Jared slowly shed his green by gaining expertise and respect on the boat. When the summer gig ended, he returned to Boston, working as a jobber on the docks, awaiting his next of three summers in Alaska.

But in the spring of 2006, Jared accepted a job to settle down, teaching high school math. "I was young and strong. I loved the work, and I also admired the men and women who harvested food. But it was a time, man, when regulation and other things started showing its teeth. Nobody seemed happy, and I wasn't sure if this was my path," Jared humbly admits. Despite the comfort and steady hum of teaching, the sea still beckoned. "I was up at night messing around with seafood entrepreneurship, tinkering on my ideas for years," says Jared. "In 2008 I drew my line in the sand—and that's when I started Red's Best."

To understand the entrepreneurial undertaking, one must also grasp the industry. As we make our way around the operation, from unloading, shipping, butchering, and processing areas, Jared consistently interrupts my industry education with compliments to his employees, a few phone calls from local fishermen, and a stop to show me the local haddock that's sitting on ice.

"It all starts with the fishermen—those men and women going out each day to supply the market. When they come in, there's gotta be somebody to accept the fish. These are the unloaders who take the fish without paying, until they work with the market makers who set the price on behalf of the fishermen to sell at fair market or better. From there, you have combinations of processors, distributors, and wholesalers, who eventually put the fish into the hands of consumption. It's a wicked business," says Jared.

I jokingly have to admit that it's the first "wicked" I've gotten out of him thus far. I digress.

Jared made his debut working as an unloader, arranging to pick up and unload fish from small boats out of Woods Hole, Massachusetts, earning the trust that he could move the product quickly and at a fair price to the fishermen. From there, he would make markets at night from his one-bedroom apartment in Southy, calling and vetting prices to move as much fish as quickly as possible.

"We got really good at unloading lots of small boats," says Jared—keen also to acknowledge childhood friend and CFO Adam Barr, who helped create a software system to manage the unloading, compliance, and aggregation of supply. "Our competitors have been around since the 1800s, man. They only have to unload one boat with everything they need. We had to find a way to unload a lot more smaller boats, effectively maintaining the trust of thousands of fishermen, boasting better quality, fresher fish due to the shorter duration of the trips, as well as the local pride of the fishermen," says Jared.

The technology was a differentiator, but it's the human element that attracts me the most. "It's all about the fishermen," says Jared. "They are the ones who trust me to take care of them in a

variable supply market, with essentially fixed demand." The CEO side starts to shine, even though Jared is wearing an orange pair of Grundéns that fall outside the typical fashion of the role. "I'll never forget taking a microeconomics class in college, and I knew I needed to find a way to create flexible demand," he says.

"Our technology allowed us to become storytellers and brand builders." For example, Red's Best was one of the first to enable a QR code that would allow the end user to know the fisherman, the boat, and the exact catch on hand. This experiment took hold with Harvard University's dining system. Traditionally, menus and markets were set months in advance—and with variable supply and pricing, demand remained relatively flat. When students demanded better, Jared stepped in with a catch-of-the-day program to sell the university fresh fish, often nontraditional species such as dogfish, porgy, skate, and mackerel. These newly "made markets" allowed Jared to provide better terms to the fishermen without placing a ceiling on their ability to still profit from the big catch.

"Now that we are over a decade in, we are starting to do the fun stuff," says Jared as clouds of "smoke" reminiscent of something out of *Back to the Future* billow out of a -120°F super freezer. Jared hands me a perfect portion of toro from the belly of a bluefin tuna. "I'm really excited about this—I used to catch a striper right off the dock

and eat it. But honestly, man, I like the flavor and texture I get from this 'superfrozen' stuff nearly as much. This allows me to once again create flexible demand by expanding the market to serve perfect bluefin from Massachusetts to guys like you living in Nashville," says Jared. "I'll show you."

He suggests packing our things and heading over to the Boston Public Market, where Red's Best has a retail footprint for customers to purchase fish or enjoy a cooked-to-order scallop roll, among other specialties. As we are leaving, stomachs grumbling, I notice dozens of pictures of local fishermen—their faces and names proudly adorn the hallways of Red's Best corporate offices.

"We work with thousands of fishermen, and each and every day, they have a choice who they want to sell to. There are no contracts, only trust," says Jared as he stares into one of the photos. "Every day I wake up, I enjoy the challenge of having my back up against the wall."

"What a life, what a story, what a commitment," I say.

"Yeah, man," says Jared. "I'll always be here for the fishermen, for my people. I'm not going anywhere." ∎

SCALLOP ROLLS with CORNICHON TARTAR SAUCE

When I asked Jared Auerbach, CEO and founder of Red's Best, about his cooking skills, he laughed and told me that he's the guy who brings the fish to the party. Fair statement. But he shared that everything that's cooked at Red's Best locations, including the Boston Public Market and Boston Logan Airport, is done to honor and celebrate the ingredient. I was instantly intrigued by the scallop roll, the lesser-known cousin of the New England lobster roll, so I suggested we give it a shot. Boy, am I glad I did. The beautiful, local sea scallops are quickly fried, leaving them sweet in taste and nearly medium rare in texture. When the scallops are dressed with a tangy house-made tartar sauce and sandwiched in a soft, buttered roll, I'm pretty sure this beats the lobster version.

Serves 2	Hands on: 10 minutes	Total: 10 minutes

CORNICHON TARTAR SAUCE
- ☐ 2 cups mayonnaise, preferably Duke's brand
- ☐ 2 tablespoons finely minced cornichons
- ☐ 1 tablespoon capers, drained and finely minced
- ☐ 2 teaspoons lemon juice
- ☐ 1 tablespoon finely chopped fresh parsley

SCALLOP ROLLS
- ☐ Vegetable oil, for frying
- ☐ 10 ounces sea scallops, foot removed and patted dry
- ☐ 2 cups clam fry mix, such as Golden Dipt
- ☐ 2 tablespoons unsalted butter
- ☐ 2 top-split hot dog buns, such as Piantedosi brand
- ☐ Lemon wedges, to serve

1 Prepare the tartar sauce. In a large bowl, mix together the mayonnaise, cornichons, capers, lemon juice, and parsley until thoroughly combined. Cover and keep cold in the refrigerator. Note: This recipe will produce an excess yield of tartar sauce, which can be stored up to 10 days in the refrigerator for other use.

2 Fill a dutch oven with vegetable oil, roughly 3 inches of oil when measured from the bottom of the pot. Over medium heat, bring the temperature of the oil to 350°F.

3 Lightly dredge the scallops in the clam fry mix, shaking off the excess to ensure a very light coating. Place all the scallops into the oil and fry for 2 minutes, turning occasionally to ensure the scallops do not stick together. Remove the scallops from the oil and drain on a paper towel–lined plate.

4 Meanwhile, place a skillet over medium heat, add the butter, and let melt. Place the buns in the skillet and turn the buns in the butter to coat and slightly toast.

5 Slather a generous portion of the tartar sauce in each of the buns. Divide the scallops between the buns. Serve with lemon wedges.

FRIED CALAMARI ⬤with
CHERRY PEPPER AIOLI

"People shouldn't be afraid of squid. There's so much of it and it's easy to cook," says Jared Auerbach, founder of Red's Best. In New England waters, Loligo is the most commonly found species, and most markets and fishmongers sell the tubes and tentacles already cleaned. I prefer to buy them cleaned and whole, butchering them into slices at home, as the presliced tubes can be a bit tougher in texture.

At Red's, the sliced tubes and tentacles are soaked in buttermilk for a few hours to help make them even more tender and delicious. The key here is to get your hands involved in the dredging process—you want to make sure the mix gets into the tentacles, as well as into the inner portion of the rings, so spend a few moments rubbing the dredge into the squid. After that, these little guys fry up in just one minute. They are delicately tender and delicious on their own, but the cherry pepper aioli takes these to the next level.

Serves 2	Hands on: 10 minutes	Total: 2 hours

FRIED CALAMARI
- ☐ 1 cup buttermilk
- ☐ 1 pound fresh squid, tubes cut into ½-inch-thick slices and tentacles portioned into bite-sized pieces
- ☐ Vegetable oil, for frying

- ☐ 2 cups clam fry mix, such as Golden Dipt
- ☐ Lemon wedges, to serve

CHERRY PEPPER AIOLI
- ☐ 1 clove garlic, finely minced
- ☐ 1 tablespoon lemon juice

- ☐ ¼ cup finely minced cherry peppers
- ☐ 1 teaspoon smoked paprika
- ☐ 2 cups mayonnaise, preferably Duke's brand
- ☐ ¼ teaspoon kosher salt

1 Place the buttermilk into a medium bowl, add the squid, and toss until incorporated. Cover the mixture and place in the refrigerator for at least 1 hour, up to 4 hours.

2 Prepare the aioli. In a medium bowl, mix the garlic, lemon juice, cherry peppers, paprika, mayonnaise, and salt together until thoroughly combined. Cover and keep cold in the refrigerator. Note: The recipe will produce an excess yield of aioli, which can be stored up to 10 days in the refrigerator for other use.

3 Fill a dutch oven with vegetable oil, roughly 3 inches of oil when measured from the bottom of the pot. Over medium heat, bring the temperature of the oil to 350°F.

4 Remove the squid from the buttermilk mixture, discarding the buttermilk. Dredge the squid in the clam fry mix, making sure the coating reaches all parts of the tentacles as well as the insides of the rings. Place the squid into the oil and fry 1 minute, turning to ensure the pieces do not stick together. Remove the squid from the oil and drain on a paper towel–lined plate.

5 Arrange the calamari on a serving platter with the cherry pepper aioli on the side. Serve with lemon wedges.

CRISPY FISH SANDWICHES

One can't visit New England without getting a bite of local cod or haddock, the traditional varieties most commonly harvested from the surrounding areas. In this version, we opted for the haddock since it's what had just come into the shop. At the Red's Best Boston Public Market counter, the fish is labeled and tagged to celebrate the fishermen who caught it. The haddock used for this sandwich on the day of my visit came from Gloucester, Massachusetts, and was harvested by the *Santa Rita* fishing boat.

You can source sustainably caught fish from Red's Best at their market location or online—or, of course, from your own supplier of choice. The fish meets a batter that is made better with local beer, and it's fried crispy to order. America has its hamburgers, but New England has its fish sandwiches. I suggest doubling down on the beer, enjoying a Narragansett or two on the side while you chow down.

Serves 2	Hands on: 10 minutes	Total: 15 minutes

BEER BATTER
- ☐ 2½ pounds fish fry mix, such as Golden Dipt, plus more as needed
- ☐ One 16-ounce can Narragansett lager
- ☐ 2 cups water, plus more as needed

FISH SANDWICHES
- ☐ Vegetable oil, for frying
- ☐ Two 5- to 6-ounce haddock fillets, or cod fillets
- ☐ Cornichon Tartar Sauce (page 74)

- ☐ 2 country rolls, such as Piantedosi brand, or hamburger buns, warmed
- ☐ Romaine lettuce leaves, to serve (optional)
- ☐ Sliced tomatoes, to serve (optional)

1 Prepare the beer batter. Add the fry mix to a medium mixing bowl. Add the beer, whisking vigorously, followed by the water, continuing to whisk until combined. The batter should coat the back of a spoon. If it's too thin, add more fry mix, and if it's too dry, add more water. Note: The batter will yield enough for 8 to 10 sandwiches, or it can be used as a batter for other seafood items such as shrimp and scallops. The excess batter can be kept, covered, in the refrigerator up to 2 days—mix the reserved batter well before reusing, to incorporate air back into the mixture prior to dredging.

2 Fill a dutch oven with vegetable oil, roughly 3 inches measured from the bottom of the pot. Over medium heat, bring the temperature of the oil to 350°F.

3 Dredge the fish fillets in the beer batter and place in the oil. Fry the fillets for 2½ to 3 minutes, turning once. Remove the fillets from the oil when crispy and golden brown, and drain on a paper towel–lined plate.

4 To assemble the sandwiches, spread a generous layer of tartar sauce on both of the split sides of the rolls. Place a fish fillet on the bottom portion of each roll, add lettuce and tomato, if desired, and finish with the tops of the rolls. Serve.

SALMON POKE-STYLE BOWLS

While Red's Best features an array of cooked-to-order items, one of the most popular to-go dishes is their poke-style bowl. Fresh salmon is cubed and served alongside fresh cucumber, pickled toppings, nori, and the like, and made into a hearty meal when served over sushi rice. The visual presentation of the offering is stunning, and the flavors come together into a seamless and delicious healthy lunch or dinner. Typically you can find most of the ingredients already prepared, but if you wish to do some of your own pickling or grating of wasabi at home, be my guest. The star of the show is the fresh salmon. The rest is supporting the cast. Get it?

Serves 1	Hands on: 10 minutes	Total: 10 minutes

- ☐ 1½ cups cooked and chilled short-grain white rice, or other rice
- ☐ ¼ pound fresh salmon, cut into ¼-inch cubes

- ☐ ¼ small cucumber, thinly sliced
- ☐ 1 tablespoon thinly sliced pickled shallots
- ☐ 1 tablespoon thinly sliced pickled ginger

- ☐ 1 teaspoon prepared wasabi
- ☐ Sliced nori
- ☐ 1 teaspoon toasted sesame seeds

Place the chilled rice in the bottom of a small serving bowl. Artfully add the salmon, cucumber, shallots, ginger, wasabi, and nori around the bowl. Sprinkle with the sesame seeds. Serve.

BLUEFIN TORO CRUDO

Technology and innovation are not only on the supply side of Red's Best. Founder Jared and operations manager Ryan Rasys also have fun experimenting with their catch. In 2019 they bought laboratory-rated, ultralow-temp freezers, boasting temps as low as -120°F, and began superfreezing portions of fish. The idea was to perfectly preserve and, in some instances, enhance the flavor and texture of the fish for folks to enjoy all around the country (these super-frozen creations can be purchased and shipped directly to you from Red's online store).

Toro comes from the belly of a bluefin tuna, and due to its proximity to the thinner portion of skin, it contains a good bit of fat to help insulate the fish. That fat translates into incredibly rich flavor and a butter-like consistency. Rasys treats this beautiful portion of fish as it should be treated—basically on its own, adorned with just a few simple enhancements such as lemon zest, salt, and scallion. If this is the future of food, we are all in good hands.

Serves 2	Hands on: 10 minutes	Total: 2 hours, 10 minutes

- ☐ One 4- to 5-ounce portion ultrafrozen bluefin toro
- ☐ 1 teaspoon lemon zest
- ☐ 1 teaspoon thinly sliced scallion, cut on the bias
- ☐ 1 teaspoon very good quality olive oil
- ☐ 1 pinch sea salt

1 The toro portions come ultrafrozen, so place the portion on a counter for approximately 2 hours to thaw.

2 Thinly slice the toro into ⅛-inch-thick slices and arrange on a serving platter.

3 Sprinkle the toro with the zest and scallion. Drizzle the fish with the olive oil, and season with the salt. Serve.

LEIGHANN SMITH AND DANIEL JACKSON, PIECE OF MEAT

New Orleans, LA

"We're just a bunch of shifty critters, out here trying to have a good time," says Leighann Smith, co-owner and butcher of Piece of Meat in New Orleans, Louisiana. Standing on Bienville Street in the Mid-City neighborhood, Leighann, her co-owner, Daniel Jackson, and I are enjoying just "one more" cold beer after a day of butchering, cooking, eating, and drinking. After all, this is New Orleans, and there's always room for one more anything.

But in this city, not everything follows a script. Take for example the car-sized hole in the street that's outside the entrance to the shop. "These guys came from the city and dug that up three months ago, saying they'd be back on Friday to fix it," says Leighann with a sarcastic cadence. Dan and I try to make the most of the functioning dysfunction, suggesting that the pair go so far as to cook and host their next famous pig roast in said hole.

But changes and flexibility are required in this city. I learn that firsthand when Leighann calls me just days prior to my arrival to let me know that the shop would be closed for remodeling during my visit. I roll with it, suggesting that we press on without the customers. Turns out, not having a set plan has its benefits, and I spend my day discovering the craft and food that has made Piece of Meat a mainstay not only in New Orleans but throughout the rest of the country. While I'm reveling in my own touristic gluttony (I'm jonesing for another bologna sandwich), I don't think the neighbors got the message. I soon find out that being "closed" is also off-script for these two.

Customers descend upon the shop throughout the day, and each are greeted as though they are family. "Dan, give those guys the steaks—the big ones," says Leighann as a local couple walks in to pick up last-minute items for an evening dinner. I'm not even sure they pay for the 2½-inch-thick grass-fed rib eyes I'd watched Dan cut by hand just hours earlier. Another customer, also seemingly unaware of the closed status, pops his head in, requesting heart and liver for a carnivore diet he's "trying out." Leighann and Dan seem to act like this request is routine, scrambling to serve. I slowly sense that the doors here are never closed, and Piece of Meat remains always open, serving as a local heartbeat in a city that never sleeps.

"I hired him," says Leighann when I ask how the duo got their start. A native of California's Bay Area, Leighann got serious about her culinary exploits around the age of eighteen, bouncing

84 BUTCHER ON THE BLOCK

between the San Francisco and Miami food scene until she found her way to New Orleans. "I didn't like my boyfriend or my job," she says, "so, I came to New Orleans, found Mimi's in the Marigny, and I've never wanted to be anywhere else."

Timing is everything, and within four months of settling in New Orleans, Leighann got her start as a sous chef at the venerable institution that is Cochon, but begged for a meat-cutting job, even though she knew it would be drastically harder, with less pay. She got more than she bargained for by taking over the meat program, a period she describes as an interesting learning curve of anxiety while mastering the details of the trade, including the making of cured meats.

As for Dan, he holds on to a part of his home, proudly sporting a Buffalo Bills cap, although he's been in New Orleans since attending college at Tulane University. He was an English and philosophy major, but his heart tugged more toward glassblowing, as it provided an outlet "outside of reading books and writing papers." While spending a decade or so in and around art studios, Dan got his start in retail, butchering at the Whole Foods on Magazine Street and finally winding up at Cochon Butcher, where Leighann hired him on as part of the team.

But the dream for Leighann was always to open something of her own, so she recruited Dan to join a local start-up market, and that began their journey of entrepreneurship. I quickly learn that the market gig was a stepping-stone to another side hustle. The two purchased their first Black Warrior smoker, parking it outside of bars and events to serve up whole pigs, sausage sandwiches, or crawfish. "I was bartending two days a week, and selling sausage on sidewalks the rest of my time," says Leighann. "It was the most money I had ever made in my life."

While on a camping trip, a friend of a friend who owned real estate expressed interest in using some vacant property to create a local butcher shop—Leighann caught word, and together with Dan, Piece of Meat was born in 2018.

Piece of Meat is more than just a butcher shop or a restaurant, for that matter: It is uniquely an experience. "If you come into the shop any day, there's a good chance you will likely see an

animal head," says Leighann. Her message is true. The custom Boos butcher block stands in the center of the room where the work of whole animal butchering takes place, while diners sit around an open bar amid the meat cases and aging room, enjoying a snack with the show. I take it all in stride as a culinary lesson—after all, Dan says, "Quality is a top priority. The main reason why we do what we do is to educate why people should eat local, from small farms—to know where your meat comes from."

Beyond the commitment to quality and locality, I ask the pair what is necessary to become great at the craft, and Leighann tells me decisively that it's all about "drive and desire." "Butchering is typically a lower-paying, labor-intensive job. It has to be a passion project or it doesn't work. Just look at me—I've been doing this over ten years

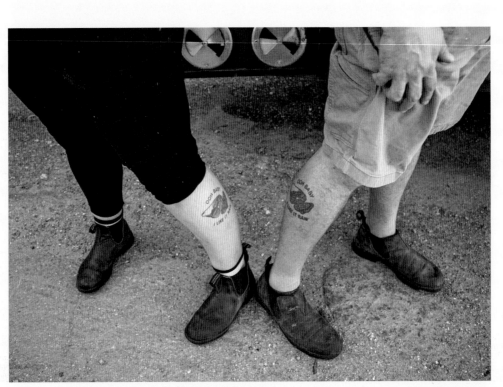

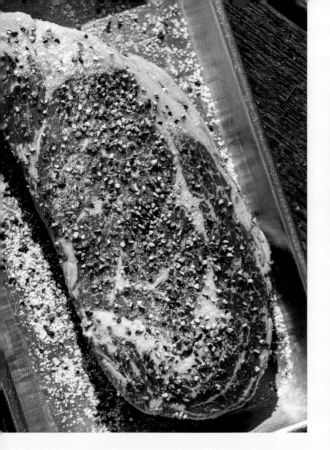

and I've not even scratched the surface on all there is to learn."

"It's gotta be hands-on," says Dan as he relays the difficulty of the physical aspect of the job. "Sometimes you don't know what you are doing until you get an animal on the board and a knife in your hand. Since the beginning, Leighann has had the vision and ambition. She shared her knowledge to help me learn by doing."

Leighann counters by telling me that the two "work together so well because they are polar opposites," and she points out the fact that Dan is a good "listener, even-keeled, and a hard worker."

Despite the practical pairing, business remains tough, often supplemented by the better restaurant margins that must be coupled with artistic butchery to survive. In a historic town like New Orleans, butcher shops once dominated a local block-by-block perspective, but nowadays, as Dan says, "We are one of the only true butcher shops left."

New Orleans remains a uniquely American yet foreign city, forging old traditions against new, surrounded by a complex milieu of experience and atmosphere. My time with Leighann and Dan reminds me that we are all advocates of moving forward while honoring the past. I share this observation with Dan and Leighann—perhaps it's the moment, maybe it's the beers, but Leighann shares a thought that sums up the time we've savored.

"This is our little place, our mission. One at a time, we have made a friend everywhere," she says.

Imagine if we all strived to do the same. ◾

BOUDIN EGG ROLLS

Travel and experience are sometimes the best motivation, but that's really the truth when it comes to this Piece of Meat classic. As co-owner Leighann shares, "I was driving to Shreveport, pulling over at Opelousas, and I stopped at Billy's to pick up some cracklin'. They had this concoction of boudin—a Creole classic that blends together portions of liver, spice, and rice (pardon the rhyme)—made into an eggroll." While boudin is traditionally served in link form, the egg roll format turned out to be the perfect medium for Leighann to enjoy. "After eating a couple of those egg rolls, I was an hour's drive away from my destination, but I actually pulled around (adding another few more hours to the commute), and drove back for more," says Leighann.

You can now enjoy Leighann's own interpretation of the dish, as the house-made boudin is formed around a big hunk of pepper jack cheese and then wrapped in a wonton wrapper and deep-fried. You can source the duo's boudin online or at local markets, or sub it out with your own variety.

Serves 4	Hands on: 15 minutes	Total: 25 to 30 minutes

SRIRACHA MAYO
- ☐ 1 cup mayonnaise, preferably Duke's brand
- ☐ ¼ cup sriracha

EGGROLLS
- ☐ Vegetable oil, for frying
- ☐ 2 links boudin, 4 to 6 ounces each, cut in half, casings removed

- ☐ 8 ounces pepper jack cheese, cut into four 2 x ½-inch sticks
- ☐ 4 large wonton wrappers
- ☐ 1 large egg, beaten

1 Prepare the sriracha mayo. In a small bowl, stir together the mayonnaise and sriracha until evenly combined. Cover and place in the refrigerator until ready to use. The mayo will keep, refrigerated, for up to 1 week.

2 Add vegetable oil to a dutch oven until it measures approximately 4 inches from the bottom of the pot. Over medium heat, bring the temperature of the oil to 335°F.

3 Make a patty out of each half link of boudin. Place a stick of the pepper jack cheese into each patty and, using your hands, form the boudin around the cheese to create a cigar-like shape. Lay out the wonton wrappers. Place a patty, long edge facing, about 1 inch from the bottom of a wrapper. Roll the patty in the wrapper to cover completely, fold the ends into each other, and continue to roll until the wrapper is tightly secured around the boudin to create an egg roll–style shape. Use the beaten egg to seal the wrapper, and repeat with the remaining patties and wrappers.

4 Place 2 of the egg rolls into the heated oil and fry for 5 to 7 minutes, turning on occasion, until golden and crispy. Remove from the oil and drain on a paper towel–lined plate. Repeat with the remaining egg rolls. Allow the egg rolls to cool for 3 to 5 minutes, slice on the bias, and serve with the sriracha mayo for dipping.

SMOKED PORK CHOPS
with GRITS and RED-EYE GRAVY

On Saturdays and Sundays, Piece of Meat transforms from a daily butcher shop and casual eatery to a full-on brunch experience. As co-owners Dan and Leighann share, this dish serves as a regular favorite, as the coffee-spiked gravy, creamy grits, and smoky pork chop allow you to forget nearly whatever happened the night before, which comes in handy in a city like New Orleans. The key here is an aromatic brine, in which the pork chops sit for a couple of hours to take on even more deliciousness. The pork is then smoked until it reaches a rare temperature, and seared off in cast-iron for good measure and to catch its drippings for the delicious gravy. For the comforting grits, Leighann shares a Southern secret: "I use an offensive amount of butter." Ain't nothing wrong with that.

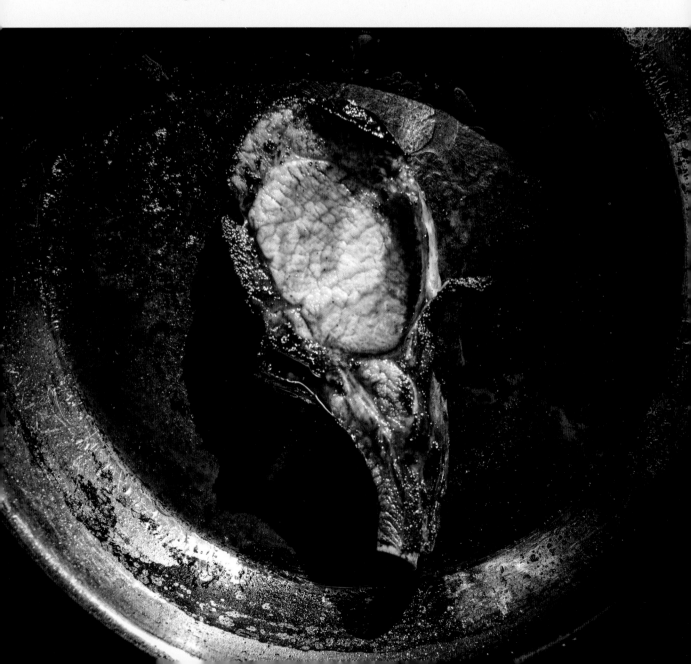

PORK CHOPS AND BRINE

- ☐ 1 cup kosher salt
- ☐ ½ cup granulated sugar
- ☐ ½ cup packed brown sugar
- ☐ 8 cups water
- ☐ 4 sprigs fresh thyme
- ☐ 2 cloves garlic, sliced
- ☐ 2 bay leaves
- ☐ 1 tablespoon whole black peppercorns
- ☐ ½ tablespoon crushed red pepper
- ☐ Ice, for cooling

- ☐ Four 8-ounce bone-in pork chops, approximately 1½ inches thick
- ☐ 2 tablespoons unsalted butter

GRITS

- ☐ 4 cups whole milk, plus more as needed
- ☐ 1 cup (2 sticks) unsalted butter
- ☐ 1 teaspoon kosher salt, plus more as needed

- ☐ ½ teaspoon fresh-cracked black pepper, plus more as needed
- ☐ 1 cup Ansom Mills grits, or stone-ground grits

GRAVY

- ☐ ½ cup black coffee
- ☐ ½ cup chicken stock
- ☐ 2 teaspoons granulated sugar

1 Place the salt, sugars, water, thyme, garlic, bay leaves, peppercorns, and red pepper into a large stockpot over medium heat. Bring the brine to a slow simmer, stir, and remove from the heat. Place ice cubes into the brine to cool completely. Add the chops and allow to sit for 2 hours, keeping the brine cold by adding more ice as necessary.

2 Preheat a smoker or grill to 200°F. Remove the chops from the brine, discard the brine, and pat the chops dry. Place the chops on the smoker over indirect heat and cook until their internal temperature is 125°F. Remove the chops from the smoker and place on a rimmed baking sheet to rest.

3 Meanwhile, make the grits. Combine the milk, ½ cup of the butter, the salt, and black pepper in a medium saucepan over medium-high heat. Once the mixture reaches a medium simmer, add the grits in a slow, steady stream, stirring constantly to ensure no lumps form. Reduce the heat to medium low. Whisk the grits regularly, adding a splash or two of milk as necessary to loosen the mixture until the grits

are tender, about 35 to 40 minutes. When the grits have reached a tender consistency, fold in the remaining ½ cup of butter and season with additional salt and black pepper to taste. Cover the grits and keep warm over low heat.

4 Finish the chops by melting the butter in a large cast-iron skillet over medium-high heat. Sear the pork chops, including the fat cap, for about 2 minutes per side, for a total of 6 to 7 minutes, or until golden brown. Remove the chops from the pan and keep warm.

5 Make the gravy. Deglaze the skillet by adding the coffee, using a wooden spoon to scrape up any of the browned bits from the bottom. Add the stock and sugar, return to a simmer, and reduce the mixture by half, 4 to 6 minutes. Remove the gravy from the heat and allow it to slightly cool and thicken.

6 Place a generous portion of the grits into four shallow serving bowls. Top with the seared pork chops and the gravy. Serve.

SEARED RIB EYES with BLUE CHEESE BUTTER and BEEF-FAT POTATOES

I get it, another rib eye recipe, right? But there's a reason the rib eye is the most beloved cut of butchers, because it combines the right mix of fat, muscle, and flavor to make it the coup de grâce of all things steak. Co-owner of Piece of Meat Leighann Smith takes it a step further, using tallow, or beef fat, which you can procure at any butcher, to make pillowy soft, decadent potatoes to serve alongside these perfectly cooked steaks. Everyone has their own method for the perfect steak preparation, but I appreciate Leighann's dedication to the black pepper, opting for a coarse-ground, almost brisket-like consistency to ensure you get that flavor and texture into each and every bite. The blue cheese butter is even more decadent. If you have some left over, it will keep for weeks, to use on that next steak-house night, or spread generously over warm, toasted bread the morning after.

Serves 4	Hands on: 1 hour	Total: 2 hours

BLUE CHEESE BUTTER
- ☐ 5 tablespoons unsalted butter, softened
- ☐ ¾ cup crumbled blue cheese

BEEF-FAT POTATOES
- ☐ 2½ pounds Yukon gold potatoes, diced into 1-inch cubes

- ☐ 3 cups beef tallow
- ☐ 2 sprigs fresh rosemary
- ☐ 4 sprigs fresh thyme
- ☐ 1 tablespoon kosher salt
- ☐ ½ tablespoon fresh-cracked black pepper

RIB EYE STEAKS
- ☐ 2 cups beef tallow

- ☐ Four 8- to 10-ounce rib eye steaks, 1¼ to 1½ inches thick
- ☐ 1 tablespoon kosher salt
- ☐ 1 tablespoon fresh-cracked black pepper
- ☐ 3 tablespoons unsalted butter

1 Make the blue cheese butter. In a small bowl, combine the butter with the cheese and mix until evenly combined. Turn the mixture out onto a sheet of plastic wrap and form the butter into a small log-like shape. Wrap it in the plastic wrap, and keep in the refrigerator until ready to use, up to 2 weeks.

2 Next, make the potatoes. Fill a dutch oven just over three-quarters with water and place over medium-high heat. When the water reaches a boil, carefully add the potatoes and parboil for 7 to 8 minutes, until the potatoes are just tender when punctured with a fork. Drain the potatoes in a colander and let them sit until the steam dissipates, 15 to 20 minutes.

3 Meanwhile, preheat the oven to 425°F. Add the tallow to a deep roasting pan, place it into the oven, and allow the tallow to completely render, until it begins to smoke, 8 to 10 minutes. Remove the pan from the oven, very carefully add the potatoes to the tallow, and toss to combine. Place the pan back in the oven and roast for 25 to 30 minutes, tossing on occasion, and adding the rosemary, thyme, salt, and pepper halfway through. The potatoes should be golden brown.

4 Make the steaks. Melt the tallow in a large cast-iron skillet over medium-high heat. Season the steaks liberally on both sides with the salt and pepper. Working in batches if necessary to avoid overcrowding, panfry the

steaks on both sides, including the fat cap, for 2 to 3 minutes, until the internal temperature reaches 125°F. Add the butter to the pan and allow it to quickly melt and foam. Using a spoon, pour the melted butter over the steaks and continue to cook for about 2 minutes, until the steaks reach an internal temperature of approximately 130°F. Remove the steaks from the heat and let rest, 5 minutes.

5 Serve the steaks alongside the roasted potatoes. Top the steaks with ½-inch-thick slices of the blue cheese butter.

PIECE OF MEAT BOLOGNA SANDWICHES

There is perhaps no sandwich more ubiquitous from my childhood than that of a bologna sandwich. Whether panfried with ketchup or served on spongy white bread with mustard and American cheese, this variety of processed "meat" is always something I've enjoyed. Nowadays bologna is getting the respect it deserves, especially co-owner of Piece of Meat shop Leighann Smith's version. It first caught fame when Mason Hereford, chef and owner of Turkey and the Wolf restaurant and James Beard nominee, used it in his homage to the bologna sandwich. While I visited the Piece of Meat shop in New Orleans, I witnessed Hereford on his weekly run, picking up more than a dozen milk cartons piled full of tubes of bologna just for one week's worth of service. While Turkey and the Wolf might have put this bologna on the critical culinary map, I lovingly also enjoy the version being served at Piece of Meat, made even more special with crispy fried onions and co-owner Dan's secret recipe for sweet BBQ sauce. You can purchase the famous bologna online, or source your own and slice it thick, to emulate this childhood, yet grown-up-appropriate, favorite.

Serves 2	Hands on: 30 minutes	Total: 1 hour

FRIED ONIONS
- ☐ Vegetable oil, for frying
- ☐ 1 cup all-purpose flour
- ☐ 1 cup cornstarch
- ☐ 1 Vidalia onion, sliced into very thin rings
- ☐ 1 teaspoon kosher salt

- ☐ 1 teaspoon fresh-cracked black pepper

BOLOGNA SANDWICHES
- ☐ 2 tablespoons unsalted butter
- ☐ 6 thick slices bologna, about ½ inch thick

- ☐ 4 slices provolone cheese
- ☐ 2 tablespoons sweet barbecue sauce
- ☐ 2 onion buns, sliced lengthwise
- ☐ 2 tablespoons mayonnaise, preferably Duke's brand
- ☐ 1 cup shaved iceberg lettuce

1 Add vegetable oil to a dutch oven until it measures approximately 3 inches from the bottom of the pot. Over medium heat, bring the temperature of the oil to 335°F.

2 In a shallow bowl, combine the flour and cornstarch until evenly mixed. Dredge the onion rings in the mixture and add to the heated oil, working in batches to not overcrowd. Fry, turning on occasion, until golden brown, about 3 minutes. Transfer the fried onion rings to a paper towel–lined plate and season evenly with the salt and pepper.

3 Meanwhile, start the sandwiches. Heat a large cast-iron skillet over medium heat and add the butter. When the butter begins to melt and foam, add the bologna and fry until slightly browned, about 3 minutes per side. Arrange 3 slices of the bologna so they overlap in the skillet. Repeat with the remaining 3 pieces of bologna. Top each bologna arrangement with 2 slices of cheese and 1 tablespoon of barbecue sauce. Turn off the heat, and allow the residual heat to melt the cheese.

4 Toast the buns, if desired, and divide and spread an even layer of mayonnaise over each half of the toasted buns. Divide the shaved lettuce between the bottoms of the buns, top each with bologna and melted cheese, and generously pile fried onions over that. Finish with the tops of the buns and serve.

KAREN BELL, BAVETTE LA BOUCHERIE

"Let me guess, you also worked for the CIA?" I ask Karen Bell in a half-joking manner as I'm scarfing down a paper-thin slice of beef carpaccio she's just put in front of me. It's an honest question, something I decide to ask since I'm finally getting a chance to sit down and enjoy a bit of respite after trancing around the butcher block all morning at Bavette La Boucherie in Milwaukee's Historic Third Ward. Just trying to keep up with Karen is its own task, but tracking down her story is even more challenging.

A Wisconsin native, Karen grew up in the idyllic Whitefish Bay area just north of Milwaukee. "I like to tell people that I fell in love with restaurants before I fell in love with cooking," says Karen. Though her parents had no connection to the restaurant industry, they made regular time to enjoy meals as a family, often cooked at home, or at former city institutions like Karl Ratzsch's. At sixteen, Karen landed her first waitressing job and instantly embraced the culture and atmosphere of the restaurant scene.

I start to follow the zigzag of Karen's time after graduating from college, building her gastronomic résumé in various restaurants from Chicago to San Francisco. But burnout is a real thing—the pressure to climb the culinary ladder juxtaposed with the sixteen-hour days and constant demand eventually took its toll after several years. "That's when I broke up with my boyfriend, sold my car, and moved to Spain," says Karen.

Such a move might seem curt and ill prepared, but Karen's sister Jessica had also undergone a quarter-life transition, ditching her job as an investment banker in New York City post 9/11 to take advantage of the laid-back lifestyle that Madrid could offer.

The new environment and culture provided a chance for the sisters to revel in the experience. "There is no time limit," says Karen as she explains the way Spaniards approach mealtime, which often starts around 8:30 or later in the evenings. Originally intending to supplement this sojourn by teaching English, Karen soon found out there were not any available positions.

"I had no intention of ever going back to work as a chef," Karen shares. "So I realized quickly that I had two choices: go back to the kitchen, or return to the States." A friend of a friend knew an American who owned a small five-table bistro, and Karen got back to work. "That's where I found a renewed passion for cooking—from sourcing the local markets in the morning to cooking in the evening." The chef life that Karen could pursue in Spain offered not only flexibility but also inspiration. When her sister Jessica returned to the States to chase love and a new career, Karen

doubled down by opening her own restaurant, Memento, a thirty-two-seat restaurant and bar, bringing more of an internationally focused cuisine to Madrid.

Karen tells me that she spent about three and a half years running her restaurant before moving to Venezuela to take on responsibilities of a "restaurant consultant." That's when my suspicions of her clandestine operations begin to take shape, but Karen assures me it was simply a path taken to follow her then-husband back to his home country.

Eventually relationships and gigs expire, and Karen's story winds back to the beginning—Milwaukee. These changes coincided with family pressure from her mom about having all the kids back in town.

Within a few hours, I gain a sense that Karen is one of the more ultimate doers I've ever come across in my travels. From pursuing a career path

less welcoming to women to dancing around the country and the world while taking on entrepreneurship and risk, nothing seems to raise Karen's blood pressure or level of stress. She is measured—meek and mild, dare I say—but confident in her execution and resolve.

A strong sense of confidence and self-worth was necessary for Karen to take on her next and current project. "I had no experience as a butcher," says Karen when she tells me about the idea she dreamed up for Bavette La Boucherie. "I originally intended to open a butcher shop with a small café, but in reality, we are a restaurant with a small butcher shop."

Days prior to the opening of the shop, the *Milwaukee Business Journal* ran a story of the new concept, prompting Bill Kreitmeier, a seventy-two-year-old German native and lifetime butcher, to leave a voicemail for Karen to inquire about a job. "Bill had a lifetime of experience working in

grocery stores, even having his own place in the public market," says Karen, "but his skill was no longer being offered in-house by the stores. They had outsourced the butchering, or stopped offering it altogether."

Before customers arrived, they got in a whole hog and went to work, Karen picking up on Bill's mastery and learning the trade along the way. While Bill showed Karen the traditional methods of making Italian and Polish sausages, she taught him a thing or two about employing different seasonings and flavors to churn out favorite varieties such as their in-house merguez. For years prior to retiring, Bill handled the butchering while Karen managed the cooking. Nowadays Karen employs and manages a robust staff to keep up with the demand. The place is packed on a Saturday lunch service, with folks dining at the tables and bar as well as call-in orders for specialty cuts from the butcher case.

Milwaukee and its surrounding areas provide a rich format to source quality livestock and vegetables, which Karen embraces in her seasonal and local cooking philosophy. "To focus on whole animal butchering, I knew there had to be a cooking aspect to introduce people to the foods they wouldn't normally procure," she says. As I walk the floor at lunchtime, I see about half of the people delighting on a beef tongue–Reuben sandwich, chatting and smiling, passing half-cut sandwiches across the table for others to take a bite, heads nodding up and down to signal that they wished they had ordered the same thing. Whatever Karen dreamed up, it is working, so much so that she intends to transition to a larger space just after my visit.

In the old days, Milwaukee's Historic Third Ward began as a working neighborhood, populated mostly by Irish immigrants who gave it the nickname of the Bloody Third due to the number of fistfights. Fires ravaged the industrial neighborhood at the turn of the century, with mostly Italians taking over the warehouse businesses and streets. Eventually, in the 1960s, the construction of the I-794 freeway caused a once-prominent neighborhood to fall by the wayside. In the early 2000s, folks like Karen began to dig back into the area, reinvesting in the vision of locality, quality, and honesty. It is now one of the most vibrant areas of the city.

After I fill my face to the brim on tongue and sausage, and down an entire bottle of "Butcher" wine, my full belly and liquid courage implore me to ask if we can pardon the freezing temperatures and walk up the street to go look at Karen's hands.

My cowboy boots slip and slide in the snow as we walk a few blocks, but I keep asking questions, and Karen shares that she's recently become a mother to a daughter. When I question the balance of work and motherhood, Karen tells me she wants her daughter to see a strong, independent working woman, to know she can do whatever she wants to do. The wind whips across the intersections as we finally make our way to the PH Dye House, a place that once housed and manufactured women's hosiery.

I look up to see a six-story mural painted by German artist Case Maclaim. While her face is not visible, Karen was chosen to sit for the mural,

wearing a white apron, hands in lap, with one placed over the other. "It's meant to celebrate working women," Karen tells me. A sense of humble satisfaction holds in her upward gaze.

Without her face, the piece of art—and Karen for that matter—is meant to represent every woman: the possibilities, the challenges, and the sacrifices. I ask the title, and upon Karen's response, I forget all about the cold and stand and admire in respectful silence.

"The Unsung Hero." ∎

BEEF CARPACCIO ⓦ PARMESAN, CAPERS, ⓐⓝⓓ ARUGULA

Owning a whole butcher shop and restaurant ensures Bavette La Boucherie proprietor Karen Bell the ability to make use of all the odds and ends of the animal. But odds and ends also are made from primary, more expensive cuts. Take, for example, the beef tenderloin. While some butchers might utilize and tie the entire head and tail sections of the cut for steaks (like on pages 8 and 9), Karen trims these portions and keeps them frozen for use in this delicious carpaccio. The key here is to let the beef shine. It's tender, thinly sliced, and will melt in your mouth. The accompanying ingredients are really all about enhancing the flavor, with a punch of acidity, creamy saltiness, and spicy, peppery notes from the arugula. Of course you don't need odds and ends, or a whole tenderloin, to pull this off—a fillet of beef will work just fine for this classic.

Serves 2	Hands on: 20 minutes	Total: 30 minutes

- ☐ 5 ounces beef fillet, frozen
- ☐ 1 teaspoon capers, drained and chopped
- ☐ 1 tablespoon finely sliced basil

- ☐ 2 pinches coarse sea salt
- ☐ 2 teaspoons extra-virgin olive oil
- ☐ 1 small handful arugula
- ☐ 1 lemon, cut in half

- ☐ 1 ounce Sartori parmesan cheese, or Parmigiano-Reggiano cheese, shaved

1 Using a meat slicer or a very sharp knife, carefully slice the beef as thin as possible, about 1/16 inch thick. Arrange the beef on a serving platter.

2 Distribute the capers, basil, salt, and 1 teaspoon of the oil evenly over the sliced beef. In a small bowl, dress the arugula with the remaining 1 teaspoon of oil and a squeeze of lemon, and place the dressed arugula in the center of the dish. Sprinkle with the cheese. Serve.

ROASTED DELICATA SQUASH, PEAR, (and) BEET SALAD (with) PICKLED CURRANTS, GOAT CHEESE LABNEH, (and) 'NDUJA HONEY

A feast for both the eyes and the mouth, the roasted offerings in this salad are fit for a meal of their own, but combined with the creamy, pungent labneh and meaty, sweet 'nduja, this is a main course standout that aims to please. If you are unfamiliar with 'nduja, well, get with it, folks. This spicy, spreadable Italian salami hails from the Calabria region, and it can be schmeared over toasted bread or crackers, added to a cheese and charcuterie board, or as in this recipe, served warm and sweetened by a touch of honey for a sweet heat element. Honestly, is this really a salad?

You can certainly expedite and reduce some of the preparation of this dish by picking up a premade labneh and vinaigrette. The currants can also be subbed with some dried raisins or cranberries. Whether you go full-on or take it easy, the combination of flavors, textures, and tastes are worth chasing.

Serves 4	Hands on: 1 hour	Total: 12 hours

GOAT CHEESE LABNEH
- ☐ 4 cups plain Greek yogurt
- ☐ 1 tablespoon kosher salt
- ☐ 2 tablespoons lemon juice
- ☐ 1 cup crumbled goat cheese

PICKLED CURRANTS
- ☐ 1 cup currants
- ☐ 1 cup water
- ☐ 1 cup white wine vinegar
- ☐ 2 tablespoons sugar
- ☐ ½ tablespoon salt
- ☐ ¾ teaspoon pickling spice

SQUASH, PEAR, AND BEET SALAD
- ☐ 1 golden beet, peeled and cut into eighths
- ☐ 1 white pear, such as a Ya pear or Chinese white pear, peeled and cut vertically, seeds and stem removed, and cut into eighths
- ☐ 1 delicata squash, cut vertically, seeds removed, and sliced into ½-inch-thick half-moons
- ☐ 2 tablespoons extra-virgin olive oil
- ☐ 1 teaspoon kosher salt

- ☐ 4 cups arugula

LEMON VINAIGRETTE
- ☐ 1 cup extra-virgin olive oil
- ☐ ⅓ cup lemon juice
- ☐ 1 teaspoon dijon mustard
- ☐ 1 clove garlic, finely minced
- ☐ 1 teaspoon kosher salt
- ☐ ½ teaspoon fresh-cracked black pepper

'NDUJA HONEY
- ☐ ½ pound 'nduja
- ☐ 1 teaspoon extra-virgin olive oil
- ☐ 2 tablespoons honey

1 Make the labneh. At least 12 hours prior to serving, combine the yogurt, salt, and lemon juice in a bowl until evenly mixed. Transfer the mixture into a fine-mesh strainer lined with cheesecloth and place the strainer over the bowl. Let sit overnight in the refrigerator. Discard the liquid from the bowl. Mix the strained yogurt mixture with the goat cheese and keep chilled until ready to serve.

2 At least 12 hours prior to serving, make the pickled currants. Put the currants in a medium bowl. In a small saucepan, combine the water, vinegar, sugar, salt, and pickling spice and bring to a boil over high heat. Remove the pan from the heat and strain the liquid over the currants in the bowl. Cover and refrigerate overnight. The next day, strain the liquid from the currants, discard the liquid, and allow the

currants to air-dry on a plate in the refrigerator prior to serving.

3 Make the salad. Preheat the oven to 400°F. On a large rimmed baking sheet, add the beet, pear, and squash, keeping the ingredients separate. Drizzle the ingredients with the oil and season with the salt. Place the pan in the oven and roast until each ingredient is bite-tender, removing the squash and pear after 15 to 20 minutes and the beet after 55 to 60 minutes. Allow all three to cool to room temperature.

4 Prepare the vinaigrette. In a small bowl, whisk together the olive oil, lemon juice, mustard, garlic, salt, and pepper. Set aside.

5 Prepare the honey. In a nonstick skillet over medium heat, combine the 'nduja and oil and

cook, breaking up the 'nduja into a fine mixture similar to ground beef. Add the honey and continue to stir and mix until evenly combined and warmed.

6 Prepare the salads by spreading a generous portion of labneh at the base of each plate. Next, add the arugula to a bowl, dress with half the vinaigrette, and place 1 cup on top of each labneh. Next, add the squash, pear, and beet into a small bowl and dress with the remaining vinaigrette and arrange, dividing the mixture by four, evenly over the top of each salad. Top each salad with approximately 1 tablespoon of pickled currents, and drizzle a tablespoon or two of the warmed 'nduja honey around the plate. Serve.

LAMB MERGUEZ MEATBALLS with PURÉED CAULIFLOWER and RAISIN-ALMOND RELISH

When Karen Bell first started Bavette La Boucherie, her time spent with lifetime butcher Bill Kreitmeier in the shop allowed her to meld his old-school knowledge of classic Midwest and German sausage specialties with the warm, bright flavors she craved from her time spent in Spain. I particularly loved her idea of making sausage, removed from its casing, into something different—a meatball. You could adopt this technique for shortcutting spaghetti and meatballs by using an Italian sausage as the base for breadcrumbs, eggs, and other seasonings (a real time-saver for a classic).

This satisfying, flavorful dish is daringly health conscious, with lean spiced lamb and puréed cauliflower utilized in the form of comfort food. The star of the show, however, is the curried relish of almonds and raisins, spiked with some acidic vinegar, which sings all things sunshine and Madrid. You can pick up preserved lemons at most specialty grocers or online—you should use them for that sweet-and-sour punch in this dish, as well as with seafood and grilled vegetables.

Serves 4	Hands on: 1 hour	Total: 1 hour

CAULIFLOWER
- ☐ 1 head cauliflower, destemmed and cut into bite-sized florets
- ☐ 2 cups whole milk
- ☐ 4 tablespoons unsalted butter
- ☐ 1 teaspoon kosher salt, plus more as needed
- ☐ ½ teaspoon fresh-cracked black pepper, plus more as needed

MEATBALLS
- ☐ 1 pound lamb merguez sausage, casings removed
- ☐ ½ cup seasoned breadcrumbs
- ☐ 1 large egg
- ☐ ¼ cup whole milk

RELISH
- ☐ 4 tablespoons unsalted butter
- ☐ 1 cup sliced almonds

- ☐ 1 teaspoon curry powder
- ☐ 1 cup golden raisins
- ☐ ½ cup white wine
- ☐ 2 teaspoons white wine vinegar
- ☐ 1 pinch kosher salt
- ☐ ¼ cup preserved lemons, sliced
- ☐ ¼ cup fresh mint leaves

1 Preheat the oven to 400°F.

2 In a large pot, combine the cauliflower, milk, butter, salt, and pepper and place over medium heat. Bring the mixture to a simmer, reduce the heat to medium low, and simmer until the cauliflower is tender when pierced with a knife, about 15 minutes. Using an immersion blender, or after carefully transferring to a traditional blender, purée the cauliflower until smooth. Taste the mixture, adding salt and pepper as desired. Keep warm.

3 Meanwhile, make the meatballs. In a medium bowl, add the sausage, breadcrumbs, egg, and milk and mix by hand. Form into small meatballs, about 2 ounces each. Place the meatballs on an oiled rimmed baking sheet and roast for 15 minutes, or until evenly browned.

4 In a skillet, melt the butter for the relish over
   medium heat and add the almonds. As the
   butter browns, toast the almonds, stirring
   occasionally, until they produce a nutty aroma
   and brown specks form, 5 minutes. Remove
   the pan from the heat and stir in the curry
   powder and raisins. Place the pan back over
   the heat until the butter begins to bubble again
   and add the white wine. Reduce the mixture

for 2 to 3 minutes. Add the vinegar and salt
and cook for 1 minute.

5 Divide the puréed cauliflower among shallow
   bowls. Divide the meatballs and relish and
   place on each serving of cauliflower. Top with
   the preserved lemons and garnish with the
   mint. Serve.

CORNED BEEF TONGUE REUBENS

It's hard to say which dish was my favorite during my time at Karen Bell's Bavette La Boucherie, but I can tell you what seemed to be the most popular. If you don't order this sandwich, either the person sitting across from you or at the table next to you will be *ohhh*ing and *ahhh*ing at it, passing bites for their companions to enjoy, and you'll wish you had some, too. For me, this is one of those dishes that validates the entire reasoning of why I put this book together. Take a classic sandwich, beloved by millions, and enhance it by utilizing a cut that needs more attention. Sure the idea of eating beef tongue might sound somewhat new or foreign, but it's a delicacy. More so than traditional corned beef, or pastrami, the tongue has a tender, gelatinous quality that serves as the perfect base in Bavette's sandwich. Instead of using the traditional wet-cure method, Karen skips the time and effort by simmering the tongues in a cured brine, which delivers an incredible result in nearly a third of the time.

While some butchers might have beef tongue on hand, oftentimes you have to procure a larger quantity at a time—which this recipe calls for. Meaning, you should have plenty of leftovers to enjoy a few days' worth of sandwiches, or use the meat in a scramble, hash, taco, or other specialty.

Serves 4	Hands on: 1 hour 30 minutes	Total: 6 hours

CORNED BEEF TONGUE
- ☐ 3 beef tongues, 2 to 3 pounds each
- ☐ ½ cup sugar
- ☐ 2 tablespoons pink curing salt #1
- ☐ 2 tablespoons pickling spice
- ☐ 1 head garlic, cut in half horizontally
- ☐ 2 sprigs fresh thyme
- ☐ 2 sprigs fresh rosemary

PICKLED MUSTARD MAYO
- ☐ ½ cup white wine vinegar
- ☐ ½ cup water
- ☐ 3 tablespoons sugar
- ☐ ½ teaspoon kosher salt
- ☐ ⅓ cup yellow mustard seeds
- ☐ 2 cups mayonnaise, preferably Duke's brand

REUBEN SANDWICHES
- ☐ 1 cup sauerkraut
- ☐ 2 tablespoons sriracha
- ☐ 8 slices rye bread
- ☐ 8 slices aged white cheddar
- ☐ 4 tablespoons unsalted butter

1 Place the beef tongues into a very large (16-quart) stockpot and cover completely with water. Over medium-high heat, bring the mixture to a slow simmer, skim off the scum, and add the sugar, curing salt, pickling spice, garlic, thyme, and rosemary. Reduce the heat to medium low, partially cover, and simmer until tender, about 4 hours. Remove the tongues from the brine, discard the brine, and allow the tongues to cool to the touch. Peel the skin from the surface of the tongues while still warm. Allow the tongues to cool to room temperature and then slice very thinly on a meat slicer or with a sharp knife.

2 Meanwhile, make the mayo. In a medium saucepan, combine the vinegar, water, sugar, salt, and mustard seeds and bring to a simmer over medium-high heat. Reduce the heat to low and simmer until the mustard seeds are plump and the liquid has reduced by half, 15 to 20 minutes. Remove the pot from the heat and allow the mustard seeds to cool in any remaining liquid. Place the mayonnaise in a medium bowl and fold in the mustard seeds and liquid. Refrigerate until ready to serve.

3 To assemble the sandwiches, in a small bowl, combine the sauerkraut and sriracha and mix until combined. Working in batches as necessary, spread a generous portion of the pickled mustard mayo over each slice of bread. Add a slice of cheddar on top of the mayo. Evenly divide the sriracha sauerkraut among 4 slices of the bread. On the remaining 4 slices, pile 6 to 8 ounces of the sliced tongue. Carefully put the halves together to form 4 sandwiches.

4 Heat a large skillet over medium heat. Add 1 tablespoon of butter per sandwich, if working in batches. Place the sandwiches in the skillet, and press them into the butter. Place another skillet or weighted object on top of the sandwiches to maintain pressure on them. Reduce the heat to medium low. Toast the sandwiches for 4 to 5 minutes, or until golden, remove the weighted object, flip the sandwiches, and replace the weighted object on top for an additional 3 to 4 minutes, until the cheese is melted and the sandwiches are warmed all the way through. Slice the sandwiches and serve.

NOTE: Alternatively, if using a sandwich press, cook each sandwich for 7 to 8 minutes, until the cheese is melted and the sandwich is warmed.

THE DELUCA FAMILY, VINCENT'S MEAT MARKET

The Bronx, NYC, NY

"He met her on the job," Peter DeLuca tells me when I ask how his father, Vincent DeLuca, met Silvia, Vincent's wife.

"You mean, actually in the butcher shop?" I ask Peter.

"Yes, of course, they met in the shop."

As I'm gathering the DeLuca family history, I decide to let my questions meander from the standard protocol, skipping forward a few decades. "Same question, Peter—how did you meet your wife?" The other line of the phone is silent for a quarter beat, followed by a cough or two and a rolling laugh.

"Same answer," Peter says. "I met Diana in the butcher shop!"

As I'm sitting in Peter and Diana's former apartment, a small walk-up now turned office just above and adjacent to the shop on Arthur Avenue in the Bronx, I'm taking in a multigenerational story of the American dream by telephone instead of in-person as planned, since Peter unfortunately couldn't make it in during my visit due to a cold. But early on in our conversation, I realize there is no degradation to the experience. Peter is just as jovial and gregarious over the phone as I could ever imagine in person. We press on.

"I just remember him telling me that they were really poor," says Peter when I ask about his father Vincent's childhood, growing up in the Calabria region of Italy. "They worked on a farm, grew grapes, and peddled whatever they could. My grandmother, I'll tell you, she was a hustler."

In 1945 at the close of World War II, Vincent, age seventeen, along with his mother and sister, joined his father for a better life in America. Vincent settled into the new country, bolstered by old country families and immigrants, eventually graduating from Roosevelt High School and going on to work first in the trades business, followed by a stint in construction. "He was earning just sixteen cents an hour," Peter tells me of Vincent's plight. Eventually dismayed with his career path, Vincent found his passion working in a family-owned butcher shop on 149th Street—the same spot where he met Silvia, his future bride.

"My father asked for a five-dollar raise," Peter tells me. Vincent and Silvia had recently married and were expecting their first child, Phillip. When he got turned down by the shop's owner, he set his sights on making it on his own, opening up his first butcher shop, Vincent's Meat Market, in 1954 on 151st Street.

Starting a self-made venture wasn't without its difficulties, but Vincent and Silvia persisted, going on to raise three sons, Phillip, Peter, and Vincent, in the Belmont area of the Bronx, which flourished with other Italian immigrants at the time. "It wasn't about material objects," says Peter when I ask him what he remembers from those days. "It was family. That was the best. You didn't miss what you didn't have."

"This might sound crazy—something like from the Mafia or whatever, but it's not," Peter preps me. "Holidays were big for our family—Christmas, the Easter lamb, and Palm Sundays. As kids I remember spending time with all of those families in our neighborhood, meeting our godfathers and all that kind of stuff. Vincent ensured that the neighborhood was well supplied with cuts of prime beef along with specialties brought from Italy, including sausages, dry goods, veal, and other products of quality.

"My dad had the gift of gab. He was a good businessman because he made people feel like family. He gave his customers a fair shake," says Peter. "As kids, I remember having to go to the shop in the early morning, before school, to unload the trucks with my brothers. We'd come back, wash up, and go to school." While the entire family pitched in to make Vincent's American dream flourish, it also paid back dividends by shaping the character of his children. "Not a lot of

health issues," shares Peter, "and the smaller store allowed him to slow down a bit—to enjoy."

More than a decade passed until the unimaginable. "I lost my best friend, my father, to cancer when he was just fifty years old," says Peter. Working through just telephone lines, it's hard to express the moment, but I can tell it still "lives" with Peter as he shares the loss. But ever generous and affable, Peter counters that although it was a particularly hard time, he knew that he had another blessing, his Diana. "Like I said, I met her in the butcher shop, but I wasn't ready to settle down. One of the last nights my dad was alive, she came with me to visit him in the hospital. I just knew right there and then that she was the one."

When Vincent passed, Peter stepped in to carry on his legacy. "My mother was a young widow, my older brother was studying to become a doctor, and my younger brother was still a kid. I

kids get the chance to spend time with their father," Peter tells me. "I was very blessed."

By 1964 Vincent was running more than twenty meat cutters and working sixteen- to eighteen-hour shifts. It began to take its toll, and Vincent decided to focus more on quality and custom work by moving to a smaller shop on 187th Street. "He was starting to have some

did what I had to do." But life isn't fair; more challenges were coming Peter's way.

"Our landlord came into the store on a Saturday—the store was packed. She kept trying to raise the rent. Since my father had no lease, it was out of our control." Fortunately Peter's brother-in-law knew of another shop on Arthur Avenue that might be up for purchase, but finding the capital to stay in business was less than living on easy street.

"I didn't even have two nickels to rub together at the time," says Peter. "But, you know, family is family. We support each other." With a whole lot of promissory notes, Peter went on to borrow from his mother, grandmother, and finally his brother Phillip, extending the loan into his nephew's christening money. It was an all-out effort.

Nineteen-eighty brought about the grand opening of Vincent's Meat Market in its third and final iteration on Arthur Avenue, where I'm spending my time at the current moment. It seems intuitive as to why Peter kept the business under his father's name, yet I still have to ask the "why."

"My father always taught me to take care of the customers, to do right by them. It was his shop, his teachings. It was my time to carry on the legacy. There were nights during the holidays that I knew the trucks would show up at three a.m., so I would sleep on the counters after my shift since I knew I didn't have time to make it home." It's this kind of unknown dedication that I think deserves the most attention.

I end my phone conversation, knowing I could talk to Peter for hours, but he's supplied me with everything I need. I decide to walk back downstairs, perusing Vincent's Meat Market in the middle morning as customers pour off the block to purchase an array of specialties often not seen in other markets: whole animals, like suckling pigs and animal heads; fresh, local rabbits; veal; lamb; and specialty sausages. Dozens of meat cutters are at bay to take your order, "fabricating" (as they say) a custom order as you wish. But there's also a back-of-the-house operation that's taking the old school to the new.

Peter Jr., Peter's son, is back up in the office, taking orders from a computer instead of behind the counter. Away from the whizzing band saws and cold lockers, Peter Jr., a former set designer, is now tasked with modernizing Vincent's Meat

Market to the next level. Along with his sister Silvana and high school friend Kenny Roopchand, he is taking the business from beyond the block to the rest of the world, serving up specialties to those both near and far through online ordering and social media.

I spend some time with Peter Jr. as I cook a few items from the shop—stuffed pork chops, hand-pounded veal, and a sandwich filled with the house-made sausage and peppers. As we sizzle and sear the ingredients just procured from downstairs, I sense a great deal of pride in Peter Jr.'s dark-set and clear eyes. "We are the opposite of your run-of-the-mill market—what we do is custom cut, specialty," Peter Jr. relays as he picks up on a seventy-plus-year value proposition.

Just then, my phone rings again—Peter has culled a few more items to help fill holes in my story. Over the speaker, I ask Peter bluntly and honestly, "Will you ever retire?"

"Ask my son," says Peter. Looking at Peter Jr., I see him both poised to make this business his own, while also careful to protect what has made the place so special. He is serious, he is focused. What a legacy to carry forward.

I soften the moment, telling Peter that "it seems to me like you are in great hands."

The audio on the phone gently barks back: "I think so too," says Peter. ∎

STUFFED PORK CHOPS

An in-house specialty at Vincent's Meat Market, nearly twenty meat cutters are ready at any time to take your order to custom specifications. A few years back, Jimmy Mechaca, a longtime employee credited with saving Peter when he had a heart attack in the store, whipped up this daily special to become a bestseller throughout the neighborhood and beyond. The process is fairly simple: take a thick-cut, bone-in, and frenched chop and butterfly it to create a pocket for the house-made stuffing of cheeses, spinach, and breadcrumbs. After that, sear it in some butter and finish it in a high-heat oven and you have yourself a main-course all-star that can be served up alongside some whipped potatoes and roasted vegetables.

Serves 4	Hands on: 45 minutes	Total: 45 minutes

- ☐ Four 8- to 10-ounce bone-in pork chops, frenched
- ☐ 1 cup seasoned breadcrumbs
- ☐ ½ cup grated fontina cheese

- ☐ ½ cup crumbled Gorgonzola cheese
- ☐ ½ cup grated mozzarella cheese
- ☐ 1½ cups spinach, torn by hand into small pieces

- ☐ ¼ cup chicken stock
- ☐ 4 tablespoons unsalted butter
- ☐ 1 tablespoon chopped fresh parsley

1 Preheat the oven to 400°F. Meanwhile, butterfly the pork chops. Insert a sharp knife on the side of a chop opposite from the bone, and cut along the length of the side to open up the chop, being careful to maintain an even cut to ensure the thickness remains even on both sides. Open up the chop to reveal a small pocket for the stuffing. Repeat with the remaining chops.

2 In a mixing bowl, combine ½ cup of the breadcrumbs with the fontina, Gorgonzola, mozzarella, spinach, and chicken stock. Using your hands, work the mixture together, squeezing and tearing the spinach with your hands to combine with the other ingredients. Carefully divide and stuff the mixture equally among the pockets of the butterflied pork chops.

3 Using butcher's twine, start from the backside of the bone of the chop and secure the twine around the bone at approximately a 45-degree angle. Wrap the twine back against the bone, and going in a triangle style, tie another 45 degrees in the opposite direction to secure the stuffing inside the chop. If necessary, use enough twine to ensure the stuffing is contained within the chop for cooking.

4 Sprinkle the remaining ½ cup of breadcrumbs on both sides of the chops. Heat a large skillet over medium-high heat. Working in batches of 2 chops, melt 2 tablespoons of the butter in the pan, then add the chops. Sear for 3 minutes, undisturbed. Flip the chops, sear an additional 2 minutes, and transfer the seared chops to a wire rack set inside a rimmed baking sheet. Repeat the process with the remaining 2 chops and 2 tablespoons of butter. Place the pork chops into the oven and cook for 10 minutes, until the internal temperature reaches approximately 145°F. Remove the chops from the oven and, using kitchen shears, carefully cut and remove the butcher's twine. Transfer the chops to a serving platter or plate. Garnish with the parsley and serve.

SAUSAGE ⓐ PEPPERS SANDWICHES

A longtime favorite of consumers, the specialty sausages made in-house at Vincent's Meat Market go back to the very beginning, recipes that Vincent brought over from his childhood in Italy. Once a year, the neighborhood puts on a street festival, Ferragosto, where the Vincent's team puts out a large charcoal grill to serve up these sandwiches to hungry neighbors. As Peter tells me, on average they can sell about two thousand of these sandwiches in a day, ranging from the Italian versions to sweet and hot to broccoli rabe. As I scan the butcher case during my visit, it seems as though they would never run out of these sausages, but like clockwork, nearly every person who comes in to the shop picks up a half dozen or so to take home.

For this particular recipe, I like to set up a two-zone fire to cook the sausages over indirect heat, while putting some char on the peppers and onion over direct heat. After that, I'll switch things up by getting a sear on the casings of the sausages, and moving the vegetables to indirect heat to soften and cook through.

Serves 4	Hands on: 45 minutes	Total: 45 minutes

- ☐ 6 Italian (or other variety) sausage links
- ☐ 1 large Vidalia onion, outside layer removed and sliced into ½-inch-thick rings

- ☐ 1 yellow bell pepper, cut in half and stem, seeds, and ribs removed and sliced into ½-inch slices
- ☐ 1 red bell pepper, cut in half and stem, seeds, and ribs

removed and sliced into ½-inch slices
- ☐ 4 top-split buns, or cut French bread, warmed or toasted

1 Open the bottom vent of a charcoal grill completely. Light a charcoal chimney starter filled with charcoal. When the coals are covered with gray ash, pour them onto the bottom grate of the grill, and then push to one side of the grill. Adjust the vents as needed to maintain an internal temperature of 350° to 375°F. Coat the top grate with oil; place on the grill. (If using a gas grill, preheat to medium [350° to 375°F] on one side.)

2 Place the sausage links on the grill over indirect heat, cover, and cook for 10 minutes, turning on occasion. Next, place the onion and peppers, cut sides down, over direct heat, and

cook for 5 to 7 minutes per side, or until charred. Transfer the peppers and onion to indirect heat, and place the sausages over direct heat to sear the casings, 2 to 3 minutes for each side, or a total of 8 to 10 minutes.

3 Remove the sausages, onion, and peppers from the grill and transfer to a cutting board. Roughly cut the sausages on the bias into 1-inch pieces and place into the buns. Evenly distribute the onion and pepper slices into the buns on top of the sausages. Serve.

GRILLED TOMAHAWK STEAKS

A favorite item at Vincent's Meat Market, these bone-in rib eyes are cut to perfection daily for those looking for a bit of entertainment with their steak. The name comes from the fact that the bone is frenched, leaving a large clean handle along with a solid rib eye portion of meat that resembles a tomahawk. Because it's a thicker cut, you have a few options to cook this beast, from reverse sear to sous vide to a more traditional method. For me, since the meat is prime and there's been so much effort put in by the meat cutters at Vincent's, I treat this very simply by grilling it over very high heat, letting it rest appropriately, and slicing it to perfection. Instead of a hard sear, I will spend some time searing and rotating the steaks to ensure they do not cook too deeply prior to moving them over to indirect heat to reach my desired internal temperature. Some really good salt is sprinkled over the top to finish. Remember, a meal is only as good as your ingredients. In this case, a tomahawk steak from Vincent's is all you need to ensure perfection.

Serves 4	Hands on: 45 minutes	Total: 2 hours

- ☐ 2 bone-in tomahawk steaks, 35 to 40 ounces each, set out about 1 hour prior to cooking
- ☐ 2 tablespoons vegetable oil
- ☐ 1 tablespoon fresh-cracked black pepper
- ☐ 1 tablespoon kosher salt
- ☐ Fleur de sel, or sea salt, to finish

1 Open the bottom vent of a charcoal grill completely. Light a charcoal chimney starter filled with charcoal. When the coals are covered with gray ash, pour them onto the bottom grate of the grill, and then push to one side of the grill. Adjust the vents as needed to maintain an internal temperature of 500° to 550°F. Coat the top grate with oil; place on the grill. (If using a gas grill, preheat to high [500° to 550°F] on one side.)

2 Drizzle the steaks with the oil, and season both sides liberally with the pepper and kosher salt. Add the steaks to the grill over direct heat and sear, 2 minutes per side, rotating the steaks 30 degrees per turn to ensure an even distribution of sear. Limiting the time to just a couple of minutes per side will ensure the outside of the meat sears without cooking too deeply and will help maintain an even internal temperature.

3 When the steaks have been evenly seared, 14 to 16 minutes of flipping and cooking, move the steaks to indirect heat. Cover the grill and cook the steaks, flipping once, until they reach an internal temperature of approximately 130°F, 25 to 30 more minutes.

4 Remove the steaks from the grill and rest for 10 to 15 minutes. Using a sharp knife, carefully slice the steak away from the bone. Next, slice the steak into ½-inch-thick slices. Sprinkle with fleur de sel. Serve.

VEAL PICCATA

A Vincent's Meat Market specialty, veal is a staple cut that seems to be harder to find these days, but when cooked properly, it's hard to deny the mild flavor and tenderness. Veal cutlets and chops are popular items in this particular neighborhood, but I've asked the in-house meat cutters to transform the cutlets by pounding them thin on an old butcher block to serve as the basis of this recipe. From there, a quick dredge in flour is all you need to quickly panfry these in some melted butter. To round out the meal, I deglaze the skillet with some wine and toss in some hot cooked spaghetti with fresh squeezed lemon and sliced, briny olives. The next time you are looking for a hearty meal, look no further than this recipe. If you prefer, you can sub out the veal for pounded chicken or turkey.

Serves 4	Hands on: 45 minutes	Total: 45 minutes

- ☐ Four 4- to 6-ounce top round veal cutlets, pounded ¼-inch thin
- ☐ 1 teaspoon kosher salt
- ☐ 1 teaspoon fresh-cracked black pepper
- ☐ 1 cup all-purpose flour

- ☐ 8 tablespoons unsalted butter
- ☐ 2 cloves garlic, sliced thin
- ☐ ½ cup white wine
- ☐ 1 cup chicken stock
- ☐ 12 ounces dry spaghetti, cooked al dente according to package instructions

- ☐ 1 lemon, juiced
- ☐ ¼ cup sliced manzanilla olives
- ☐ ¼ cup finely chopped fresh parsley
- ☐ Lemon slices, for garnish

1   Preheat the oven to 250°F. Meanwhile, season the veal cutlets on both sides with the salt and pepper and dredge in the flour, shaking off any excess. Working with 2 cutlets at a time, melt 2 tablespoons of the butter in a skillet over medium heat. Add the veal to the pan and sear about 3 minutes per side, until browned and crispy. Transfer to a wire rack set inside a rimmed baking sheet. Keep warm by transferring the baking sheet to the oven. Repeat with 2 more tablespoons of the butter and the other 2 veal cutlets, transferring the cooked veal to the baking sheet and keeping it warm in the oven.

2   Add an additional 2 tablespoons of butter to the skillet, followed by the garlic, and cook for 1 minute. Deglaze the skillet by adding the wine, using a wooden spoon to scrape up any of the browned bits from the bottom. Add the stock, bring the mixture to a simmer, and let it reduce by half, about 5 minutes. Reduce the heat to low and toss in the pasta with the

remaining 2 tablespoons of butter, the lemon juice, and olives. Stir the pasta to coat it in the sauce.

3   Divide the pasta among four plates, or place it on a serving platter, and drizzle the sauce over the pasta. Remove the veal from the oven and place it on top of the pasta. Sprinkle with the parsley and garnish with lemon slices. Serve.

CARA MANGINI, THE VEGETABLE BUTCHER

> ### San Francisco, CA

"Life happens at the table."

It's a Sunday morning in San Francisco, and I'm perusing the produce stands at the weekly Fort Mason Center Farmers' Market. With a burlap bag in hand, I wander to each stall with Cara Mangini. The sun drenches the tableside stands, casting the perfect light on naturally beautiful, vibrant ingredients that, in this city, remain perpetually in season. In the back of the market, a local band breaks into "Shakedown Street" by the Grateful Dead, the scent of fresh strawberries perfumes the air, and time seems somewhat suspended in the moment—until Cara breaks the silence. "Oh my gosh, they have asparagus," she says. "You have to understand," she explains, "after living nearly a decade in Ohio, I'm not used to always having these kinds of ingredients available."

As photographer Andrea Behrends captures Cara's portrait in the market, I can see that she too has picked up on Cara's excitement. "Flash me that asparagus smile," she says.

After gathering pints of fresh cherry tomatoes, bunches of purple kale, and a pair of neon green Romanescos, we stroll the path back toward Cara's place, a walk-up home in the Cow Hollow district, first built in 1932 by her great-grandfather Ernesto. "I actually come from a family of butchers," Cara shares as she relays the jobs and trades of her ancestors, many of whom settled in the Bay Area after leaving Italy at the turn of the century. Since that time, Cara's family has remained largely entrenched in both the city and surrounding suburbs, but I'm catching Cara in a current golden mean, as her family and business have recently found their way here.

Upon graduating with a degree in journalism, Cara landed an editorial assistant job with *Condé Nast Traveler*, but a temp gig with the beauty brand Bumble and Bumble never released its grasp, and Cara found herself climbing the corporate ladder as a business executive for the brand in New York for the first part of her career.

"I've had lots of mentors," Cara shares, "but one day, one of them challenged my path by asking a simple question: 'If you could do one thing on your day off, what would you do?'" Immediately Cara's heart responded, "Gather people around the table to eat."

"That was it," says Cara. "I kept waiting for my path to reveal itself, but finally my direction became clear, and I went about taking the steps to make it happen." While still juggling corporate responsibilities, Cara enrolled in the Natural Gourmet Institute, stashing her knives and apron below her corporate desk during the day, and attending culinary school and working kitchen gigs at night.

One day, an administrator at the school advised Cara about a new position in the soon-to-open food emporium of Eataly, the job description requesting a "vegetable butcher" to serve in the produce area of the market. I'll be the first to admit, the idea of butchering vegetables sounded more like a marketing angle than reality, but after Cara served as the very first of such in the market, she breathed life and authenticity into the idea. "I've made it my mission to help people work with vegetables," says Cara. "As humans, we are naturally attracted to the shapes, colors, and variety of vegetables. But as I found working in Eataly, most people lack the knowledge of properly choosing and prepping these beautiful ingredients. Fulfilling that need allowed me to bring tips and tricks to excite people to eat their vegetables."

After garnering such a hands-on experience in New York City, Cara decided to pursue her path back toward family and to the West, finding a job in St. Helena, California, working for Long Meadow Ranch. The food program at the ranch offered a true farm-to-table experience, providing Cara the ability to work the farm in the morning, followed by a stint at the afternoon market, and finally working on the line in the evenings. Throughout this tenure of growth and development, Cara continued to rely on mentors and experiences to shape her future.

I'm paying attention to Cara's winding road, when suddenly a man walks into her backyard, carrying a trove of plates, platters, and most importantly, a carrot cake. "Oh," says Cara, "this is my husband, Tom."

"Perfect timing," I say, speaking to both the cake and what I sense is the next chapter. As Tom sets plates and platters onto a backyard table, I open up my line of questioning.

"We met at the Fancy Food Show in the Moscone Center," says Tom. At the time, he was serving as one of the early executives responsible for taking a little brand, Jeni's Splendid Ice Creams, out of Columbus, Ohio, to the mainstream.

"Months earlier, I was looking at all of the new cookbook releases, and one really struck me," says Cara, layering on to the story. "When I saw a little tent for Jeni's Ice Cream, I thought, Wow, that's the book I'd been obsessing over. So I had to go over to check them out." The actual facts might vary, but from what I glean, Tom offered up a few ice cream samples, they met for lunch the next day at Zuni Café, and to steal a *Seinfeld* reference, yada yada yada, the two hit it off.

After months of bicoastal dating, Cara decided to follow her path to Columbus, bringing her cuisines inspired by California and Mediterranean produce right along with her. Within a few months, Little Eater, a pop-up concept Cara had placed in the North Market in downtown became a hit, and

Cara found herself nurturing a relationship and new business.

Over the next decade, Cara built Little Eater into a Columbus mainstay, fulfilling the dream to put vegetables at the center of the plate while also bringing awareness and joy to those seeking satisfying, healthy food. Along with the local praise, Cara's work gained further national and critical acclaim when she released her first book, *The Vegetable Butcher*, bringing her passion and awareness to a broader audience.

But the high-speed train of success doesn't come without its trade-offs. "I started my restaurant and business before kids, and as the restaurant grew, my kids were also growing." Tom and Cara recount stories of the early days, when he would have to call the restaurant to beckon Cara home in the middle of a service. The kids were still nursing and needed their mom.

Balancing passion and family is an art in and of itself, and as Cara puts it, she was already wondering what it would be like to expand outside of Columbus. But instead, March of 2020 ushered in the global pandemic that brought the world, and restaurant owners especially, to their knees. Not knowing what might lie in their future, Cara embraced the slowdown, and with Tom's collaboration, they and their two young kids packed up and settled into her great-grandfather's former home in San Francisco, the walk-up where we're now enjoying carrot cake.

"The pandemic, as tough as it was, allowed me an opportunity to shift priorities, to spend more time with my family," says Cara. "But also, and perhaps more importantly, to refocus on my mission."

"Life happens at the table?" I question, hoping to end the story as it began.

"Yes," says Cara, "but people don't always have to be in my restaurant. I'm learning that I can further my mission more, perhaps, beyond from just a restaurant."

I understand Cara's sentiment—sometimes you have to give up what you know, perhaps even what works, to create an even larger impact. In my

day spent with Cara, it's easy to see that she will continue to balance and broaden paths to further her professional success. It's also easy for me to recognize that Cara's personal success—her family—is worth savoring. After all, Cara is embracing the fact that life also happens at *her* family table. ▪

ZUCCHINI-HERB FRITTERS ⓐⓝⓓ CARROT–PINE NUT YOGURT ⓦⓘⓣⓗ CHILE OIL

I'm a sucker for anything crunchy, crispy, and fried—even vegetables. Author of *The Vegetable Butcher* Cara Mangini recommends using a box grater or handheld grater with large holes, as it can quickly shred a bunch of zucchini, potato, and carrots into the perfect base for this recipe. To up the ante, these little guys are packed with herbs, such as mint, dill, and parsley, and fried until they are crisp on the outside and tender in the middle.

If you choose, you can enjoy them on their own with a squeeze of lemon on top, but I'm a big believer in the Carrot–Pine Nut Yogurt that Cara shared from her trips to Turkey. It also doubles as a dip to enjoy with crudités and flatbread or pita chips. Alternatively, simply sub with Greek-style yogurt mixed with grated garlic and a squeeze of lemon.

Serves 6	Hands on: 1 hour	Total: 1 hour 15 minutes

- ☐ 2 large eggs
- ☐ ½ cup all-purpose flour, plus ¼ cup, as needed
- ☐ 1½ teaspoons fine sea salt
- ☐ ¼ teaspoon fresh-cracked black pepper
- ☐ 1 teaspoon chili powder
- ☐ ½ teaspoon aleppo pepper, or ¼ to ½ teaspoon crushed red pepper

- ☐ ½ teaspoon ground cumin
- ☐ 3 small zucchini (about 1 pound), trimmed
- ☐ 1 russet or Yukon gold potato (10 to 12 ounces), peeled
- ☐ 2 small carrots (about 4 ounces), trimmed and peeled

- ☐ ½ cup loosely packed mint leaves, minced
- ☐ ½ cup loosely packed parsley, minced
- ☐ ½ cup loosely packed dill, minced
- ☐ 1 cup canola oil
- ☐ Carrot–Pine Nut Yogurt with Chile Oil (page 127), to serve

1 In a large bowl, whisk the eggs, then whisk in the flour, salt, black pepper, chili powder, aleppo pepper, and cumin until a thick paste forms.

2 Over a large tea towel or piece of cheesecloth, coarsely grate the zucchini on the large holes of a box grater. Wrap up the zucchini in the center of the towel, twisting around the zucchini to enclose it. Repeatedly squeeze the zucchini over the sink to release as much liquid through the towel as possible. Place the zucchini in a separate bowl. Coarsely grate the potato and carrots and add them to the bowl with the zucchini.

3 When you are ready to make the fritters, add the grated vegetables along with the minced mint, parsley, and dill (reserving a tablespoon or so of each herb as garnish) to the egg-flour mixture. Stir with a rubber spatula to evenly combine. (You don't want the combined batter to sit long before frying.)

4 Heat the oil in a large skillet over medium-high heat until it shimmers. (Drop some batter into the oil; it should sizzle.) Nearly fill a ¼-cup measure with batter (don't pack it) and use a spoon to carefully drop the batter into the oil. Use the back of the spoon to lightly flatten the batter. You should be able to fit 6 cakes at a time. Let the fritters cook, turning once, until the cakes are lightly browned and crisp, ▶▶

2 to 3 minutes per side. Remove the cakes as they finish to a paper towel–lined cooling rack. Turn the heat down between batches. If the batter becomes runny, add more flour, a little at a time, up to ¼ cup. Turn the heat back up to medium high and repeat, cooking the remaining batter in two more batches. Turn the heat down at any time if the cakes start to brown too quickly.

5 Serve immediately to maintain crispness. Serve with the Carrot–Pine Nut Yogurt. Top the fritters with more fresh herbs if you wish.

NOTE: To reheat the fritters, place on a baking sheet and bake at 425°F, about 10 minutes, until crisp on the outside and hot through the middle.

CARROT-PINE NUT YOGURT WITH CHILE OIL

Makes 2½ cups	Hands on: 15 minutes	Total: 30 minutes

- ☐ ¾ cup extra-virgin olive oil
- ☐ 4 medium to large carrots, grated

- ☐ ⅓ cup pine nuts, or finely chopped walnuts or pistachios
- ☐ ¾ teaspoon fine sea salt, plus more as needed

- ☐ 1½ cups full-fat plain Greek yogurt
- ☐ 2 teaspoons aleppo pepper
- ☐ 1 to 2 cloves garlic

1 Heat ½ cup of the oil in a large skillet over medium-high heat. Add a pinch of the grated carrots to test: they should sizzle. Add the remaining carrots and cook, stirring frequently, until they begin to soften, about 5 minutes.

2 Add the pine nuts and salt. Reduce the heat to medium and continue cooking, stirring frequently, until the carrots are completely soft and browning in places and the pine nuts are golden, another 3 minutes or so. Place the yogurt in a medium bowl and immediately stir in the hot carrot mixture. Season to taste with salt, if needed. Transfer the yogurt to a serving bowl, or keep covered in the refrigerator up to 3 days.

3 To top the yogurt with chile oil, heat the remaining ¼ cup of olive oil in a small skillet over medium heat. Add the aleppo pepper and let it sizzle very briefly, about 20 seconds. Transfer the oil to a small bowl or liquid measure, add the garlic cloves, and let stand for at least 15 minutes to infuse the garlic. Strain the oil through a small fine-mesh strainer. Press divots into the yogurt with the back of a spoon and drizzle the oil over the top.

ROMANESCO STEAKS 𝒶𝓃𝒹 ROASTED RED PEPPER-FETA PESTO 𝓌𝒾𝓉𝒽 ARUGULA, JALAPEÑO-PICKLED CURRANTS, 𝒶𝓃𝒹 OLIVES

Admittedly there's a lot going on with this recipe, but that also means there's a lot to love. Truth be told, you could get away with just the Romanesco (think of a hybrid between broccoli and cauliflower) steaks, as I'm a huge believer in Cara Mangini's high-heat method for roasting these in the oven—literally foolproof. But the additional components, including the pickled currants and pesto, really set this dish over the top. It's something you get *oohs* and *aahs* for when you present it at the dining table. Plus, the spicy pickled currants and pesto are super versatile, and both can be used to brighten up salads, pastas, or other dishes, if you want to stretch these components.

Typically a large head of Romanesco will yield two or three steaks, as the side cuts don't hold together too well. You can still roast the florets that fall off the stalk, if you wish. If you cannot find Romanesco, large heads of cauliflower make for a great substitution.

Serves 2 or 3	Hands on: 1 hour 15 minutes	Total: 1 hour 30 minutes

JALAPEÑO-PICKLED CURRANTS
- ☐ ⅓ cup water
- ☐ ¼ cup rice wine vinegar
- ☐ 2 tablespoons apple cider vinegar
- ☐ 2 tablespoons sugar
- ☐ ¾ teaspoon kosher salt
- ☐ ½ cup dried currants
- ☐ 1 large jalapeño, quartered lengthwise, seeds and ribs removed

PESTO
- ☐ 2 large red bell peppers (about 1¼ pounds)

- ☐ ½ cup toasted pistachios
- ☐ 4 ounces feta cheese
- ☐ ½ teaspoon aleppo pepper, plus more as needed
- ☐ 1 tablespoon lemon juice, plus more as needed
- ☐ ¼ teaspoon kosher salt, plus more as needed
- ☐ 2 tablespoons extra-virgin olive oil

ROMANESCO STEAKS
- ☐ 1 to 2 large heads Romanesco, or cauliflower

- ☐ Up to 6 tablespoons extra-virgin olive oil
- ☐ 1½ teaspoons kosher salt
- ☐ 2 cups baby arugula, packed
- ☐ ½ cup pitted green olives, sliced into rounds
- ☐ Aleppo pepper, as garnish (optional)
- ☐ Chopped pistachios, as garnish (optional)
- ☐ Freshly crumbled feta, as garnish (optional)

1 Make the currants. Whisk together the water, vinegars, sugar, and salt in a wide-mouth jar until the sugar and salt dissolve. Add the currants and jalapeño, stir to combine, and let stand for at least 30 minutes or ideally overnight, or up to 7 days, covered, in the refrigerator.

2 Make the pesto. Preheat the oven to 450°F and line a rimmed baking sheet with foil. Place the bell peppers on the baking sheet and roast for 30 to 35 minutes, turning halfway through with tongs, until the peppers are soft all over and charred and blistering in places. Transfer ▶▶

them to a large bowl. Cover and briefly steam the peppers, making them easier to peel.

3 Meanwhile, place the toasted pistachios in the bowl of a food processor. Pulse and blend until they are very finely chopped.

4 When the bell peppers are cool enough to handle, peel them over a fine-mesh strainer set in the same bowl used to steam them so that the interior juices can run into the bowl and the strainer can capture the seeds and skin. As you work, transfer the peeled peppers to the food processor with the pistachios, then add all of the strained juices. Add the feta, aleppo pepper, lemon juice, and salt to the food processor and process until mostly blended. Scape down the sides of the bowl. With the processor running, stream in the olive oil. Continue to process until the pesto is well blended with some texture. Adjust the aleppo pepper, lemon juice, and salt to taste. You can make this up to 3 days in advance and keep, covered, in the refrigerator.

5 Preheat the oven to 475°F. Cut the Romanesco into steaks. Peel and snap off the outer, dark green leaves. Cut off the stalk flush with the base of the crown and stand it upright, steady, on your cutting board. Trim the sides of the Romanesco, as these pieces don't usually hold together well, and reserve them for another use (or go ahead and roast them; see headnote). Cut 1-inch-thick slices from the top of the crown down through the core. You should yield 2 or 3 steaks, or perhaps more, per head of Romanesco. Sometimes the steaks are precariously held together, so use a wide spatula to transfer the steaks off your board to one or two baking sheets. Do not overcrowd the steaks. (If you have yielded more than 6 steaks or if they are extra-large in size, you'll need two baking sheets; adjust the racks to space them evenly in the oven.)

6 Brush the steaks generously and evenly on both sides with olive oil and season with salt, carefully turning them as needed and making sure to oil in between the grooves of the stalk. Place the steaks in the oven—use the bottom rack if you're using one baking sheet and use both the bottom rack and upper rack if you are using two baking sheets. Roast the steaks for 18 to 20 minutes, turning them with a wide metal spatula halfway through cooking and rotating racks if you are using two baking sheets, until they are nicely browned on both sides and tender, but not overly soft or falling apart.

7 To serve, top the steaks with a generous spoonful of pesto and a small handful of arugula. Add some currants, draining them as you lift them from the jar, and olives. If desired, garnish with aleppo pepper, chopped pistachios, and feta.

MIXED CHERRY TOMATOES, CORN, and QUINOA with BASIL VINAIGRETTE

Cara Mangini's restaurant, Little Eater (a loose translation of her last name), was a modern, produce-inspired deli with hearty, vegetable-based sandwiches and an always-changing lineup of seasonal, prepared salads that guests could mix and match to make a meal. This is one of those standout salads, a classic and a favorite that bursts with fresh tomatoes and corn from the market, along with some hearty quinoa. Perhaps my favorite part is that when the corn is at its peak, Cara recommends just shaving it right off the cob, adding it raw to the salad. If you prefer, or if you have corn that's less than perfect, you can alternatively blanch the cobs for a couple of minutes in boiling water. The basil and honey in the tangy vinaigrette help to pull out the natural flavors from the corn and tomatoes without overpowering. This salad can be enjoyed immediately, but it's perhaps best when allowed to sit and chill for an hour or so. ▶▶

- ☐ 1¾ cups water
- ☐ 1 teaspoon fine sea salt, plus more as needed
- ☐ 1 cup tricolor quinoa, or white quinoa, well rinsed and drained
- ☐ ¼ teaspoon fresh-cracked black pepper, plus more as needed

- ☐ ½ cup Basil Vinaigrette, plus more as needed (recipe follows)
- ☐ 1 pint mixed cherry tomatoes, halved, or quartered if extra-large
- ☐ 2 cups freshly cut corn kernels (from 2 large ears of corn)

- ☐ ⅓ cup freshly crumbled feta (optional)
- ☐ Generous handful of fresh basil leaves, finely sliced or chopped

1 Bring the water to a boil in a medium-sized heavy saucepan over high heat. Add ½ teaspoon of the salt and the quinoa and give it a stir. Return the water to a boil, then reduce the heat to low and cover. Simmer, covered, for 15 minutes, or until the water has fully absorbed without burning the grains. Remove the pan from the heat and let stand, covered, for 5 minutes to continue to steam. Carefully uncover and fluff the quinoa with a fork. Allow it to cool to room temperature, uncovered. If the quinoa appears overcooked or wet, spread it out on a baking sheet to cool.

2 Transfer the quinoa to a large bowl and combine with ¼ teaspoon of the salt, the pepper, and about ½ cup of the well-stirred basil vinaigrette. Add the tomatoes and sprinkle them with the remaining ¼ teaspoon of salt. Gently stir in the corn, feta (if using), and fresh basil, reserving some for topping. Adjust the salt, pepper, and vinaigrette to taste. Sprinkle with the reserve basil.

BASIL VINAIGRETTE

- ☐ ½ cup packed fresh basil leaves
- ☐ 2 tablespoons white balsamic vinegar, or white wine vinegar

- ☐ ¼ teaspoon fine sea salt, plus more as needed
- ☐ 1 tablespoon honey, or agave or maple syrup
- ☐ ½ cup extra-virgin olive oil

Combine the basil, vinegar, salt, and honey in a blender and blend to chop the basil. With the blender running on low speed, stream in the olive oil, then cover, and turn up the speed to high. Blend until the vinaigrette is smooth and emulsified. Adjust the salt to taste.

SPICED-CARROT LAYER CAKE with BROWNED BUTTERCREAM FROSTING

With the amount of carrots in this cake, I swear I refute the sweet indulgence and convince myself I'm eating healthy. Seriously, I have had a lot of carrot cakes in my life, but this one, well, takes the cake. Author of *The Vegetable Butcher*, Cara Mangini, turns peeled, chopped, boiled, and puréed carrots into a rich confection topped with a highly addictive, silky smooth browned butter frosting and gorgeous ribbons of rainbow carrots.

Note: If you plan to top this cake with the rainbow carrot ribbons, allow the ribbons to stand for about 10 minutes on a paper towel. This will prevent their pigment from transferring to the cake.

Serves 6 to 8	Hands on: 1 hour 15 minutes	Total: 1 hour 30 minutes

- ☐ 1½ pounds carrots, peeled and coarsely cut into 1-inch pieces
- ☐ 3 cups all-purpose flour
- ☐ 2 teaspoons baking soda
- ☐ 1 teaspoon fine sea salt
- ☐ 1 teaspoon ground nutmeg
- ☐ 1½ teaspoons ground cinnamon

- ☐ ¾ cup canola oil
- ☐ ¾ cup stirred, unsweetened canned coconut milk
- ☐ 2 cups packed light brown sugar
- ☐ ½ cup granulated sugar
- ☐ ½ cup shredded coconut (optional)

- ☐ ¾ cup pecan halves, toasted and chopped
- ☐ Browned Buttercream Frosting (recipe follows)
- ☐ 3 rainbow carrots, peeled then shaved into ribbons with a vegetable peeler (optional)

1 Place the carrots in a large saucepan or dutch oven, and add enough water to cover them by 1 inch. Bring to a boil, then reduce the heat to a steady simmer and cook until the carrots are very tender, about 25 minutes.

2 Set an oven rack to the middle position and preheat the oven to 350°F. Lightly oil all sides of two 9-inch round cake pans and line the bottom of each pan with a round of parchment, smoothing out any air bubbles. Lightly oil the parchment and set the prepared pans aside.

3 In a large bowl, whisk together the flour, baking soda, salt, nutmeg, and cinnamon.

4 Drain the carrots well, transfer them to a food processor, and pulse, then process, until smooth. Scrape down the sides of the bowl and add the oil, coconut milk, and sugars.

Process until the mixture is well combined and smooth, scraping down the sides as necessary.

5 Add the carrot mixture to the dry ingredients and stir, using a rubber spatula, until just combined. Stir in the shredded coconut, if using, and the pecans. Evenly divide the batter between the two prepared pans, spreading out the batter with the spatula (it will be quite thick). Bake the cakes for 30 to 35 minutes, until cooked through the middles. The cakes should be firm to the touch and a tester should come out clean when inserted into the centers. Be careful not to overbake this cake.

6 Transfer the pans to a wire rack to cool for 10 minutes. Run a butter knife or offset spatula around the edges of the cakes. Turn the pans over to gently release the cakes out of the pans and onto the wire rack. Remove the ▶▶

parchment and let the cakes continue to cool completely.

7 To assemble the cake, place one layer, top side down, on a cake stand or plate and spoon a little less than half of the frosting on top. Use an offset spatula or a butter knife to evenly spread the frosting over the cake. (You will not frost the sides of this cake, but it's fine for frosting to spill out a bit onto the sides.) Place the remaining layer, top side up, over the frosted bottom layer. Scoop the remaining frosting onto the center of the second layer and spread it in an even layer all the way to the edge. Leave the sides bare. Top with a tangle of rainbow carrot ribbons, if you wish.

BROWNED BUTTERCREAM FROSTING

- ☐ ¾ cup (1½ sticks) unsalted butter
- ☐ 4 cups powdered sugar
- ☐ 2 teaspoons vanilla extract
- ☐ 3 to 6 tablespoons whole milk, plus more as needed

1 Melt the butter in a medium saucepan over medium heat and continue to gently simmer, stirring occasionally, until it becomes golden brown and fragrant, 8 to 10 minutes. (Solid particles should drop to the bottom of the pan and will start to brown while the clarified butter becomes golden in color.) Strain the butter through a fine-mesh strainer into a small bowl or liquid measure and let cool. Do not chill.

2 Meanwhile, sift the powdered sugar into a large bowl (or into the bowl of a stand mixer). Remove 1 cup and reserve it.

3 Add the browned butter to the large bowl along with the vanilla and beat together with an electric hand mixer (or a stand mixer) on medium speed until just incorporated. Add 3 tablespoons of milk and another ½ cup of the sugar. Beat on medium speed and then increase to high speed until the frosting is light and fluffy. Add more milk to loosen the frosting if it is too thick and lumpy, then continue to beat until you reach your desired consistency and no lumps remain. If you add too much liquid at any point, add more of the reserved sugar.

4 The frosting will keep, in an airtight container, refrigerated, for up to 1 week. Bring it to room temperature before using and add more milk if needed to thin it—beat briefly until well incorporated.

OMAR LOPEZ, CARNICERIA SPECIALTY MEATS

Enterprise, AL

Adversity.

As you make your way into Enterprise, Alabama, you'll see a monument, the only one in the world dedicated to an insect, that celebrates the kind of prosperity that can only result from adversity. At the turn of the nineteenth century, residents and farmers throughout the growing town of Enterprise had their lives threatened by an infestation of boll weevils, which destroyed the cotton crops and agrarian economy that largely supported life in this small Southern town.

But rather than lying on their backs, the farmers bound together, ditched the cotton crop entirely, and planted peanuts and other diversified crops in an effort to shore up losses and create a brighter future. The gamble paid off, and instead of damning the boll weevil altogether, the residents of Enterprise erected a statue to forever celebrate their "herald of prosperity."

Truth be told, I was unaware of this town's particular history—quirks, as we Southerners say—until I flew the Piper into town, following

directions to Carniceria Specialty Meats, located just off Boll Weevil Circle.

"You can't come back tomorrow?" says Omar Lopez. "Man, I'm very busy." Despite calling Omar weekly for the past few months to confirm my arrival, I'm not deterred—I forge ahead that today is the day. And within minutes, Omar seems to have embraced my visit, as I'm standing in the back of his butcher shop, watching him flutter between a band saw and a cleaver, chopping up pork shoulders and pig heads destined for a large copper cauldron to make the day's carnitas.

"I've been doing this since I was twelve, man," says Omar, flashing his gold teeth each and every time he laughs. Though he was born in Mexico City, Omar got his start in Veracruz, working in his uncle's butcher shop. "He taught me everything I know about cutting meat, but it was my mom who taught me how to cook." I watch as Omar stirs a large pot, nearly the size of him, containing large pieces of tender barbacoa that fall apart as he stirs. "Here, try it," he says, handing me a chunk of beef that I could make an entire meal. I scarf it down, nearly burning my tongue as the tender and spicy meat melts in my mouth. "Later, we make tacos," he says.

In those days and throughout Mexico, Omar shares that a butcher was not just responsible for breaking down the animal, but also harvesting it as well. "It was hard," says Omar. "I still remember being maybe fifteen years old, having just put down a hundred-and-twenty-five-kilo hog, and trying to push it through the streets of Veracruz in a wheelbarrow. People were laughing at me as I struggled with it in the street. I barely got it back to the shop. I kept telling myself that every time it fell, I had to get it back up and try harder."

After spending nearly a decade under his uncle's tenure, Omar struck out on his own, a period of time he refers to as being "young and dumb," when he tried to foster his own butcher trade in a highly competitive market. "I was only

making like two hundred pesos a day (less than ten dollars in today's money), working fifteen hours a day. I could barely survive," he says.

Though Omar had dreams of becoming a lawyer, he had to break the law in order to achieve his dreams. "I walked five days and five nights," he says. "Nobody understands—it is very hard." With just water and the clothes on his back, Omar took the chance to cross the border into the United States through Arizona. But Omar's hopes for prosperity promised by those who helped him make the journey were quickly dashed. "There wasn't really any work waiting for me—they took advantage of me," he says. Within a few months, Omar returned to Mexico.

A few years later, ever determined to make a life in America, Omar made the treacherous crossing once again, this time heading east to find work butchering in a chicken plant in Eufaula, Alabama. The gig was steady, the money regular, and he spent the next decade working jobs in several industries ranging from cooking to construction to landscaping. "This was my reality," Omar says. He transitioned jobs to make as much money as possible, while also supporting his family. During this period, he felt compelled to formalize his status, to give back to the country that gave him opportunities he could not find in his native Mexico. Omar explains that, after spending nearly a decade to become a legal citizen of the United States, the day he earned said citizenship "was the happiest day of my life."

In 2019 Omar doubled down on his dream, opening up his own carniceria, providing him with a chance not only to showcase his lifelong skills of butchery but to foster new tastes and opportunities in his community. As you enter Carniceria Specialty Meats and Grocery, a sign in the front reads "Eat Beef—The West Wasn't Won on Salad." After entry, an array of prepared foods lines the right side, with a clear opening to the back to view the butchering block, adjacent to a case of hand-butchered prime meats, including steaks and sausages. Though nearly all of the dry goods, sauces, and other items hail from Mexico, American flags and tributes to the Armed Forces make up the rest of the decorations. "I'm proud to share products from home, but I'm also very proud to be an American. I came here for a better life, and I'm honored to be contributing to the American dream."

As the lunch hour approaches, I gain a firsthand perspective as to why Omar couldn't take my calls—he is truly too busy. Over the course of the next few hours, I watch him grind in every role that's required of an entrepreneur, from mentoring his own boys, who are also working in the kitchen, to making custom orders for customers, to plating up tortas, tacos, and fajita platters. The line of customers stretches to the entrance as people are picking up meals to go or hand-butchered meats to grill for the upcoming weekend. Whatever you want, Omar does, and I can quickly tell that he has built his business just as much on hospitality as expertise.

Instead of trying to keep up with Omar, I decide to join the lunch crowd. I get busy making good on the offer to pile chunks of barbacoa high on house-made tortillas with fresh pico de gallo. I'm surprised to also find fresh ceviche. Because

of the proximity to the Gulf Coast, Omar likes to highlight local Gulf shrimp in a traditional dish that I prop on top of tostadas, washing them down with a cold Topo Chico, since I know I'll be having to fly my way home. For dessert, I decide to pack a bag of the house-made chicharrones to sit left seat on the flight, their crunchy and salty bites to satisfy my in-flight cravings.

As I make for my departure, Omar and I capture a few photos together outside the shop, both grinning ear to ear while Omar's contagious laughs and one-liners continue to zing past customers making their way into the shop.

"You've built something really special here, Omar," I say.

"Life is not easy, man," he says. "But now, I'm giving people the kind of opportunities I didn't have. I always tell them, it is not easy, but if you want something, you have to work for it."

It seems that adversity continues to herald prosperity for those in Enterprise, Alabama. ■

OMAR LOPEZ, CARNICERIA SPECIALTY MEATS **139**

OMAR'S CHICHARRONES

A variation on the standard chicharrones, or pork rinds, these contain tidbits of meat against the skin. It's a once-a-week specialty that Carniceria Specialty Meats and Grocery owner Omar Lopez prepares to high demand. Most butchers will be able to provide skin that you can use for this simple recipe, but the technique at home is crucial—cut the skin into pieces and allow them to dry for an hour or so prior to frying, which helps to stiffen the skin and also to remove any water from the surface area. Omar prefers to fry the skins in pork lard, which you can also source from your butcher, but vegetable or canola oil will also do the trick. The key is a double-fry method: The first fry renders the fat of the skin down some, and the second fry creates that crunchy crispiness we all crave. Be cautious not to overcook when frying—you don't want the skins to darken past a golden brown, otherwise they will get tough. I like to use a splatter screen over the frying oil to prevent any unnecessary splattering and popping.

Serves 2 or 3	Hands on: 15 minutes	Total: 1 hour, 15 minutes

- ☐ 1 pound pork skin, cut into 1½- to 2-inch squares
- ☐ Lard or vegetable oil, for frying
- ☐ 1 teaspoon kosher salt

1 Set a wire rack inside a rimmed baking sheet and place the pork skin on it. Allow to air-dry for an hour, or up to overnight, in the refrigerator. Pat the skins dry with a paper towel prior to frying.

2 Fill a dutch oven with lard until it reaches at least 4 inches up the side of the pot as measured from the bottom. Over medium heat, bring the lard temperature to 350°F. Carefully add the pork skin pieces to the pot, working in batches as necessary, stirring to ensure they are not clumped together, and fry for 4 to 6 minutes to render some of the fat of the skin.

3 Remove the pieces from the pot, and increase the heat to medium high to bring the lard to 400°F. Place the pieces back into the pot to finish frying. The pieces will pop and sizzle as they expand, so use caution or a splatter screen to prevent any splattering. Fry the chicharrones until they are just golden, 2 to 3 minutes. Remove them from the pot and place them on a paper towel–lined baking sheet to absorb the excess grease. Season with the salt. Serve.

GULF SHRIMP CEVICHE

I was somewhat surprised to find an array of seafood at Carniceria Specialty Meats and Grocery, but given its proximity to the Gulf Coast, owner Omar Lopez is happy to carry fresh fish, shrimp, and whatever else his customers demand alongside his prime meats. While watching the lunch crowd, I polled many of the customers waiting in line about what I should try, and most exclaimed that they had come for the ceviche—even though it has a reputation for having a bit of spice. While there are thousands of variations on ceviche, Omar includes ingredients like carrot and cucumber that are less common, adding both color and crunch that make this version incredibly satisfying. "I make this fresh every day. It's good to eat it nearly right after it's been made—don't wait, dig in," says Omar.

While ceviche is traditionally served alongside chips, I take Omar's advice to not wait and heap it on top of tostadas, and crunch into every bite with a smile.

Serves 4	Hands on: 25 minutes	Total: 45 minutes

- ☐ 1 pound extra-large Gulf shrimp, peeled, deveined, and cut into bite-sized pieces
- ☐ ¼ cup very finely diced red onion
- ☐ ¼ cup very finely diced white onion
- ☐ ¼ cup very finely diced cucumber

- ☐ ¼ cup very finely diced carrot
- ☐ ½ jalapeño, seeds and ribs removed and very finely diced
- ☐ ½ avocado, peeled, pitted, and finely diced
- ☐ 2 cloves garlic, minced
- ☐ ½ cup chopped fresh cilantro

- ☐ 2 limes, juiced, plus more as needed
- ☐ ¼ cup orange juice
- ☐ 1 teaspoon kosher salt, plus more as needed
- ☐ 1 teaspoon fresh-cracked black pepper
- ☐ 8 corn tostadas

1 In a large bowl, add the shrimp, onions, cucumber, carrot, jalapeño, avocado, garlic, cilantro, lime and orange juices, and salt and pepper and stir together to ensure even distribution. Cover and refrigerate for 10 to 15 minutes. Remove from the refrigerator and stir again. The shrimp should be just slightly firm from sitting in the citrus juices. Taste, adding more salt or lime juice, as needed.

2 Pile the ceviche generously on the corn tostadas. Serve immediately.

OMAR'S TORTA

In my time spent with Omar Lopez, owner of Carniceria Specialty Meats and Grocery, I quickly realized that Omar has a generous heart when it comes to portions. Take, for example, this "steak sandwich," as he calls it. When he hands me a torta shaped like a football and weighing what has to be a few pounds, I sense that this sandwich has more than just steak, and I start looking around to see if it also comes with three friends to help devour it.

Omar tells me that in Mexico City, this kind of street food is some of the most exciting cuisine in the country. And while this torta is a skirt steak sandwich, it also has ham, hot dogs, queso, and the rest of the trimmings. The torta roll is buttery soft with toasted edges. I nearly have to unhinge my jaw to try to get everything in one bite, and despite the massive undertaking, it's cheesy, meaty, and savory all at the same time. I can see why this is a late-night favorite best shared.

Serves 2	Hands on: 25 minutes	Total: 25 minutes

- ☐ 1 tablespoon vegetable oil
- ☐ 6 ounces skirt steak, sliced very thin
- ☐ ½ teaspoon kosher salt
- ☐ ½ teaspoon fresh-cracked black pepper
- ☐ ½ teaspoon garlic powder
- ☐ 1 slice thick-cut ham

- ☐ 2 beef hot dogs, split in half lengthwise
- ☐ 2 to 3 thin slices red bell pepper
- ☐ 2 to 3 thin slices green bell pepper
- ☐ 1 tablespoon mayonnaise
- ☐ 1 large torta-style roll, split and toasted

- ☐ 1 cup grated Oaxaca cheese, or white American cheese
- ☐ 1 tablespoon finely diced white onion
- ☐ 1 tablespoon finely chopped fresh cilantro

1 Heat a large cast-iron skillet over medium-high heat. When the pan begins to just smoke, add the oil, swirling it in the pan to ensure an even coat. Add the skirt steak and season with the salt, black pepper, and garlic powder. Cook the steak for 2 minutes per side. Remove the steak to a plate to rest and add the ham, hot dogs, and bell peppers to the skillet. Cook, stirring on occasion, for 4 to 6 minutes, until brown.

2 Remove all the ingredients from the skillet to a plate and reduce the heat to medium. Spread the mayonnaise on the bottom half of the torta roll and place it, mayo side up, in the skillet. Pile the steak, ham, hot dogs, and bell peppers onto the roll. Layer the cheese on top of the meat and peppers and cover the skillet for 1 to 1½ minutes to melt the cheese.

3 Remove the torta from the skillet and sprinkle the onion and cilantro over the cheese. Finish with the top half of the torta roll, cut the sandwich in half, and serve immediately.

BARBACOA TACOS

The first taste I got during my visit to Carniceria Specialty Meats and Grocery was straight from owner Omar Lopez's hands—a chunk of the barbacoa meat that had been stewing in a large pot throughout the morning. Just a few hours later, all of it was devoured by those coming in for a quick lunch or those taking the meltingly tender meat to go. There are no shortcuts to Omar's success, and the same could be said for his cooking. Omar uses tougher, less utilized cuts of beef and cooks them low and slow, allowing time and temperature to do their magic, churning out this delicious meat that can be enjoyed on its own or piled into tacos, quesadillas, tortas, or tamales—all of which you can ask Omar for, despite the fact there isn't a menu in his shop.

Serves 6 to 8	Hands on: 1 hour	Total: 6 hours

BRAISING SAUCE
- ☐ 4 cups chicken stock, plus more as needed
- ☐ ½ cup orange juice
- ☐ ½ cup lime juice, plus more as needed
- ☐ 1 tablespoon apple cider vinegar
- ☐ 3 cloves garlic, smashed
- ☐ 1 small yellow onion, cut into chunks
- ☐ 3 chipotle chiles in adobo sauce
- ☐ 5 dried guajillo chiles, stems and seeds removed
- ☐ 1 dried ancho chile, stem and seeds removed
- ☐ 1 teaspoon ground cloves
- ☐ 1 tablespoon ground cumin
- ☐ 1 tablespoon dried oregano
- ☐ Kosher salt

MEAT
- ☐ 3 pounds chuck roast, cut into large chunks with any large portions of fat removed
- ☐ 1 pound beef cheeks, cut into large chunks
- ☐ 1 tablespoon kosher salt
- ☐ 1 tablespoon fresh-cracked black pepper
- ☐ 1 tablespoon garlic powder
- ☐ 2 tablespoons vegetable oil
- ☐ 2 bay leaves

PICO DE GALLO
- ☐ 2 cups finely diced tomatoes, seeds and ribs removed
- ☐ 1 cup finely diced and seeded cucumber
- ☐ ½ cup finely diced yellow onion
- ☐ ¾ cup chopped fresh cilantro
- ☐ 2 cloves garlic, minced
- ☐ ½ jalapeño, seeds and ribs removed and finely dice
- ☐ 4½ teaspoons lime juice
- ☐ 1 teaspoon kosher salt

- ☐ 18 to 24 corn tortillas, to serve

1 In a large pot, add the stock, orange and lime juices, vinegar, garlic, onion, chiles, cloves, cumin, and oregano and bring to a simmer over medium-high heat. Reduce the heat to low and allow the braising sauce to simmer while preparing the meat. As the process for browning the meat finalizes, turn off the heat, and carefully use an immersion blender (or regular blender) to process the ingredients until smooth. Taste the sauce, adding salt or lime juice if necessary.

2 Meanwhile, arrange the meat on a large rimmed baking sheet and season evenly with

the salt, pepper, and garlic powder. Place a large heavy-bottomed stockpot or oversized dutch oven over medium-high heat and add the oil. Working in batches to avoid overcrowding the pot, brown the meat on all sides, 2 to 3 minutes.

3 Transfer all of the cooked meat back into the pot and ladle in the braising sauce until it completely submerges the meat. Note: Additional chicken stock or water may be added if needed to cover. Place the bay leaves into the pot and allow the mixture to come to a slow simmer.

4 When the mixture reaches a simmer, cover the pot, reduce the heat to low, and simmer the beef until it is easily-pulled-apart tender, 4 to 6 hours. Remove the beef from the pot and cover with foil to keep warm, and reserve braising liquid.

5 While the beef simmers, prepare the pico de gallo. In a medium bowl, combine the tomatoes, cucumber, onion, cilantro, garlic, jalapeño, lime juice, and salt. Refrigerate until ready to use.

6 To assemble the tacos, warm the tortillas in a cast-iron skillet over medium heat for 30 seconds per side. Pull and portion the reserved barbacoa meat into each taco and top with pico de gallo and reserved braising liquid as desired. Serve.

VINCENT DISALVO, DISALVO'S RESTAURANT AND LOUNGE

Williamsport, PA

For business travelers, there's an unspoken rule that comes from a life of travels. When you call your spouse on the road and they ask how the trip is going, you must always answer, "The weather is terrible and there's nothing good to eat."

I explained to my wife early in the evening that snow would keep me from getting out of Williamsport, Pennsylvania, that night. Tired, hungry, and hung-up wet, I walked the streets, finding myself on the outskirts of downtown when a *Purple Rain*–like sign reading DiSalvo's in cursive print lured me in like a beacon in the night. I suppose I was partially truthful—the weather, after all, was bad for flight, even for sturdy Lycoming aircraft engines, for which the town is known. But if I am to come clean, when I called my wife back to say goodnight, I failed to mention that I had just eaten a rigatone alla bolognese that had me praying the snow might continue so I might have another meal there.

Sidling up to the large bar, I find myself in a bit of hiatus, garnering hunting and fishing tales from the local diners over rounds of stiff cocktails. But on this evening, I had no idea that my friendly overtures and atmospheric misfortunes would lead to something greater.

"We make this in-house—give it a try," says Vincent DiSalvo, sporting a crisp white chef coat and graying hair tied tightly behind in a ponytail. In his hands he showcases a plate piled high with house-made coppa, prosciutto, and dry sausage. It takes only a few bites, and a few minutes, to realize that Vince is a kind spirit, willing to share his passion for food and joie de vivre to anyone, even to those strangers like me who are "stuck" in town.

"My grandfather Antonio came here in 1903, emigrating from Messina, Italy, to find a better life in America," says Vince. As a shoemaker, Antonio quickly found work and success in his vestige trade, but he also decided to broaden his ventures by partnering and creating the Williamsport Macaroni Company in 1905. Providing staples like spaghetti, ziti, capellini, vermicelli, rigatoni, and tagliarini, the company supplied the growing Italian immigrant community with homeland favorites and also fueled the lumberjacks of the northern tier counties. Sadly with the onslaught of larger competitors and the Great Depression, the pasta company shut down after nearly thirty years.

"This is the family table," Vince shares as he's recounting the unique family history and photos to me as we walk toward the back corner of DiSalvo's Restaurant. The large round family table sits in a direct sight line to the kitchen, where Vince has spent the majority of his lifetime preserving family tradition.

On my first chance encounter with Vince, he romanticized over the family traditions he has carried on since his childhood. With a rich family history in the area, Vince grew up spending time with his grandfather Antonio, father Vince, uncle Nick, and cousins, hunting and fishing from the vast expanse offered in the hidden valleys and Allegheny mountain ranges in this lush part of central Pennsylvania. As Vince lays fifty-year-old Polaroids on the counter, I witness bucks and hogs hanging and being butchered by men and women who are no longer on this soil, but it's a valid precursor to honor the moment.

As we prepare to butcher the pig in family tradition, Vince's son Vincenzo has flown up from his current base in Charleston, South Carolina, to foster the family tradition, along with cousin Stefano. A hog weighing more than 120 pounds dressed sits ready for the butcher block. Instead of waiting on the young bucks, Vince grabs it by the quarters, slushing it across the kitchen counter and onto the wooden block. Before his son and Stefano can say a word, Vince squares them both in the eye, saying, "Dad's not dead yet."

We wheel the pig out into the courtyard of DiSalvo's, lighting a fire as Vince goes to work on butchering the hog in the traditional style. There is a pause, however, in the cool, crisp Pennsylvania spring air. With bluebird skies, clutching a boning knife in hand, Vince stares at the kids, savoring the bounty at hand, the crackling of the fire, and the smell of smoke in the air. "I can feel my dad here," he says.

Guided by memory, experience, and perhaps spirits, Vince gets to work crafting the primal cuts of the hog, making quick work of the shoulders, hams, and loins, some of which will become our immediate pleasure. He follows with those cuts destined for curing that will last the rest of the year. The fire cracks, beckoning some of the trimmings from the butchering process. "Go get the cast-iron skillet," says Vince. The skillet is rested upon glowing embers, with pieces of meaty pork fat sizzling away as we finalize our more distinct cuts, like guanciale and loins destined for coppa. As the pork finishes, we break for a moment, nearly burning our hands as we all poke for the meaty pieces in the skillet. "What's for breakfast?" I say.

In less than an hour, Vince has broken down the whole animal—he might not be a butcher by trade, but he is a perfect example of how tradition, practice, and preservation are hallmarks of what have made this country, and its people, so incredibly interesting.

At the surface level, I've known Vince only in the right here and now. As I dig a bit further, I find a deeper background, one on a tuna clipper in the South Pacific after spending time studying

biology at Wilkes University. After a few years at sea, he returned to Williamsport and worked in the nightclub trade as he supported his new and growing family.

But tradition never dies, and it was Vince's mom, Mariannina, who had immigrated in 1956 and revived the families' 1900s tradition by restarting DiSalvo's Pasta in 1984. Vince returned to his roots, working for his mother as they nurtured a business that grew to multiple locations and offered family classics beyond pastas to a hungry crowd throughout the region. In 1992 Vince took the vision further, opening a smaller café under the family name, until he finally settled on his flagship in 1997. I walk the grounds of the DiSalvo's property on East 4th Street as Vince seems intent on a new expansion.

"You aren't getting tired?" I ask.

"Never," says Vince. "I need to learn something new every day," he says.

We walk back inside the restaurant, and perhaps reflecting on our conversation, Vince goes about ensuring that I learn something new as well. The whole pork belly that he's expertly butchered hours earlier lies on a service table. Vince goes to work chopping an array of garlic, herbs, and bacon that will find their way inside of

this belly. "I don't share this with a lot of folks," says Vince as he melds together a concoction of baking soda and vinegar to ensure a crispy skin. "But I trust you," he says, both half-serious and convincingly.

Serious or not, I'm honored to have earned Vince's trust. My time spent in Williamsport reminds me that life can throw everything at you, but it is meant for good. You just have to be open to finding it.

As I depart DiSalvo's, this time with weather in perfect conditions, I ask Vince for any sage advice or parting words, until the next time.

"Don't close yourself off—you stop growing," he says. "My goal is to learn and teach. If I can share something I learn with someone else, well, that's priceless." ∎

PORCHETTA

The traditional style of butchering the hog is the key to authenticity here. Instead of preserving the ribs, the entire loin section is sliced from the ribs, providing a lay-flat loin that's perfectly suited for this Italian classic. Of important note, at DiSalvo's, the actual tenderloins are removed from the belly for making other cured delicacies, and the rib portions of meat are all saved to make in-house sausages. The best method, from my perspective, is owner Vince DiSalvo's technique to help dry and set up the skin for that beautiful crispy and crunchy reveal. He rubs baking soda over the skin and lets it sit prior to activating it with vinegar. Use caution and make sure the reaction stays with the skin, and not on the meat. All good things must rest, so it's important to let the entire porchetta rest prior to slicing and serving. This is a Sunday roast on steroids—wow, just wow.

Serves 8 to 10	Hands on: 1 hour	Total: 2 hours 30 minutes

- ☐ 6 pounds pork belly, skin on
- ☐ 2 pounds uncured smoked bacon, chopped
- ☐ 10 cloves garlic, minced
- ☐ 2 bunches fresh flat-leaf parsley, chopped

- ☐ 2 tablespoons kosher salt
- ☐ 2 tablespoons fresh-cracked black pepper
- ☐ 1 fennel bulb, stems removed and thinly sliced
- ☐ ½ cup baking soda

- ☐ 1 cup white vinegar
- ☐ 8 sprigs fresh rosemary
- ☐ ½ cup dry white wine

1 Preheat the oven to 350°F. Lay the pork belly, skin side down with long side parallel to the surface edge, on a work surface. In the bowl of a food processor, add the bacon, garlic, and parsley and pulse until it becomes a paste consistency. Evenly smear the belly with the paste, and season with 1 tablespoon salt and 1 tablespoon pepper. Next, evenly distribute the fennel on top of the paste.

2 Roll the belly tightly from bottom to top, with the seam on the bottom to finish. Truss or tie the rolled belly in 1-inch intervals from end to end, using butcher's twine.

3 Rub the outside skin liberally with the baking soda, and let it sit for 15 minutes. Carefully rinse the baking soda with the white vinegar, keeping the vinegar from washing onto the meat. Season the rolled belly on all sides with the remaining tablespoon salt and tablespooon pepper. To finish, secure the rosemary sprigs under the butcher's twine.

4 Place the pork belly roll on a wire roasting rack set inside a roasting pan. Roast, checking every 30 minutes and rotating on occasion for even browning, for 1½ hours, or until the internal temperature reaches 140°F. Remove the porchetta from the oven and allow it to rest for 30 minutes before slicing.

5 While the porchetta is resting, place the roasting pan over medium heat. When the drippings begin to bubble, deglaze the pan by adding the white wine and using a wooden spoon to scrape up any of the browned bits from the bottom. Reduce the heat to medium low, and reduce the mixture by half, about 15 minutes.

6 Slice the pork between trusses and serve with the pan sauce.

MAKING
PORCHETTA

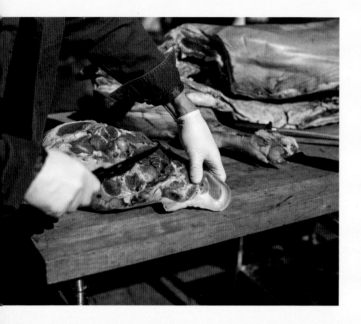

PORK BREAD

Pane con Ciccioli

In the old days, Vince and family would enjoy cooking up bites and trimmings from the pig right as it was being butchered for the family. Those cast-iron bites, whatever was left over for that matter, were destined to be folded into some bread with tangy peppers and cooked to perfection. While I've never seen this particular dish before, it's the kind of thing I know is important if only because Vince's son continuously asked about the right chop on the ingredients, as well as the ratio of pork to peppers. This is, my friends, a family classic, and it's important to make it right. I can say, the day you butcher a whole hog, enjoy its trimmings for breakfast, and essentially roll the rest into a pizza-style dough as laid out here is a day well spent. Secret is out. This is delicious.

Serves 2 or 3	Hands on: 1 hour	Total: 1 hour

- ☐ 1 pound pork shoulder trimmed of fat, cut into ½-inch cubes
- ☐ 1 cup pickled banana peppers
- ☐ 1 teaspoon kosher salt
- ☐ 1 teaspoon fresh-cracked black pepper
- ☐ ½ cup dry white wine
- ☐ All-purpose flour, for dusting
- ☐ 1 pound fresh bread dough, such as pizza dough
- ☐ ¼ cup extra-virgin olive oil

1 Place a cast-iron skillet over medium heat. When the skillet begins to slightly smoke, add the pork and brown on all sides until well browned and cooked through, 12 to 14 minutes. Drain the excess fat from the pan, add the banana peppers, season with the salt and black pepper, and toss to incorporate the peppers and seasoning into the browned pork.

2 Add the wine to deglaze the skillet, using a wooden spoon to scrape up any of the browned bits from the bottom. Reduce the heat to low, and cook until most of the wine is evaporated, about 3 minutes. Remove the skillet from the heat.

3 Meanwhile, preheat the oven to 350°F. Dust a surface with flour and roll out the bread dough into roughly a 6 x 12-inch rectangle. Spoon the pork mixture evenly over the stretched dough. Very carefully roll the dough lengthwise into a pinwheel and place the rolled dough, seam side down, onto a baking sheet.

4 Brush the dough with the olive oil and place it into the oven. Bake until golden brown, 25 to 30 minutes. Remove the bread from the oven and let rest 10 minutes. Slice the bread and serve.

PACCHERI PASTA with FRESH SAUSAGE

Paccheri con Salsiccia Fresca

While we all might not have a meat grinder at home, don't fret—you can still pull off this simple, rustic style of cooking to provide a great family meal. Pasta is at the heart and soul of Italian cooking, and these short, tubular paccheri shapes make the perfect conduit for the fresh basil and loose Italian sausage. When I say loose, I mean it—sans casings. You can chop the pork collar entirely by hand, or if equipped, process the marinated pieces even finer by using a meat grinder. This is a very simple, satisfying dish that's held together by a perfect cut of pork, and a process of cooking up beautiful pasta. It's a meal to stop you in your tracks.

Serves 4	Hands on: 1 hour	Total: 13 hours

LOOSE ITALIAN SAUSAGE

- ☐ 1 pound trimmed pork collar, or trimmed pork shoulder
- ☐ ¼ cup dry white wine
- ☐ 1 teaspoon fennel seeds
- ☐ 1 tablespoon kosher salt
- ☐ ½ teaspoon crushed red pepper
- ☐ ½ teaspoon fresh-cracked black pepper
- ☐ 1 clove garlic, minced

PASTA

- ☐ 1 tablespoon plus 1 teaspoon kosher salt
- ☐ 12 ounces uncooked paccheri pasta, or rigatoni
- ☐ 2 tablespoons extra-virgin olive oil
- ☐ 1 medium sweet onion, finely minced
- ☐ ¼ teaspoon crushed red pepper
- ☐ ¼ teaspoon fresh-cracked black pepper
- ☐ ¼ cup dry white wine
- ☐ 1 bunch fresh flat-leaf parsley, finely chopped
- ☐ 4 to 6 leaves fresh sweet basil, roughly chopped
- ☐ One 14.5-ounce can whole San Marzano tomatoes, squeezed by hand with juices reserved
- ☐ ½ cup grated Parmigiano-Reggiano cheese

1 Prepare the sausage by dicing the pork into small cubes, about ¼ inch in size. In a sealable container, place the pork and add the wine, fennel seeds, salt, red pepper, black pepper, and garlic. Toss to combine. Place in the refrigerator and marinate overnight. Note: If desired, the marinated pork can be further broken down in a meat grinder, using a ⅜-inch plate.

2 For the pasta, over medium-high heat, bring a large pot of water to a boil. Add the 1 tablespoon of salt and the pasta to the water. Cook the pasta al dente, according to the instructions. Reserve one-quarter cup of pasta water and drain.

3 Meanwhile, add the olive oil to a large sauté pan over medium-high heat. Add the marinated sausage and brown, stirring often, for 6 to 8 minutes. Next, add the onion, the remaining 1 teaspoon of salt, the red pepper, and black pepper. Sauté the onion until caramelized, stirring often, for 4 to 6 minutes. Deglaze the pan by adding the wine, using a wooden spoon to scrape up any of the browned bits from the bottom. Add the parsley, basil, and tomatoes with their juices, bring the mixture to a slow simmer, and reduce the heat to medium low, simmering the mixture for 5 minutes.

4 Add the cooked pasta to the pan, along with the reserved pasta water. Stir the pasta as the mixture returns to a simmer, 2 minutes. Add the cheese, and stir to combine. Serve immediately.

NONNA'S DEER

Cervo à la Nonna

I questioned Vince DiSalvo, owner of DiSalvo's, what recipe one might not get to enjoy at his restaurant. An avid hunter and outdoorsman, Vince always has perfectly butchered and preserved wild game cuts on hand. Thus he took the time to whip up a childhood classic, once prepared by those lovely ladies who came before him. The backstrap, or loin, is one of the most prized cuts and often the easiest to harvest after field-dressing a deer. In this dish, it's treated both respectfully and simply. After a quick pan-sear to rare, it's allowed to finish over julienned onion and bell pepper. A stew-like dish, this classic begs to be sopped up with crusty bread and a good house wine.

Serves 4	Hands on: 30 minutes	Total: 45 minutes

- ☐ 2 pounds venison backstrap, trimmed of any silver skin and sliced into ½-inch-thick medallions
- ☐ 1 tablespoon kosher salt, plus more as needed
- ☐ ½ tablespoon fresh-cracked black pepper, plus more as needed

- ☐ 1 cup all-purpose flour
- ☐ 2 tablespoons extra-virgin olive oil
- ☐ 1 small sweet onion, julienned
- ☐ 1 red bell pepper, julienned
- ☐ 4 San Marzano canned tomatoes, squeezed by hand with juices reserved

- ☐ 1 bunch fresh flat-leaf parsley, roughly chopped, with a few tablespoons reserved for garnish
- ☐ ¼ cup dry red wine
- ☐ ¼ teaspoon crushed red pepper
- ☐ Italian-style or sourdough bread, to serve

1 Season the venison with the salt and black pepper on both sides. Add the flour to a shallow bowl and dredge the medallions on both sides, shaking off any excess flour.

2 Place a large cast-iron skillet over medium-high heat. When the skillet begins to slightly smoke, add the oil and swirl the pan to ensure the oil evenly coats the bottom and sides. Add the venison medallions and sear until brown, about 2 minutes on both sides. Next, add the onion and bell pepper and stir to combine. Using tongs, place the venison on top of the onion and bell pepper to prevent the venison from overcooking. Allow the onion and pepper to caramelize, 6 to 8 minutes, stirring as needed to bring the onion and pepper in contact with the surface of the pan.

3 Add the tomatoes with their juices, the parsley, and wine and stir. Bring the mixture to a simmer, reduce the heat to medium low, and continue to cook for 4 to 5 minutes to thicken the sauce. Taste the mixture, adding additional salt and black pepper as needed. Add the red pepper and garnish with the reserved parsley.

4 Remove the skillet from the heat. Serve the venison with warmed bread for dipping.

VINCENT DISALVO, DISALVO'S RESTAURANT AND LOUNGE   161

ABRAHAM SAMUEL DENNIS, DENNIS FOOD STORE

Valdosta, GA

Devoted. Faithful. Kind.

These are the traits for which I remember my grandfather Abraham Samuel Dennis—or as I lovingly called him, Giddy.

When people pass, we are left with their tangibles, like his F. Dick–brand chef's knife that still to this day carries a sharper blade than any of my own. I treasure that item—it isn't hidden away in a box not to be seen or used. Rather it sits on a magnetic steel to the side of my stove. It is something I see every day. Tangibles stoke the fire of memory and, even better, legacy. They remind us not only of what was but, perhaps more importantly, what to carry on.

At the turn of the century, life in our family's native Beirut, Lebanon, offered very little opportunity, so seeking a better life, my great-great-grandfather Jim went about changing the course of our family history. Initially Jim spent a few months in France, only to cross the ocean to America, through Ellis Island. Not speaking any English, Jim made ends meet by selling dry goods on the railroad lines, traveling from town to town, until he eventually procured enough funds to move his wife, Mary, and the rest of his family to join him in America.

It was on South Patterson Street in Valdosta, Georgia, where Jim went about building his own version of the American dream, starting with a small gas station and fruit stand, growing the business into a small store with his son Sam and

Sam's new bride, Sophie. My great-grandfather Sam and Sophie had married at an early age, as was custom in those years, soon after meeting at a first communion in Birmingham, Alabama. The pair went on to foster the first generation to be born on American soil, including my grandfather Abraham and his siblings, David and Mary.

But South Patterson Street was no easy street. My grandfather Abe recalled having to live with the family in the back of the store in the early days and spending many a night sleeping on the floor. Through the Great Depression, the family survived, with the kids working alongside their parents, doing whatever it took to make ends meet. Eventually the war broke out in Europe again, with both my grandfather and his brother, David, taking up arms to preserve freedom.

When Abe and David returned from the war, America was teeming with new opportunity. Capitalizing on the butchering skills my grandfather had perfected during his time in the service, he and his siblings, David and Mary, pushed the envelope, expanding the Dennis Food Store into the first supermarket of its time—known for having the best meats in town—in Valdosta.

A few years later, Abe met a woman at a family wedding in Jacksonville, Florida. As the story goes, Blanche played hard to get, until finally deciding amidst an old-school flicker film at a classic theater that he was the one. If you knew her for just one minute, the "playing hard to get

part" was just her way of having a good time! My grandmother Blanche and Abe were married in Jacksonville, Florida, in 1949. They were together for more than fifty years, and had four kids: Marcia, Yvonne (my mother), Jim, and Jeanne.

Upon Sam's passing in 1963, the responsibility of running the store was inherited by the next generation. Since my grandfather was the oldest, the preservation of the business fell primarily on his shoulders. That said, it was a family business, and David, Mary, and Sophie each played a vital role in expanding and maintaining the livelihood that preserved each family.

As my uncle Jim recalls, my grandfather would sharpen his knives in the early mornings with a long steel, looking as though he was a surgeon ready to attend to a procedure. Weekly, my grandfather accepted deliveries of beef sides delivered to the back door by an Armour-brand meat truck. The delivery man, dressed in a white coat with a cap and sash, would drop them at the door for weighing, and Abe and David would sign off on the order before hanging them in the aging coolers. While Abe would go to work breaking down the custom cuts, David would go about his

duties, including spicing the house-made sausage sold by the pound and, on occasion, preparing link sausages on request. On Saturdays a soundtrack of Paul Harvey could be heard in the background on the radio, with David and Abe eating lunch—cooked hot dogs with my aunt Mary's famous tomato, onion, and mustard relish—habitually at high noon. There were always enough dogs left over, wrapped in wax paper, for anyone lucky to drop in.

For me, these are habitual family rituals that I've only gleaned through discovery. While I was growing up, my parents lovingly recounted many stories of the old store, like the time my older sister, Ashley, had her first sip of a Coca-Cola before she could walk. When I came around, four years later, the store had changed hands. In retirement, ever devoted, my grandfather Abe spent his time serving the Knights of Columbus, a Catholic organization focused on charity and faith, to better his community spiritually in the same way he gave to his community throughout his professional career.

My fondest childhood recollections come from our regular visits to Valdosta, of us sitting

together at the small circular kitchen table, eating a breakfast of fresh-squeezed orange juice, boiled eggs, and labneh, supplemented by cold, leftover stuffed grape leaves. Perhaps my favorite memories come from an Easter tradition. While most kids were chasing about the house finding treats from the Easter Bunny, Giddy and I would scour through dozens of hard-boiled eggs that had been dyed and decorated the night before. With the sound of oil rolling in cast-iron pans as my grandmother, who we called Sitty, cooked her famous fried chicken, we searched for "strong" eggs, as we deemed them. The game was to try to crack the opponents' eggs by popping each by hammering the opposing eggs together by hand to determine whose egg was the strongest—those that wouldn't crack under pressure. Often mine were the first to crack because Abe would encircle his egg so tightly with his fist that I was never able to make contact with the surface. Until, of course, I got a bit older and caught on to the technique. It was our tradition, and not an Easter goes by where I don't think of those memories.

I count myself fortunate to not only have known both sets of my immediate grandparents but to have spent quality time with them, even

into my early adult years. But in the early winter of 2004, our family knew it was time for my Giddy to reach the heavens. In his final days, our family came together in Valdosta, and in our faith, we witnessed both the sacrifice and blessing of one's transition.

My aunt Jeanne so lovingly eulogized and captured every moment, including my grandfather's final words:

"I would like to say, only to say, just one thing in the world, that we always have, we have one thing to say, one thing to do—that we love, love, love each other.

"I want you all to stay together, be together. Love each other, love, love, love; always be together."

While I struggled for quite some time to find the right words to encapsulate a life and a family patriarch, I have chosen to simply go back to his own words. This experience of posthumously revisiting my own family history has allowed me a deeper connection with my own aunts and uncles.

I think my grandfather got it all right. Despite all of his giving, his sacrifices, and his talents, I think simply his final words were his best words.

After all, we just need to love, love, love. ◼

KIBBEH NAYYEH

كبة نيئة

In our family, there is probably no dish more celebratory than kibbeh nayyeh, an iconic Lebanese dish. When I was a kid, the savory meat mixture, usually made with beef or lamb and eaten sandwiched between thin Syrian bread, would always be on the cocktail table amidst an array of hummus, olives, and cheeses to kick off a holiday meal.

It wasn't until I reached my adolescence that I realized I was actually eating raw meat. While the meat is raw, much care goes into preparing this dish to consume it without worry. That starts first by selecting a portion of lean top round steak. Typically this is sourced in the early morning from the butcher—it should be the first cut that is ground, usually three times, on clean blades. You should never use beef that has been ground prior, or on blades that have not been sanitized. In my own home, I have a specific hand grinder that I use just for making kibbeh. Fine bulgur and onion is then added to the ground meat and melded together, seasoned simply with salt and pepper. Ice water, on the side, will allow you to keep your hands chilled and keep the meat from sticking to them while incorporating the ingredients and shaping the kibbeh.

Typically kibbeh nayyeh is served alongside breads, sliced onions, and fresh mint. This nayyeh (raw) version of kibbeh should be consumed immediately, with any leftovers used for baked or fried kibbeh varieties (see page 169).

Serves 4 to 6	Hands on: 30 minutes	Total: 30 minutes

- ☐ 1½ pounds top round steak
- ☐ 1 cup #1 bulgur wheat
- ☐ 1 white onion, peeled and ends removed

- ☐ ½ tablespoon kosher salt, plus more as needed
- ☐ 1 teaspoon fresh-cracked black pepper, plus more as needed

- ☐ Ice water, for dipping
- ☐ Scallion green, as garnish

1 Trim the fat cleanly from the steak: no white portions of fat or sinew should remain. Next, grind the steak three times using a meat grinder with sanitized fine blades. Keep the meat very cold throughout the process and place the ground meat in a large bowl to mix freely.

2 Under cold water, rinse the bulgur two or three times in a fine-mesh strainer. Place the rinsed bulgur over the top of the meat. Next, process the onion in a food processor until finely puréed. Alternatively, the onion can be grated by hand on the small holes of a box grater. Add the onion on top of the bulgur. Season the meat with the salt and pepper.

3 Next, dip your hands in the ice water, and use your hands to combine the meat with the bulgur, onion, and salt and pepper. As necessary, dip your hands in the ice water to prevent the mixture from sticking to your hands, while also adding a bit of water to keep the meat moist, as the bulgur will absorb some of the moisture. Taste, adjusting the salt and pepper as needed.

4 To serve, once again dip your hands in the ice water and transfer the kibbeh to a platter, shaping it into an oval shape, and using the side of your hand to indent a cross shape, as is traditional, if desired. Garnish with the fresh scallion green and serve immediately.

KIBBEH BIL SANIEH (BAKED KIBBEH)
كبّة بالصينيّة

This is a meat-lover's dream, made by layering a large helping of the raw kibbeh nayyeh with another meat mixture, househ, which is fresh ground meat sautéed with onion, pine nuts, and cinnamon. Once the layers are pressed together, the signature crosshatch pattern is cut into the top, and pats of butter are arranged on top so that the layer will brown and slightly crisp when baked. The mixture is baked (or can also be deep-fried in smaller portions) and delivers a meaty bite that instantly brings me back to my childhood. Typically this dish is prepared after folks have had their fill of kibbeh nayyeh. It's a way to safely use any leftovers from a big batch (we normally tripled the recipe on page 166 on holidays, cooking the kibbeh nayyeh to preserve and enjoy in another variation). Whether consumed warm, at room temperature, or cold—this is one of my favorite snacks to enjoy days after the feast.

Serves 8 to 10	Hands on: 45 minutes	Total: 1 hour 30 minutes

HOUSEH
- ☐ 1 tablespoon extra-virgin olive oil
- ☐ 1 small yellow onion, finely diced
- ☐ ½ cup pine nuts
- ☐ ¾ pound ground top round

- ☐ ½ teaspoon ground cinnamon
- ☐ 1 teaspoon kosher salt
- ☐ ½ teaspoon fresh-cracked black pepper

KIBBEH NAYYEH LAYER
- ☐ 1 recipe prepared Kibbeh Nayyeh (page 166)
- ☐ Ice water, for dipping
- ☐ 4 tablespoons unsalted butter, cut into thin slices

1 Preheat the oven to 400°F. Place a cast-iron skillet over medium heat and add the oil. Add the onion and cook until the onion is tender and soft, 6 to 8 minutes. Add the pine nuts and cook for an additional 2 minutes. To finish, add the top round, cinnamon, salt, and pepper and brown the beef in the onion mixture, stirring with a wooden spoon and breaking up the pieces of meat, until no longer pink, 6 to 8 minutes. Remove from the heat and allow the mixture to cool.

2 In a 9 x 13 x 2-inch pan, preferably stainless-steel and not glass or coated, press about half of the raw kibbeh nayyeh mixture into the bottom, dipping your hands in ice water as needed to keep the meat from sticking to your hands. Next, evenly add the cooked househ on top, using the wooden spoon to press the househ into the kibbeh. To finish, use the remaining kibbeh nayyeh and press a smooth, flat layer to completely cover the top of the househ.

3 Use a knife to cut a crosshatch diamond pattern about ¼-inch deep into the top. Layer the butter evenly on top of the kibbeh and bake for 50 to 60 minutes, until the baked kibbeh has achieved a nice mahogany brown tone. Remove from the heat and allow to cool for 15 to 20 minutes prior to serving.

NOTE: The baked kibbeh can be cooled to room temperature, covered, and stored in the refrigerator for 3 to 5 days.

SHISH KEBABS

شيش كباب

My grandfather would often use trimmings and other butcher cuts to make shish kebabs (skewers) and feed the family for Sunday lunch. While some folks use beef or lamb tenderloin, I argue it's completely unnecessary for this recipe. The more affordable sirloin provides plenty of tenderness and, dare I say, a bit more flavor and texture when cooked properly. Of course, a marinade is key here—up to twenty-four hours if you can. But I've also turned out a great kebab that's only had half an hour to soak up the acidic and garlicky marinade.

Whenever you're making kebabs, the key is to cut the meat and vegetables to consistent size. That way everything cooks evenly. Perhaps equally important, you don't want to overcrowd your skewers—I prefer to leave a bit of daylight in between the pieces so that the heat can reach every part of the surface, creating that rich Maillard reaction of browned meat. Otherwise, you will end up with a lackluster sear. You can use this same marinade and technique if substituting lamb, poultry, or pork. Typically I round out the rest of this meal with some basmati rice and tabbouleh.

Serves 4	Hands on: 30 minutes	Total: 1 to 24 hours and 30 minutes, depending on marinating time

- ☐ 1½ pounds sirloin, trimmed of any fat and cut into 1-inch cubes
- ☐ 1 large Vidalia onion, cut into 1-inch cubes
- ☐ ½ cup extra-virgin olive oil
- ☐ ⅓ cup red wine vinegar
- ☐ 1 tablespoon Worcestershire sauce
- ☐ 4 to 6 cloves garlic, smashed
- ☐ 1 tablespoon dried oregano
- ☐ 2 to 3 sprigs fresh thyme
- ☐ 1 tablespoon kosher salt
- ☐ ½ tablespoon fresh-cracked black pepper
- ☐ 1 teaspoon ground cinnamon
- ☐ ½ teaspoon ground allspice
- ☐ ½ teaspoon crushed red pepper
- ☐ 6 to 8 long metal skewers

1 At least 30 minutes prior to cooking, and up to 24 hours in advance, combine the sirloin, onion, oil, vinegar, Worcestershire, garlic, oregano, thyme, salt, black pepper, cinnamon, allspice, and red pepper in a ziplock bag. Toss the ingredients to combine, and place in the refrigerator to marinate, turning on occasion to ensure even distribution.

2 Open the bottom vent of a charcoal grill completely. Light a charcoal chimney starter filled with charcoal. When the coals are covered with gray ash, pour them evenly onto the bottom grate of the grill. Adjust the vents as needed to maintain an internal temperature of 500° to 550°F. Coat the top grate with oil; place on the grill. (If using a gas grill, preheat to high [500° to 550°F] on all sides.)

3 Remove the beef and onions from the marinade, discarding the marinade, and skewer the kebabs, adding a few meat pieces followed by an onion piece, being careful not to overcrowd the kebabs.

4 Grill the kebabs, uncovered, for 2 to 3 minutes per side for a total of 10 to 12 minutes, until the internal temperature reaches 130°F for medium rare. Remove from the grill, rest for 5 minutes, and serve.

FATAYER (MEAT PIE)

فطاير

Nearly every culture and cuisine has a version of bread stuffed with meat, but of course I'm a bit biased that my family's fatayer is the best of them all. The ground beef is studded with fresh parsley and acidic lemon juice, which creates a craveable bite that ensures you can never stop with just one. Although you can serve these hot, like most traditional Lebanese food, they can be enjoyed—even preferred—at room temperature or cold.

Since my grandparents have passed, my aunt Marcia has largely taken on the legacy of making meat pies for most family gatherings, as well as during my visits to see her in Sarasota, Florida. I learned the lesson the hard way, but for the perfect dough, the flour really matters—you don't want too soft of a consistency. Spend time kneading the dough; it should be firm and not sticky. After that, you can put your Lebanese grandmother skills to the test by shaping meat pies into your preferred form, either round or a triangle. Truthfully this is one of those dishes that I don't think I'll ever master as well as my Sitty (grandmother), but I never tire of practicing, and my own girls seem happy with the results.

Serves 8 to 10	Hands on: 1 hour 30 minutes	Total: 3 hours

DOUGH
- ☐ 6 cups all-purpose flour, preferably Gold Medal brand, plus more as needed
- ☐ 1 tablespoon kosher salt
- ☐ 1¼ cups Crisco shortening, cut into small squares
- ☐ 2¼ cups ice water
- ☐ 1 cup cornmeal

FILLING
- ☐ 2½ pounds ground beef
- ☐ 1½ Vidalia onions, finely diced
- ☐ 3 tablespoons dried mint
- ☐ ¾ cup finely chopped fresh parsley
- ☐ 6 medium lemons, juice

- ☐ 1½ teaspoons kosher salt, plus more as needed
- ☐ 1 teaspoon fresh-cracked black pepper, plus more as needed
- ☐ ½ teaspoon ground cinnamon
- ☐ ½ teaspoon ground allspice

1 Prepare the dough. Combine the flour and salt in a large bowl. Cut the Crisco into the flour until small pea-like shapes form. Gradually add the ice water in ½-cup increments until incorporated. Knead the dough by hand on a floured surface, adding a bit of flour as needed if it's sticking, for 15 to 20 minutes. Let the dough rest for 1 hour.

2 Meanwhile, prepare the filling by placing a cast-iron skillet over medium heat. Add the beef, using a wooden spoon to break up the beef into smaller portions. After 2 to 3 minutes, add the onions and cook the beef and onion mixture together, stirring on occasion, until the onions are tender and translucent and the beef is cooked through, 5 to 7 minutes. Add the mint,

parsley, lemon juice, salt, pepper, cinnamon, and allspice, stir to incorporate, and cook for 4 to 5 minutes, to let the flavors meld. Taste the mixture, adding more salt and pepper if needed. Remove from the heat and set aside.

3 Preheat the oven to 450°F and set a rack in the bottom and the top. Pinch off a portion of the dough and shape it into a 1½-inch ball. Dust a solid surface with cornmeal and lay the ball on the cornmeal and repeat with the remaining dough. Let the dough balls rest for 20 minutes while the oven heats. Grease 2 rimmed baking sheets and set them aside.

4 After the dough has rested, form the dough ball into a thin circular shape by pressing on the ball

with your hands and stretching slightly into a larger circular shape. Pick up the dough and rest it in the palm of your hand. Using your other hand, add approximately 2 tablespoons of the filling to the center of the circle. Using your hands, pull the bottom portion up toward the center, and crease the two sides together to join, using pressure by pinching the dough together to form a triangle shape. Alternatively you can place the circular dough in your hands, add filling and squeeze the filling in the palm of your hand, and create a circular shape by pinching the sides together to form a round meat pie.

5 Place the filled pies on the prepared baking sheets and bake, working in batches as necessary on the bottom rack until the pies are puffed and slightly golden, raising to the top rack in the last few minutes of cooking to get a browned color on the outside of the pies, 12 to 16 minutes. Remove from the oven and serve immediately, or let cool and serve at room temperature.

NOTE: The meat pies can be cooled to room temperature and frozen up to 6 months. To thaw, place in the refrigerator overnight and serve cold or at room temperature, or heat gently as desired.

FRIDAY LUNCH

A family tradition, a light lunch on Fridays, was always something put together quickly by my Giddy and his brother, David, not only for themselves and family but for any of the sales folks fulfilling orders at the store. Per Catholic tradition, meat was not to be consumed on Fridays, so a spread of canned fish, boiled eggs, and potatoes would fall on butcher paper, along with slices of tomatoes, onion, cheese, and crackers. A choose-your-own-adventure style of graze, this is one of those dishes that I "rediscovered" when discussing old family traditions with my own mother. What a great tradition to revive—and trust me, no cheese and cracker will ever be the same without tomato and onion! Better yet, laying all of this out on butcher paper means it's a quick cleanup. I can almost hear Abe saying, "Get back to work!"

Serves 4 to 6	Hands on: 30 minutes	Total: 30 minutes

- ☐ 4 to 6 large eggs, boiled in water for 6 to 8 minutes, cooled, and cut in half
- ☐ 12 small potatoes, boiled in water for 10 to 12 minutes, until tender, and cut in half
- ☐ One 5-ounce can tuna packed in olive oil
- ☐ One 5-ounce tin sardines, packed in olive oil
- ☐ 1 pound sharp cheddar cheese, cut into thin slices
- ☐ ½ Vidalia onion, sliced thin
- ☐ ½ cup kalamata olives
- ☐ 1 to 2 roma tomatoes, sliced thin
- ☐ 24 saltine crackers
- ☐ Kosher salt
- ☐ Fresh-cracked black pepper

Arrange the eggs, potatoes, fish, cheese, onion, olives, tomatoes, and crackers on butcher paper. Season with salt and pepper to taste. Serve.

PART

03

COCONUT CURRY SALMON
(PAGE 298)

RECIPES

PRIMARY CUTS

STARTERS, SALADS, AND SMALL DISHES

The following recipes are intended as starters, or perhaps to be combined together to share as part of a larger meal. Whether through technique or featured ingredient, each dish offers its own tie to the practice of butchering to help hone your skills—or you can patronize your local shop to create a memorable dish to enjoy.

SMOKED SAUSAGE
PLATTER
(PAGE 180)

SMOKED SAUSAGE PLATTER / PHOTO ON PAGE 179

While you can certainly tackle making your own sausages at home, this practice is likely alive and well at your local butcher. Since most butchers are working from whole animals or larger cuts, the ability to use trimmings and scraps is a perfect practice for not letting anything go to waste, while also producing delicious varieties of sausage. Keep in mind that every shop will vary with its specialty or familial recipe, and that certain items and stock might change daily based on what is on hand. Instead of being married to a certain item, I would encourage you to buy a variety of whatever you can find, smoking them for good measure, and serving them on a platter for folks to choose their own adventure. This makes for a great appetizer, but it can also be a fun tapa or shareable main to go alongside some of your favorite sides or snacks. One last note: I prefer to buy fresh, raw varieties instead of those that might have been par-cooked or smoked prior, as they are usually juicier and more tender since they are freshly made and prepared.

Serves 4 to 6	Hands on: 30 minutes	Total: 3 hours

- ☐ 10 links, approximately ¼ pound each, raw specialty sausage, 2 links from 5 different varieties, such as

Italian, Polish, bratwurst, andouille, makanek, chorizo, merguez, and turkey or chicken varieties

- ☐ 1 cup whole-grain mustard
- ☐ Toothpicks, to serve

1 Open the bottom vent of a charcoal grill completely. Pour a large pile of charcoal onto the bottom grate on one side of the grill. Light a charcoal chimney starter filled halfway with additional charcoal. When the coals are covered with gray ash, pour them onto the pile of existing charcoal. Adjust the vents, nearly closing them, as needed to maintain an internal temperature of 200° to 225°F. Coat the top grate with oil; place on the grill. (If using a gas grill or smoker, preheat to low [200° to 225°F] on one side.)

2 Place the sausages over indirect heat, cover the grill, and smoke the sausages for 2 to 3 hours, turning every 45 minutes or so, until the internal temperature reaches 160°F. Remove the sausages from the grill and rest for 10 minutes.

3 Slice the sausage links into 1-inch pieces and arrange on a board with a bowl of the mustard for dipping and toothpicks for serving. Serve.

TOSTADA NACHOS / PHOTO ON PAGE 183

A vegetarian-friendly option that can be dressed up or down as much as you like, or made meaty with some leftover cooked protein and broiled until crispy and warm. You might ask, Where's the butchering? But this recipe will put your knife skills to work, slicing and dicing the toppings to arrange on the tostadas after they come out of the oven. I'm a huge fan of using tostadas instead of individual tortilla chips, as spreading the beans becomes a much more efficient process on a much larger canvas. This is a great go-to for a quick appetizer, light meal, or of course, late-night snack. Be creative with your toppings—you don't need to limit yourself to just the items below. I will usually throw in other odds and ends I might find in the fridge to add to the mix. The contrast of the crispy tostada, creamy beans, and warm cheese to the crisp cool freshness of the toppings is hard to beat.

Serves 6	Hands on: 20 minutes	Total: 20 minutes

- ☐ One 16-ounce can refried beans
- ☐ 12 corn tostada shells
- ☐ 3 cups grated extra-sharp cheddar cheese
- ☐ 1 roma tomato, seeds removed and very finely diced

- ☐ ½ cup pitted green manzanilla olives, sliced thin
- ☐ ¼ cup sliced scallions
- ☐ ½ cup very thinly sliced romaine lettuce, preferably from the heart of the romaine

- ☐ 1 avocado, peeled, pitted, and cut into ¼-inch pieces
- ☐ ¼ cup taco sauce
- ☐ Sour cream, to serve

1 Set an oven rack in the middle of the oven, and preheat the oven to broil.

2 Spread a generous, even layer of the refried beans over each tostada shell, and place on two baking sheets with an inch or so of space between each tostada.

3 Sprinkle the cheese evenly over the top of the beans on each tostada. Place one of the baking sheets into the oven and broil until the cheese is bubbly and slightly browned, about 2 minutes, being careful not to burn the tostadas. Remove from the oven and repeat with the other baking sheet.

4 Garnish the tostadas evenly with the tomato, olives, scallions, lettuce, and avocado. Drizzle the taco sauce over the tops of the tostadas and serve with sour cream on the side.

"LEFTOVER"
QUESADILLAS
(PAGE 210)

TOSTADA
NACHOS
(PAGE 181)

SHRIMP SCAMPI ⊕ ⓣⓗⓔ HALF SHELL

Abilene, Texas, is probably the last place you'd expect to find fresh, delicious seafood, but at the local hotspot The Beehive, this dish, grilled over mesquite, happens to be one of my favorites and one of the most unique ways of preparing shrimp. Instead of removing the shell altogether, the legs are removed, and the shrimp is butterflied, a half-shell-style butchering technique that allows the shell to protect the delicate meat while also imparting even more flavor. It also presents beautifully.

Inspired by my friends at The Beehive, I've put my own version of this dish together so you can share in the goodness. I like to use the largest, freshest Gulf shrimp I can find, about ten per pound, as the larger shrimp is easier to butcher in this manner—not to mention you get a big, delicious bite! After cooking the shrimp quickly over a hot fire, I brush these with a garlic-herb butter to emulate that classic scampi flavor. You can serve these on their own as a beautiful appetizer, or fold them into some buttered linguine for a delicious supper.

Serves 2 or 3	Hands on: 15 minutes	Total: 30 minutes

- ☐ 10 extra-large shrimp, shells and tails on
- ☐ ½ cup (1 stick) unsalted butter
- ☐ 2 cloves garlic, minced
- ☐ ¼ cup finely chopped fresh parsley
- ☐ 1 lemon, cut into quarters, to serve

1 Open the bottom vent of a charcoal grill completely. Light a charcoal chimney starter filled with charcoal. When the coals are covered with gray ash, pour them onto the bottom grate of the grill, and then push to one side of the grill. Adjust the vents as needed to maintain an internal temperature of 400° to 450°F. Coat the top grate with oil; place on the grill. (If using a gas grill, preheat to medium high [400° to 450°F] on one side.)

2 Using your hands, carefully remove the legs from the shrimp, taking care to keep the shells and tails on. Lay a shrimp on a steady surface, shell side down, and use a paring knife to butterfly the meat from where the legs were removed, being careful to not cut all the way through the shell. Rub the butterflied flesh using your index and middle finger to help flatten the shrimp as evenly as possible. Repeat with the remaining shrimp.

3 Place a small stainless-steel saucepan over direct heat, add the butter and keep the pan over direct heat until the butter is melted. Add the garlic and cook in the butter for 1 minute. Carefully transfer the pan to indirect heat, add the parsley, stir and keep warm.

4 Place the shrimp on the grill over indirect heat, shell sides down. Cover the grill and cook the shrimp for 5 minutes. Uncover the grill and begin basting the shrimp constantly with the warmed garlic-herb butter. Continue to cook until the shrimp are just firm, 2 to 3 more minutes. Remove the shrimp from the grill and serve with the lemon wedges.

COUNTRY SAUSAGE WONTON BITES

Most locally owned butcher shops specialize in a variety of in-house sausages, but usually it's the country sausage, or breakfast sausage, that's found ground fresh, without casings, and sold in quantities to your liking. I always enjoy having a pound or two of this style sausage on hand to griddle up next to fried eggs in the morning or, in this instance, to put together in a super-simple appetizer. I make use of store-bought wonton wrappers to stuff into muffin tins (you can get creative on your shapes by folding them into ovals, triangles, or whatever you prefer) and prebake them to better encase the meaty, cheesy bites. If you need to plan ahead, you can cook the stuffing a day or two in advance and keep it refrigerated until ready for use. You can easily double the recipe and cook it in two batches if serving a larger crowd.

Serves 4 to 6	Hands on: 20 minutes	Total: 20 minutes

- ☐ One 12-ounce package wonton wrappers, about 50 wontons depending on the package
- ☐ 1 pound country sausage, or ground bulk pork sausage

- ☐ ¼ cup finely diced green bell pepper
- ☐ ¼ cup finely diced red bell pepper
- ☐ ¼ cup sliced black olives
- ☐ 2 scallions, finely minced

- ☐ 2 cups grated sharp cheddar cheese
- ☐ ½ cup ranch dressing

1 Preheat the oven to 400°F. Grease two 24-cup mini-muffin tins and place the wonton wrappers in the wells. Place the wontons in the oven and bake for 4 to 6 minutes, until lightly browned. Remove the wontons from the oven and set aside in the tins. Leave the oven on.

2 Meanwhile, in a skillet over medium heat, brown the sausage, using a wooden spoon to break the meat up into crumbles, about 8 minutes. Drain the excess fat from the pan. Add the bell peppers, olives, scallions, cheese, and ranch dressing and stir until incorporated. Remove the skillet from the heat, and spoon the filling into the wonton shells. Place the shells back into the oven and bake until golden and bubbly, 6 to 8 minutes. Serve.

BACON BUTTERMILK CORNBREAD

When I was growing up in the South, our supper table often included a hearty protein, an array of fresh vegetable sides, and of course, cornbread, a staple for most Southern families. I add bacon for a smoky, meaty twist to make this a savory and decadent side that I personally could make my entire meal. Nowadays bacon has been transformed from a breakfast staple to a prized ingredient in every meal or dish. Of course, you can often find locally cured and smoked bacon at your favorite butcher shop to use as the base ingredient of this dish. The key to making this recipe is a well-seasoned cast-iron skillet and literally "frying up" the bread in the bacon drippings. The result is miraculous. Serve this up as a side dish to practically any meal, or save it all for yourself—I won't tell anybody.

Serves 6	Hands on: 30 minutes	Total: 1 hour

- ☐ ½ pound sliced bacon, cut crosswise into ¼-inch-thick lardons
- ☐ 1½ cups stone-ground yellow cornmeal
- ☐ 1 cup all-purpose flour

- ☐ 1 tablespoon baking powder
- ☐ 1 teaspoon kosher salt
- ☐ 2 tablespoons sugar
- ☐ 1½ cups buttermilk
- ☐ 2 large eggs, beaten

- ☐ 8 tablespoons unsalted butter, melted
- ☐ 1 cup grated sharp cheddar cheese
- ☐ ¼ cup finely chopped fresh chives

1 Preheat the oven to 400°F. In a 12-inch cast-iron skillet over medium heat, fry the bacon until crispy and browned, 8 to 10 minutes, stirring as needed to avoid burning. Remove from the heat. Using a slotted spoon, transfer the bacon to a plate lined with paper towels. Leave about 1 tablespoon of bacon drippings in the skillet and discard the rest or save for another use.

2 Meanwhile, in a large bowl, mix together the cornmeal, flour, baking powder, salt, and sugar. In another bowl, stir together the buttermilk, eggs, butter, cheese, and chives. While stirring the dry ingredients, slowly pour the buttermilk mixture into the dry ingredients until combined, being careful not to overwork the batter. Add the reserved cooked bacon and stir to incorporate.

3 Place the skillet over medium-high heat and heat for 2 minutes, carefully swirling the bacon drippings around the pan and up to about 1 inch on the sides. Pour the batter into the hot skillet and use a wooden spoon to distribute it evenly. Cook, without stirring, for 2 minutes.

4 Transfer the skillet to the oven and bake for 25 minutes, or until the edges turn brown and the cornbread pulls away from the sides of the skillet. Let stand for 10 minutes before cutting into wedges. Serve.

ROASTED BONE MARROW with COUNTRY BREAD

The fatty, gelatinous yield from the insides of beef bones is some of the best, most nutritious fat you will ever find. Filled with iron and other nutrients, bone marrow dishes are now more de rigueur than exception at restaurants all over the country. Truth be told, making this dish at home couldn't be simpler, especially when sourcing from your favorite butcher. When time permits, I prefer soaking the bones overnight in salted water to purge any remaining blood and impurities. It's best to request that your butcher supply the cut (whatever your preference) from the middle portion of the leg, to produce the most yield. Served up with some crusty bread, this is a go-to for a nice bottle of wine or a start to a celebratory meal.

Serves 4	Hands on: 30 minutes	Total: 30 minutes

- ☐ 3 or 4 marrow bones, cut into 1- to 1½-inch portions
- ☐ 1 teaspoon kosher salt
- ☐ 1 teaspoon finely minced fresh parsley
- ☐ Country bread, cut into slices and warmed, to serve
- ☐ Small serving spoons, to serve

1 Preheat the oven to 450°F. Arrange the bones on a rimmed baking sheet with the marrow facing up. Place into the oven and roast the bones until the marrow is puffed and just slightly bubbling, 20 to 25 minutes.

2 Remove from the oven, season evenly with the salt and garnish with the parsley. Serve with bread and spoons.

TURNIP GREENS ⓐ COUNTRY HAM

A Southern boy like me has a few vices: a love for Mama, a cold beer and/or a neat bourbon, and a good tune from the Allman Brothers. But we also must discuss food—country ham and greens being at the top of the Southern food echelon. I can rarely count a Southern carnivore who won't happily wallop a bowl of hearty greens, so long as they are studded with salty, savory country ham, and maybe with a bit of pepper, vinegar, and cornbread to boot. Country hams are prevalent down in my part of the world, but if you can't find one—well then, you should ask your butcher to procure!

If you've never cooked greens, this is why you will find them in my butchering book. They take a bit of work. Washing them clean of sand and dirt is the first key step, but even more so for this "quick cook" recipe, you have to rip apart the greens from the stems and rough chop them so they are ready to braise. If you think you have too many greens, just wait—the cooking process will reduce the volume by about five times, so always buy more than you think you need. Isn't that true for everything?

Serves 4 to 6	Hands on: 45 minutes	Total: 2 hours

- ☐ ½ pound country ham, cut into cubes
- ☐ ¼ cup apple cider vinegar
- ☐ ¼ cup bourbon

- ☐ 1 tablespoon crushed red pepper
- ☐ 1 teaspoon kosher salt
- ☐ 1 Vidalia onion, very thinly sliced

- ☐ 1½ pounds turnip greens, stems removed and roughly chopped
- ☐ 4 cups chicken stock

1 Heat a very large stockpot over medium high. Add the ham and cook until slightly seared and browned, 4 to 6 minutes, stirring on occasion. Next, add the vinegar and bourbon to deglaze, using a wooden spoon to scrape up any of the browned bits from the bottom of the pan. Add the red pepper, salt, and onion, stirring to combine, and sauté until the onion is just translucent, about 5 minutes.

2 Add the greens, stirring them into the mixture to allow the greens near the heat to wilt and folding in those greens at the top of the pot to reach the heat. Continue in this stirring manner, until the volume of the greens in the pot has reduced by half. Add the stock, stir to combine, and bring the mixture to a simmer.

3 When the mixture reaches a simmer, reduce the heat to medium low and allow the greens to simmer and reduce for 1 to 1½ hours, until most of the stock is reduced and the greens are tender to the bite. Serve.

GRILLED CORN "RIBS"

Call it what you may, but a cob of corn sliced into four "ribs" happens to be one of my favorite summer sides. Fresh corn on the grill is synonymous with every backyard cookout, and serving the corn in this manner ensures there's plenty to go around, not to mention that it's fun to eat. The key is a sharp knife, a steady surface, and some patience when it comes to slicing the ears of corn. After that, it's all about grilling these ribs over direct heat to get some smoky char and tender kernels. Instead of drizzling these with butter, I like to spread a light layer of mayo over the grilled corn. It's a sticky and savory base that captures the grated cheese and parsley. Give this a try the next time you want a fun spin on a classic.

Serves 4 to 6	Hands on: 30 minutes	Total: 1 hour

- ☐ 4 ears fresh corn, husks and silk removed
- ☐ 2 tablespoons extra-virgin olive oil
- ☐ 1 teaspoon kosher salt

- ☐ ½ teaspoon fresh-cracked black pepper
- ☐ ½ cup mayonnaise, preferably Duke's brand

- ☐ ½ cup grated parmesan cheese
- ☐ ¼ cup finely chopped fresh parsley

1 Open the bottom vent of a charcoal grill completely. Light a charcoal chimney starter filled with charcoal. When the coals are covered with gray ash, pour them onto the bottom grate of the grill, and then push to one side of the grill. Adjust the vents as needed to maintain an internal temperature of 400° to 450°F. Coat the top grate with oil; place on the grill. (If using a gas grill, preheat to medium high [400° to 450°F] on one side.)

2 Using a sharp knife on a secure and steady surface, lay an ear of corn on its side and make a perpendicular cut near the stem of the cob to create a flat end. Stand the cob up vertically and rest the flat end on the steady surface. Carefully cut the cob vertically in half. Place both halves, cut sides down, on the surface, and cut each half again lengthwise to create 4 "ribs." Repeat with the remaining ears of corn. Drizzle the ribs with the olive oil and season with the salt and pepper.

3 Place the corn ribs, kernel sides down, over direct heat and grill for 4 to 5 minutes, or until slightly charred. Transfer the ribs to indirect heat, flip so the cut sides are down, and grill, covered, for an additional 4 to 6 minutes, or until tender.

4 Remove the corn from the grill and brush the kernels with a light layer of mayonnaise. Sprinkle the corn ribs with the parmesan cheese and parsley. Serve.

SMASHED FRIED OKRA with BANANA PEPPER RANCH

There is perhaps no vegetable more loved in my family than okra. Whether it's bountifully served in gumbo or accompanied by a pot of butter beans, grilled or roasted, okra is one of my favorite ingredient mainstays. All that said, I believe fried okra is prophetic, made especially out of this world when smashed, then fried. Such a technique releases some of the natural starchiness while also tenderizing the pods. But the best part is that this butchering technique creates more surface area, ensuring crispy-crunchy little pods that are as amusing and addictive to eat as a bowl of popcorn. Always be sure to source young, tender pods, no more than a few inches in length.

This simple dipping sauce made with pickled banana peppers is also highly addictive. It can be used for any of your other favorite fried foods, à la chicken fingers, wings, fish, cauliflower, etc.

Serves 4 to 6	Hands on: 30 minutes	Total: 1 hour

BANANA PEPPER RANCH
- ☐ ½ cup buttermilk
- ☐ ½ cup sour cream
- ☐ ½ cup mayonnaise
- ☐ 2 cloves garlic, minced
- ☐ 1 teaspoon dried dill
- ☐ 2 teaspoons red wine vinegar
- ☐ 2 tablespoons finely chopped fresh chives
- ☐ 2 tablespoons finely chopped jarred mild banana peppers
- ☐ 1 to 2 dashes hot sauce

OKRA
- ☐ Canola oil, for frying
- ☐ 2 pounds young, tender okra
- ☐ 3 cups buttermilk
- ☐ 3 cups yellow cornmeal
- ☐ Kosher salt
- ☐ Fresh-cracked black pepper

1 About an hour prior to cooking, make the ranch. In a large mason jar, combine the buttermilk, sour cream, mayonnaise, garlic, dill, vinegar, chives, banana peppers, and hot sauce. Cover the jar with the lid and shake vigorously until combined. Place the jar in the refrigerator until ready to serve. Note: The dressing will keep for up to 1 week in the refrigerator.

2 Fill a dutch oven with enough oil to reach approximately 3 inches of depth as measured from the bottom. Heat the oil to 350°F over medium heat.

3 Meanwhile, using either a cleaver or meat mallet, smash the okra pods from tip to end. Pour the buttermilk and cornmeal into two separate shallow containers. Working in batches of 10 to 12 pods at a time, first dip the okra in the buttermilk and then dredge in the cornmeal. Add the okra to the dutch oven and fry for approximately 3 minutes, flipping once, until browned and crispy. Use a slotted spoon or spatula to remove the okra to a wire rack set inside a rimmed baking sheet and season generously to taste with salt and pepper. Repeat with the remaining okra.

4 Serve the fried okra with the banana pepper ranch on the side.

EGG DROP SOUP ⬤ₘᵢₜₕ PORK BELLY CRACKLIN

I must confess, the idea of taking one of America's favorite takeout dishes to the next level with fried pork belly might sound ambitious—or perhaps gluttonous—but nevertheless I believe in sacrificing for the greater good. As a kid, I grew up downing bowls of egg drop soup from Jade Dragon, our local Chinese food takeout spot in Lilburn, Georgia. As I got older, making egg drop soup at home became surprisingly easy. But since I can never leave good enough alone, I continued to tweak this recipe, craving something a little bit extra. Enter deep-fried squares of pork belly. Yes, my friends, it's like the fried wonton noodles but meatier.

Serves 4	Hands on: 30 minutes	Total: 1 hour

- ☐ 8 cups chicken stock
- ☐ 1 teaspoon sesame oil
- ☐ 1 teaspoon soy sauce
- ☐ ½ teaspoon white pepper
- ☐ ½ teaspoon turmeric
- ☐ ⅔ cup hot water
- ☐ 6 tablespoons cornstarch
- ☐ 6 eggs, lightly beaten
- ☐ ½ cup thinly sliced scallions
- ☐ Pork Belly Cracklin (recipe follows)

1 Combine the stock, sesame oil, soy sauce, white pepper, and turmeric in a dutch oven over medium-high heat and bring to a medium simmer, 12 to 15 minutes, stirring on occasion. When the mixture is simmering, combine the water with the cornstarch in a small bowl and stir vigorously to create a slurry, making sure there are no lumps of cornstarch.

2 While stirring the stock, still simmering, slowly pour in the cornstarch slurry. If a thinner consistency is desired, use only half of the slurry. Allow the mixture to return to a medium simmer, then cover and reduce the heat to low. Simmer for 5 minutes.

3 Turn off the heat and let sit, covered, for 5 minutes. This will help get perfect "egg flowers," as they are often called. Remove the cover, and while stirring the soup, slowly pour in the beaten eggs. Ladle the soup into serving bowls and top with the sliced scallions and pork belly cracklin. Serve.

PORK BELLY CRACKLIN

Serves 4	Hands on: 30 minutes	Total: 1 hour

- ☐ 1 pound boneless pork belly, skin on
- ☐ 6 cups peanut oil
- ☐ 1½ teaspoons kosher salt

1 Using an extremely sharp knife on a sturdy surface, carefully cut the pork belly into approximately 1-inch cubes. Pat the pieces dry using a paper towel.

2 Pour the oil into a dutch oven and over medium-low heat bring the oil to a low frying temperature of 225°F. Add the cubes of pork belly into the oil carefully, stirring to ensure they don't clump together, and fry until lightly

browned, 20 to 25 minutes. Transfer the cooked pork belly to a paper towel–lined baking sheet and allow to cool for 10 minutes.

3 Increase the heat to medium high. When the oil reaches 425°F, add the pork cubes back into the oil and fry until the skin begins to bubble and crack, 4 to 5 minutes. Transfer the fried cubes to a fresh paper towel–lined baking sheet, season with the salt, and allow to cool. Reserve for use in soup, or for a snack!

WHITE BEAN ⓐⓝⓓ HAM SOUP

A requirement of most home cooks should be that a leftover ham bone is in the freezer at all times for putting up a pot of greens or a comforting and hearty white bean and ham soup. Of course, if you don't have a bone laying around from a holiday feast, you can always call in a favor from your local butcher. For best results I prefer using the bone from a smoked ham—the flavor is that much more nuanced—but frankly any ham bone will do. Boiling the bone for a couple of hours will reveal a solid portion of meat that, when cooled, can be pulled away by hand from the bone and added to the soup.

This is one of those recipes you will want to start preparing the night before, primarily to soak the beans—and if using a frozen bone, to thaw overnight in the refrigerator. After that, this is a really simple, humble dish that pleases time and time again.

Serves 4 to 6	Hands on: 1 hour 30 minutes	Total: 16 hours

- ☐ 1 to 1¼ pounds dried great northern beans
- ☐ One 2- to 3-pound ham bone
- ☐ 3 carrots, finely diced

- ☐ 1 large Vidalia onion, finely diced
- ☐ 3 cloves garlic, peeled
- ☐ 1 tablespoon Louisiana hot sauce

- ☐ 1 tablespoon Creole seasoning, plus more as needed
- ☐ 10 sprigs fresh thyme, stems removed
- ☐ Kosher salt

1 The night before serving, add the beans to a large bowl and cover with cold water by two times the depth. Allow the beans to soak overnight. If using a frozen ham bone, place the bone in the refrigerator overnight to thaw.

2 When ready to prepare, place a 12-quart stockpot over medium-high heat. Add the ham bone and cover completely with water, about a gallon. Bring the water to a boil, reduce the heat to medium, and simmer for 2 hours, or until the meat pulls easily from the bone. Remove the bone from the pot and place it onto a rimmed baking sheet to cool.

3 Add the carrots, onion, garlic, hot sauce, Creole seasoning, thyme, and soaked beans to the pot. Allow the mixture to come back to a medium simmer, cover, and reduce the heat to low. Cook the beans until tender, 1½ to 2 hours. In the last 30 minutes of cooking, use your hands to pull off any meat from the bone and shred into bite-sized pieces. Place the ham into the pot with the beans and cook for the final 30 minutes. Taste, adding more salt and Creole seasoning, if needed. Serve.

PORK CHILI VERDE

I'm a huge fan of any chili, but this tangy, slightly sour chili brimming with meaty pork and warm, green, roasted hatch chiles is one of my favorites throughout the fall season. This recipe calls for a few different "techniques" to maximize flavor, yet it comes together rather easily. I prefer to roast whole tomatillos, onion, and garlic until softened and slightly caramelized. After poaching the pork to tender perfection, we blend all of the vegetables together to create a thick, hearty stock. From there, we fold in some roasted hatch chiles and the shredded pork. I typically like to use country-style ribs, which are cuts from the pork shoulder. Serve this up with some warm tortillas to sop up all of the goodness

Serves 4 to 6	Hands on: 35 minutes	Total: 2 hours, 30 minutes

- ☐ 12 medium tomatillos, outer husks removed and cut in half vertically
- ☐ 1 large Vidalia onion, peeled and quartered
- ☐ 6 cloves garlic, peeled

- ☐ ¼ cup vegetable oil
- ☐ 1 teaspoon kosher salt
- ☐ 8 cups chicken stock
- ☐ 1½ pounds country-style pork ribs
- ☐ 4½ teaspoons ground cumin

- ☐ 2 tablespoons chili powder
- ☐ 1 lime, juiced
- ☐ 24 ounces jarred roasted hatch green chiles
- ☐ Warmed tortillas, to serve

1 Preheat the oven to 450°F. Arrange the tomatillos, onion, and garlic on a large rimmed baking sheet. Drizzle with the oil and season with the salt. Roast the vegetables until tender and caramelized, 35 to 40 minutes. Remove from the oven and cool slightly.

2 Meanwhile, combine the stock, pork, cumin, and chili powder in a dutch oven over medium-high heat. Bring to a medium simmer, cover, and reduce the heat to low. Allow the pork to simmer in the broth for 1 hour. Remove the pork and set it aside on a plate to cool.

3 Add the roasted vegetables to the stock. Using an immersion blender (or regular blender), carefully purée the mixture until completely broken down and smooth. Add the lime juice along with the chiles. Increase the heat to medium and allow the mixture to slowly simmer, uncovered, for 30 minutes, reducing slightly.

4 Using two forks, shred the cooled pork into pieces, discarding any bones. Add the shredded pork back into the dutch oven until warmed through. Serve alongside tortillas.

SPAGHETTI SQUASH ⬤ BROWN BUTTER

For those seeking a low-carb substitute to pasta, spaghetti squash screamed onto the scene years back as a tasty alternative, whether you use it in place of pasta or as the star of its own show (as in this recipe). I promise this is a simple dish to prepare time and time again. The key to making the hearty vegetable emulate the pasta texture we all love is the roasting method, which helps eliminate water—nobody wants soggy "noodles." For this recipe, I take it a step further by cooking the noodles in some toasty brown butter. This preparation makes for a solid side dish to any grilled protein.

Serves 4	Hands on: 10 minutes	Total: 1 hour, 15 minutes

- ☐ 1 large spaghetti squash
- ☐ 2 tablespoons extra-virgin olive oil
- ☐ 1 teaspoon kosher salt, plus more as needed

- ☐ 1 teaspoon fresh-cracked black pepper, plus more as needed
- ☐ 3 tablespoons unsalted butter

- ☐ 1 tablespoon finely chopped fresh parsley

1 Preheat the oven to 425°F. Lay the squash horizontally on a sturdy cutting surface, finding a position where the squash lies flat. If the squash literally rolls in each direction, folded towels placed on either side of the squash can help secure it. Using a sharp knife, cut the squash in half lengthwise. Use your hands to remove any seeds or extra-stringy pulp.

2 Arrange the squash, cut sides up, on a baking sheet and drizzle with the olive oil. Season both sides with the salt and pepper and place the squash into the oven to roast, uncovered, for 30 minutes.

3 Using tongs, carefully flip the squash to cut sides down, and roast for an additional 15 minutes, or until slightly browned and the surface is dry.

4 Remove the squash from the oven and allow to cool 5 minutes. Using a fork, scrape the meaty part of the squash onto a plate (spaghetti-like noodles will form).

5 Heat a large nonstick skillet over medium heat and add the butter. When the butter begins to foam and slightly turn brown, add the squash. Saute the squash for 3 minutes. Adjust the salt and pepper to taste. Garnish with the parsley and serve.

ROASTED TOMATOES with FUNKY FETA

There's something incredibly rich and decadent about this warm, comforting side dish that always pleases. I like to use an array of colorful heirloom cherry tomatoes, as the mix of colors adds a vibrant "pop" that provides a nice change of pace from the standard red varietal. Of course, if you can't find the colorful versions, the standard red tomatoes will do the trick. The key to this dish is to not go cheap on the feta. My daughter Vivienne always tells me she wants the creamy, funky feta—not the dry, cheap stuff! She would suggest a good Greek, Bulgarian, or French feta that's packed in brine. Roasting all of this together is a breeze, and the side can be served along any protein, schmeared on bread, or placed atop some hot, cooked rice or pasta. A real winner here, folks.

Serves 4	Hands on: 10 minutes	Total: 20 minutes

- ☐ 2½ cups heirloom cherry tomatoes, sliced in half vertically
- ☐ 8 ounces feta cheese packed in brine, cut into ½-inch cubes
- ☐ 4½ teaspoons extra-virgin olive oil
- ☐ 1 teaspoon kosher salt
- ☐ ½ teaspoon fresh-cracked black pepper
- ☐ 4 large fresh basil leaves

1 Preheat the oven to 425°F. Line a rimmed baking sheet with foil and arrange the tomatoes and feta on it. Drizzle with the olive oil and season evenly with the salt and pepper. Place the pan into the oven and roast, uncovered, for 12 to 15 minutes, or until the tomatoes have slightly charred and softened.

2 Remove the pan from the oven and allow to cool slightly. Transfer the mixture to a serving dish.

3 Stack the basil leaves on top of one another, roll into a cigar shape, and use a sharp knife to slice, or chiffonade, the basil into small, thin ribbons. Garnish the tomatoes and feta with the fresh basil. Serve.

ROASTED HASSELBACK POTATOES

The technique of "butchering" small, fanlike cuts into a potato is nothing new (popularized in Sweden in the 1950s), but that doesn't mean I can't put my own spin on it! These spuds are one of my favorite side dishes to round out a steakhouse dinner party since they are foolproof, beautiful, and delicious. Superior to just a plain ole baked potato, this spud has more surface area, meaning you get crispy, fry-like texture where the cuts are made, combined with the softer baked potato–like texture in the rest of the interior. My trick? Spooning the seasoned butter and garlic mixture into the cuts throughout the cooking process, which further embellishes this technique, providing moisture and seasoning at the same time. Though you could stop there, for extra indulgence I like to finish these potatoes by wedging some sharp cheddar cheese into the slits, melting that away, and then topping with crispy bacon, scallions, and tangy sour cream. Can I get an AMEN? I will often cook a few extra potatoes when entertaining, as leftovers are great for a morning hash of steak and eggs.

Serves 6	Hands on: 30 minutes	Total: 1 hour 30 minutes

- ☐ 6 russet potatoes
- ☐ 4 tablespoons unsalted butter, melted
- ☐ ¼ cup extra-virgin olive oil
- ☐ 1 tablespoon kosher salt

- ☐ 1½ teaspoons fresh-cracked black pepper
- ☐ 1½ teaspoons garlic powder
- ☐ 8 to 10 slices deli-style cheddar cheese, cut into 1-inch squares

- ☐ 1 cup sour cream
- ☐ ½ cup crumbled cooked bacon
- ☐ ½ cup thinly sliced scallions

1 Preheat the oven to 450°F and line a baking sheet with foil. Rinse the potatoes and pat dry. Place one of the potatoes on a cutting board or a flat surface, and place a chopstick (or fork stem) on each side of the potato to use as a guide to not cut entirely through the potato. Working from about ½ inch from each end, carefully make ¼-inch vertical slices into the potato until the cuts are made across the entire side. Place the potato onto the prepared baking sheet. Repeat the process with the remaining potatoes.

2 Combine the butter, olive oil, salt, pepper, and garlic powder in a small mixing bowl. Brush half of the butter mixture all over the potatoes, using care to slightly open the slits and get even more of the mixture inside of the potato.

3 Bake the potatoes for 55 minutes total, removing the potatoes from the oven at the 20-minute and 40-minute mark to quickly brush with more of the butter mixture. When done, the potatoes should be tender to the touch, with crispy edges on the slices.

4 Remove the potatoes from the oven and allow them to sit for 5 to 10 minutes. Leave the oven on. Carefully insert the cheese squares into each cut of the potatoes and return to the oven to cook for 5 more minutes, or until the cheese is melted.

5 Remove the potatoes from the oven and top with a dollop of sour cream, followed by a generous sprinkle of crumbled bacon and scallions. Serve.

"LEFTOVER" QUESADILLAS / PHOTO ON PAGE 182

There's probably no better culinary concept to catch leftovers than a quesadilla. A toasted tortilla, made better by cheese, creates a blank canvas on which you can throw together whatever you have on hand, from proteins, beans, and legumes to vegetables, and make an honest quick snack, appetizer, or meal within just a few minutes. To ensure success, the items should be chopped down to similar sizes and precooked, if necessary. For example, you don't want to throw hunks of raw steak into the fold of this quesadilla, or raw veggies that haven't given up their goodness and tenderness for the process. Oftentimes I put together quesadillas with leftover steak, chicken, or seafood kebabs because I have an ample amount of protein and veggies on standby that I can put to "new" use. For those looking for a bit of portion control, this can be your leftover savior—I mean it. Stash away a few bits of last night's dinner to serve as the base to tomorrow's lunch, and that's stretching both the meal and budget without adding to the waistline.

Serves 4	Hands on: 20 minutes	Total: 35 minutes

- ☐ ¾ pound leftover protein, such as steak, chicken, pork/ham, or seafood
- ☐ 1½ cups leftover vegetables, such as onions, peppers, or greens

- ☐ 4 large burrito-style flour tortillas
- ☐ 2 cups grated cheese, such as cheddar, Monterey Jack, or Swiss
- ☐ 1 cup beans, such as black beans or pinto beans

- ☐ 4 tablespoons (½ stick) unsalted butter
- ☐ Salsa, to serve (optional)
- ☐ Sour cream, to serve (optional)

1 Chop or slice the leftover protein and vegetables into similar sizes, roughly a ¼-inch dice.

2 Lay 2 of the tortillas flat. On the bottom half of each of these tortillas, sprinkle ¼ cup of cheese in a thin layer. On top of the cheese, add a fourth of the protein, vegetables, and beans. Top each with an additional ¼ cup of cheese. Fold the top halves of the tortillas down over the cheese to create a half-moon shape.

3 Heat a large cast-iron skillet over medium heat. Add 1 tablespoon of butter, and allow the butter to gently melt. Add the 2 folded quesadillas to the skillet and cook, undisturbed, for 2 minutes. Flip the quesadillas, add an additional 1 tablespoon butter and swirl it around the pan to reach each quesadilla. Cook an additional 4 to 5 minutes to create a golden-brown crust on each side of the tortillas. If the cheese isn't melted, reduce the heat to low and cover the skillet with a sheet of aluminum foil or a cover. Cook for an additional 30 to 45 seconds per side until the cheese is melted.

4 Remove the quesadillas from the skillet, and transfer to a plate tented with foil to keep warm. Repeat the procedure with the remaining ingredients for 2 additional quesadillas. When ready, slice the quesadillas into quarters, and serve with salsa and sour cream, if desired.

SHAVED ASPARAGUS SALAD / PHOTO ON PAGE 213

The vibrant green color of asparagus becomes even more enhanced when quickly blanched in some simmering water, followed by a shock in ice water. For this recipe, I chose to use a vegetable peeler to shave the asparagus into fine little strips. Not only are these strips beautiful in color, but they are crunchy and delicious. Since the cut end of the asparagus is often tough and discarded, I will hold the end in my hand and peel toward the tip, turning and repeating until I've used as much of the vegetable as possible. I like to toss these together with some shaved brussels sprouts, shredded kale, and some tangy goat cheese, all fortified with a light and bright vinaigrette.

Serves 4	Hands on: 20 minutes	Total: 40 minutes

- ☐ 1 pound asparagus
- ☐ 1 cup finely shredded brussels sprouts
- ☐ 1 cup finely shredded kale
- ☐ 1 cup crumbled goat cheese

- ☐ ¼ cup red wine vinegar
- ☐ ½ cup extra-virgin olive oil
- ☐ 1 teaspoon kosher salt
- ☐ ½ teaspoon fresh-cracked black pepper

- ☐ ¼ teaspoon crushed red pepper
- ☐ ¼ teaspoon smoked paprika

1 Heat a large saucepan filled halfway with water to a slow simmer over medium-high heat. Meanwhile, fill a large mixing bowl with ice and water. When the water reaches a slow simmer, add the asparagus and blanch in the water, turning as needed to ensure each spear is submerged for 30 seconds in total—do not cook beyond 30 seconds. Immediately transfer the asparagus to the ice water to quickly cool. Turn off the stove and discard the blanching water.

2 When the asparagus is fully chilled, about 5 minutes in the ice bath, drain from the ice water and pat dry with paper towels. Working one at a time, grab each spear by the cut end and use a vegetable peeler to shave small strips toward the top of the spear. Rotate the asparagus 20 to 30 degrees and continue to create strips from all sides of the spear, including the tips if possible.

3 Transfer the strips and remaining tip portions to a medium serving bowl. Add the brussels sprouts, kale, and goat cheese.

4 Combine the vinegar, oil, salt, black pepper, red pepper, and paprika in a small mason jar (or another container that can be sealed) and shake until well combined. Pour the dressing over the vegetables, and gently toss to combine, being careful not to break up the goat cheese.

5 Allow the salad to sit and marinate for 10 minutes prior to serving.

SMOKED CARROT "SALAD" (PAGE 215)

POLISH CUCUMBER SALAD (PAGE 214)

SHAVED
ASPARAGUS SALAD
(PAGE 211)

POLISH CUCUMBER SALAD / PHOTO ON PAGE 212

A creamy, crunchy side staple you'll find at any venerable Polish establishment throughout the country, this cucumber salad is a mainstay that's simple to prepare at home. The key to making this dish perfect is to "butcher" the cucumber correctly. Common garden and kirby cucumbers typically contain larger seeds, and more of a soft interior. If that's your cuke of choice, it's a good idea to slice them lengthwise and use a spoon to scrape out all of the middle. After that, you can cut the cucumber into half-moons. Persian and English cucumbers typically have a firmer texture and smaller seeds, saving you some of the work since you wouldn't necessarily need to remove the core unless desired. I like to add just a touch of vinegar to the mixture to cut the thick, creaminess of the sour cream. This dish pairs especially well with grilled foods, as a cool, refreshing summertime side.

Serves 4 to 6	Hands on: 10 minutes	Total: 40 minutes

- ☐ 4 kirby cucumbers, seeded and sliced into ½-inch half-moons (see headnote)
- ☐ 1½ cups sour cream
- ☐ ½ clove garlic, finely minced
- ☐ 1 tablespoon red wine vinegar
- ☐ 2 tablespoons chopped fresh dill
- ☐ 1 teaspoon kosher salt
- ☐ ½ teaspoon fresh-cracked black pepper

Combine the cucumbers, sour cream, garlic, vinegar, dill, salt, and pepper in a large serving bowl. Using a large spoon, gently toss the ingredients to combine until evenly incorporated. Place the bowl in the refrigerator for 30 minutes to chill prior to serving. This salad is best if served within 4 to 6 hours of preparation, to prevent the cucumbers from losing their crunch.

SMOKED CARROT "SALAD" / PHOTO ON PAGE 212

I'm a big believer that if you have open space on a grill or smoker, it should be used accordingly. That's how this dish came about—one day when I was smoking a brisket, a rack of ribs, and a pork butt. I realized I had just enough square inches to properly throw one more item on the grill. Cleaning out the fridge, I found a pound or so of carrots and decided, Why not? The result was tender, smoked carrots that I cooled to room temperature and dressed as a bit of salad or side. It was a hit both in taste and presentation. I believe that such experiments are the essence of furthering your cooking repertoire—it provides a chance to try new things while also expanding your horizons. Typically I do not peel my carrots, but for this recipe I find that peeling them allows more of the smoke flavor to penetrate while also providing a livelier color to the carrots after cooking for better presentation.

Serves 4 to 6	Hands on: 15 minutes	Total: 2 hours

- ☐ 2 pounds carrots, ends trimmed and peeled
- ☐ ¼ cup thinly sliced red onion
- ☐ ½ cup red wine vinegar
- ☐ ½ cup crumbled feta

- ☐ ¼ cup chopped fresh parsley
- ☐ 2 tablespoons extra-virgin olive oil
- ☐ 1 tablespoon good-quality aged balsamic vinegar

- ☐ ½ teaspoon kosher salt
- ☐ 1 teaspoon crushed red pepper

1 Open the bottom vent of a charcoal grill completely. Light a charcoal chimney starter filled with charcoal. When the coals are covered with gray ash, pour them onto the bottom grate of the grill, and then push to one side of the grill. Adjust the vents as needed to maintain an internal temperature of 250° to 275°F. Coat the top grate with oil; place on the grill. (If using a gas grill, preheat to medium low [250° to 275°F] on one side.)

2 Place the carrots on the indirect side of the grill, cover, and smoke the carrots, turning on occasion until tender, about 1½ hours.

3 Meanwhile, in a small mixing bowl, submerge the red onion in the red wine vinegar and allow to quickly pickle for 1 hour. Remove the onion from the vinegar and place on a paper towel to drain. Note: The onion-infused vinegar can be reused for a vinaigrette.

4 Remove the carrots from the grill and allow to cool for 15 minutes.

5 Arrange the smoked carrots in a serving bowl or platter, breaking them apart by hand into 2- to 3-inch portions, or as desired. Artfully top the carrots with the pickled red onion, feta, and parsley. Drizzle with the oil and balsamic vinegar and evenly season with the salt and red pepper. Serve.

CATCHALL SALAD

If your fridge looks like mine, there's always a slew of vegetables rolling around in the drawers, left over from other dishes. Since I've usually got only a handful of this or a single item of that, it's hard to put all of these nutritious ingredients to use. But have no fear, this catchall salad is my go-to for using up all of that goodness and creating a delicious side dish that aims to please. Brussels sprouts and corn are typically included as my base ingredients, but the rest can be subbed out with whatever you have on hand, be it zucchini, squash, kale, etc. The idea is to slice it all together, serve it up with my tangy dressing, and add as much feta as needed to make it better. One of my favorite things about this dish is that it can be prepped and dressed an hour or so in advance of serving, as the heartier vegetables stand up well and absorb the dressing without becoming soggy like traditional lettuce. So you can knock this dish out, putting your knife and butchering skills to the test, and move on to the rest of the meal.

Serves 4	Hands on: 45 minutes	Total: 1 hour, 45 minutes

- ☐ 2 ears corn, husks and silk removed
- ☐ 1 red or green bell pepper, cut in half and stem, seeds, and ribs removed
- ☐ 2 cups brussels sprouts, ends removed and sliced very thin

- ☐ 1 carrot, ends removed and sliced very thin
- ☐ 1 stalk celery, sliced very thin
- ☐ 1 cup cherry tomatoes, cut into quarters
- ☐ ¼ cup sliced kalamata olives
- ☐ ¼ cup thinly sliced scallions

- ☐ 1 cup crumbled feta cheese
- ☐ ¾ cup extra-virgin olive oil
- ☐ ⅓ cup red wine vinegar
- ☐ 1 tablespoon kosher salt, plus more as needed
- ☐ ½ tablespoon fresh-cracked black pepper, plus more as needed

1 Open the bottom vent of a charcoal grill completely. Light a charcoal chimney starter filled with charcoal. When the coals are covered with gray ash, pour them onto the bottom grate of the grill, and then push to one side of the grill. Adjust the vents as needed to maintain an internal temperature of 400° to 450°F. Coat the top grate with oil; place on the grill. (If using a gas grill, preheat to medium high [400° to 450°F] on one side.)

2 Place the corn and pepper halves over direct heat on the grill, charring on all sides, for 2 to 3 minutes per side. Transfer the grilled corn and pepper to a baking sheet to cool. Using your hands, peel away the charred skin of the pepper and discard, and use a knife to dice the grilled pepper. Place the flat end of the corn on a sturdy cutting board surface and, using a knife, carefully cut the kernels off the ear of each corn. Transfer the cut kernels and diced pepper to a large serving bowl.

3 Add the brussels sprouts, carrot, celery, cherry tomatoes, olives, scallions, feta cheese, olive oil, red wine vinegar, salt, and pepper to the serving bowl and toss until everything is well coated. Adjust the seasoning to taste. Place the salad in the refrigerator for 30 to 60 minutes. Remove the salad from the refrigerator, toss again, and serve.

MAIN CUTS

The following dishes offer hearty, satisfying preparations that can be served as the main course or expanded for entertaining when paired with some Primary Cuts (page 178) and/or Alternative Cuts (page 318). I always like to remind you that your meal will only be as good as your ingredients. So source the best-quality ingredients possible while using the following recipes to produce memorable meals and occasions.

PORK BLADE STEAKS WITH CORN RELISH (PAGE 286)

GRILLED SKIRT STEAK with TONNATO SAUCE and CAPERS

Skirt steak and tonnato sauce are two of my culinary wonder powers. The inside skirt steak has long been revered by those in Texas for its tenderness, love of high heat, and ability to boldly take on the flavors of a marinade—most importantly, it can be sliced thin and rolled into tortillas for everybody's favorite, fajitas. But instead of rolling up this delicious, tender cut into tortillas, I like to serve it as the star of the show.

If you've never made tonnato sauce, the tuna, anchovies, and capers might make you feel as though I'm putting you through a stunt on *Fear Factor*. But you have to trust me here—this sauce is anything but fishy, and everything umami. The salty and savory are a perfect combination to bring out that rich dark sear and crusty flavor from the Maillard reaction, i.e., grilling those steaks over a hot fire. I prefer to let the steaks rest for about an hour until they hit room temperature. I promise that once you try this tonnato sauce, you'll be finding ways to serve it with everything, including grilled proteins, crudités, and hard-boiled eggs, and in salad dressings too. You. Are. Welcome.

Serves 4 to 6	Hands on: 45 minutes	Total: 2 hours

TONNATO SAUCE

- ☐ One 7-ounce can tuna packed in olive oil, drained
- ☐ 1 tablespoon anchovy paste, or 4 whole anchovies packed in oil and drained
- ☐ 2 tablespoons capers, drained
- ☐ 1 clove garlic, peeled
- ☐ ½ lemon, juiced
- ☐ 1 tablespoon red wine vinegar
- ☐ ½ cup extra-virgin olive oil
- ☐ ⅔ cup mayonnaise, preferably Duke's brand
- ☐ ½ teaspoon Creole seasoning

SKIRT STEAKS

- ☐ Two ¾- to 1-pound inside skirt steaks
- ☐ ½ cup vegetable oil
- ☐ 1 teaspoon kosher salt
- ☐ 1 teaspoon fresh-cracked black pepper
- ☐ 1 tablespoon capers, drained, as garnish
- ☐ 1 teaspoon finely minced fresh chives, as garnish

1 In the jar of a blender, combine the tuna, anchovy paste, capers, garlic, lemon, vinegar, olive oil, mayonnaise, and Creole seasoning. Pulse the ingredients until a sauce is formed—the consistency should be pourable. Transfer the tonnato sauce to a covered container and chill in the refrigerator until ready for use. The sauce keeps for up to 1 week in the fridge.

2 Open the bottom vent of a charcoal grill completely. Light a charcoal chimney starter filled with charcoal. When the coals are covered with gray ash, pour them onto the bottom grate of the grill, and then push to one side of the grill. Adjust the vents as needed to maintain an internal temperature of 500° to 550°F. Coat the top grate with oil; place on the grill. (If using a gas grill, preheat to high [500° to 550°F] on one side.)

3 Brush the skirt steaks with the oil on both sides and season evenly on both sides with the salt and pepper. Grill the steaks over direct heat, 4 to 6 minutes per side, until a meat thermometer reads 135°F for medium rare. Remove the steaks from the grill, tent with foil, and rest for 45 to 60 minutes.

4 Thinly slice the skirt steaks on the bias and transfer the slices, cut sides down, onto a large serving platter. Gently spoon and drizzle the tonnato sauce over portions of the steak and empty areas of the platter, being careful not to overdress. Garnish with the capers and chives. Serve.

FLANK STEAK ROULADE

The roulade technique of pounding out a large hunk of meat, stuffing it with some of my favorite ingredients, and then rolling and tying it all together to finish on the grill is one of those experiences that keeps me excited about cooking. The entire process is super simple, but it's a combination of processes and techniques that makes spending time in the kitchen fun. Flank steak is already known for being flavorful and tender, but pounding out the steak will create more tenderness, along with an even cooking surface that holds in plenty of the goodness. By goodness, I'm stuffing this with fresh, tender spinach, bright cherry tomatoes, and tangy, salty feta. After cooking I like to slice this into individual portions, which showcase the impressive stuffing along with the perfectly cooked meat. This cut alone is almost a meal in one, but I like to round out this dish with some roasted potatoes.

Serves 4 to 6	Hands on: 45 minutes	Total: 2 hours

- ☐ 2 pounds flank steak
- ☐ 1 teaspoon kosher salt
- ☐ ½ teaspoon fresh-cracked black pepper
- ☐ 1 cup crumbled feta cheese
- ☐ 2 cups fresh spinach leaves
- ☐ 1 cup sliced cherry tomatoes
- ☐ 2 tablespoons extra-virgin olive oil

1 At least 1 hour prior to cooking, place the steak on a large cutting board lined with plastic wrap. Lay another piece of plastic wrap over the top of the steak. Using a meat mallet or pounder, assertively pound the meat in sections until you reach an even, uniform surface of meat approximately ⅓ inch in thickness. The steak will resemble a rectangular shape.

2 Open the bottom vent of a charcoal grill completely. Light a charcoal chimney starter filled with charcoal. When the coals are covered with gray ash, pour them onto the bottom grate of the grill, and then push to one side of the grill. Adjust the vents as needed to maintain an internal temperature of 275° to 300°F. Coat the top grate with oil; place on the grill. (If using a gas grill, preheat to medium low [275° to 300°F] on one side.)

3 Remove the top plastic wrap and season the steak with half the salt and pepper. Flip the steak, using your hands to maintain the wrap on the bottom of the cutting board to keep the board clean, and season the other side with the remaining salt and pepper.

4 Arrange the feta cheese evenly over the top of the steak, followed by the spinach and tomatoes. Using your hands, tightly roll the steak, starting with the short side. Be careful to keep the ingredients contained within the steak while rolling. Place the rolled steak, seamside down on the cutting board to maintain the closure. Use butcher's twine to secure the rolled steak into a tight, roast-like feature.

5 Drizzle extra-virgin olive oil over the steak and place onto the grill over direct heat for 3 to 4 minutes per side, for a total of 12 to 15 minutes. When a thermometer inserted into the center of the roast reaches 130°F, remove the steak from the grill, and allow to rest for 10 minutes on a cutting board.

6 After resting, carefully remove the butcher's twine. To serve, slice about ½ inch from the smaller end—this can be the "butcher's bite" and enjoyed before you serve your guests. Continue to slice the steak in ½- to ¾-inch segments to serve.

SCORED FLANK STEAK
🅐 DIJON 🅐 CAPER BOARD SAUCE

Flank steak has risen in popularity over the years, as it's a tender, flavorful cut that easily satisfies a crowd. Truth be told though, I've had a bit of a love-hate relationship with the cut until I improvised the following technique. You see, the natural striations of this steak, even at super-high heat temperatures, often caused me to not get that great, even sear—and thus the flavor from the beloved Maillard reaction—across the entire cut. Instead of throwing my hands, and flames, entirely in the air, I took my knife and scored small crisscross incisions on both sides of the meat. This technique not only helps impart more of the marinade, it also allows the heat to reach the meat more evenly so it can develop a dark, rich crust. As if I wasn't already giving away enough secrets, I serve this with a beautiful briny and tangy board sauce made of dijon mustard, capers, and herbs. I prefer to cook this just to medium rare plus and slice the meat on top of the sauce ingredients so the juices mix into the sauce, creating a flavor that's out of this world.

Serves 4 to 6	Hands on: 35 minutes	Total: 5 to 25 hours

STEAK
- ☐ 2 pounds flank steak, scored ¼ inch deep on both sides in cross-hatch pattern
- ☐ ¼ cup extra-virgin olive oil
- ☐ 2 tablespoons balsamic vinegar
- ☐ 2 cloves garlic, minced
- ☐ 1 tablespoon finely chopped fresh parsley
- ☐ 1 teaspoon kosher salt

- ☐ ½ teaspoon fresh-cracked black pepper

DIJON AND CAPER BOARD SAUCE
- ☐ 2 tablespoons capers, drained and minced
- ☐ 1 clove garlic, minced
- ☐ 2 tablespoons good-quality dijon mustard

- ☐ 1 tablespoon finely chopped red onion
- ☐ 1 tablespoon finely chopped fresh parsley
- ☐ 1 tablespoon finely chopped fresh tarragon
- ☐ ¼ teaspoon crushed red pepper
- ☐ ¼ teaspoon kosher salt
- ☐ ¼ teaspoon fresh-cracked black pepper

1 At least 4 hours prior to cooking, or up to 24 hours, combine the steak, oil, vinegar, garlic, parsley, salt, and black pepper in a ziplock bag and toss to combine. Allow the steak to marinate in the refrigerator—the longer the better—turning the bag over a few times during the process.

2 Open the bottom vent of a charcoal grill completely. Light a charcoal chimney starter filled with charcoal. When the coals are covered with gray ash, pour them onto the bottom grate of the grill, and then push to one side of the grill. Adjust the vents as needed to maintain an internal temperature of 500° to

550°F. Coat the top grate with oil; place on the grill. (If using a gas grill, preheat to high [500° to 550°F] on one side.)

3 Remove the steak from the marinade, shaking off any excess, and discard the marinade. Place the steak over direct heat and grill, undisturbed, for 6 to 8 minutes per side, until a meat thermometer reads 135°F for medium rare plus. Remove the steak from the grill, tent with foil, and rest for 15 minutes.

4 Meanwhile, make the board sauce. In a medium bowl, combine the capers, garlic, mustard, onion, parsley, tarragon, red pepper,

salt, and black pepper. Stir to combine. On a cutting board, liberally line the sauce in a linear direction on the board to cover, about the length of the steak.

5 Add the steak over the sauce on the board. Using a sharp knife, thinly cut the steak on the bias. Toss the sliced steak and its juices together with the board sauce until combined. Serve.

SKIRT STEAKS (with) GARLIC BUTTER

Though it's gained in popularity, skirt steak has long been one of my favorites. It's an affordable cut that delivers plenty of tenderness and big beefy flavor. Typically half the cost of a rib eye or strip steak, skirt steak is a thin, longer cut that comes from the plate or diaphragm area, just under the rib section. I prefer the outside cut, which is longer and thicker than the wider, thinner inside cut. In terms of comparing it to its cousin, the flank steak, both are great cuts, but the grains run lengthwise on a flank steak, and across the width on a skirt steak. On the whole, flank steaks are also typically thicker with less flavor.

The main thing to consider with skirt steaks is that they should be cooked super hot and rather quickly, then cut against the grain to achieve filet-like tenderness. Traditionally used for fajitas, the skirt steak takes well to marinades, and when sliced thin and on the bias, it can stretch to feed a crowd. For this particular recipe, I'm treating the steak as the star of the show, portioning it into individual steaks and topping it with a simple, garlicky compound butter to finish. It serves best with french fries, a simple green salad, and a good Côtes-du-Rhône blend.

Serves 4	Hands on: 25 minutes	Total: 1 hour

GARLIC COMPOUND BUTTER
- ☐ ½ cup (1 stick) unsalted butter, softened
- ☐ 1 tablespoon lemon juice
- ☐ 1 tablespoon minced garlic
- ☐ 1 tablespoon chopped fresh parsley
- ☐ 1 teaspoon kosher salt

- ☐ ¼ teaspoon crushed red pepper

STEAK
- ☐ 1 outside skirt steak, about 2 pounds in total, 1½ inches thick

- ☐ 1 tablespoon extra-virgin olive oil
- ☐ 1 tablespoon kosher salt
- ☐ 1 tablespoon fresh-cracked black pepper

1 In a small bowl, combine the butter with the lemon juice, garlic, parsley, salt, and red pepper. Use a fork to smash and fold together the ingredients. Cover the bowl and place in the fridge for 1 hour to firm up. This keeps up to 1 week in the refrigerator, or it can be wrapped in plastic and frozen for up to 3 months.

2 Open the bottom vent of a charcoal grill completely. Light a charcoal chimney starter filled with charcoal. When the coals are covered with gray ash, pour them onto the bottom grate of the grill, and then push to one side of the grill. Adjust the vents as needed to maintain an internal temperature of 500° to 550°F. Coat the top grate with oil; place on the grill. (If using a gas grill, preheat to high [500° to 550°F] on one side.)

3 Cut the steak into four 8-ounce portions. Drizzle the steaks with the oil to coat and season evenly on both sides with the salt and black pepper.

4 Grill the steaks for 2 minutes over direct heat. Rotate the steaks 45 degrees and grill an additional 1 minute. Flip the steaks and cook for 2 more minutes (if the steaks are thinner, reduce the cooking time by 1 minute), or until internal temperature reaches 130°F for medium-rare. Remove the steaks from the grill and rest for 5 minutes on a cutting board or plate.

5 Remove the garlic butter from the refrigerator and use a tablespoon to scoop a dollop of butter over each steak. Serve.

RIB EYE CAP STEAKS

Yes, my friends, it's possible to have your cake and eat it too. There's very little debate that the tenderloin is the most tender of all steaks, and perhaps some debate that rib eye steaks have the most flavor. But did you know that the cap of the rib eye, the *spinalis dorsi* as it's referred to in proper anatomy, or calotte steak in French, is a one-two punch of flavor and tenderness that makes it one of the most prized steaks in the universe? If you are staring at a standard-cut rib eye, the cap will be the portion of meat that literally circles the round shape over the fatty "eye" portion of the steak. Some butchers trim this entire portion whole, turning out a steak that's just over a foot long, about half a foot wide, and an inch or so in thickness. Others, like in this recipe, will trim this portion of a thick-cut rib eye steak off, tying it together to form a mock filet for the grill. Whatever you do, be prepared to enjoy one of the most tender, flavorful cuts of meat that you will ever have in your entire life! Because this is the holy grail of steaks, I like to treat it as simple as possible, with high heat, and a touch of salt to dry brine and finish. This is the steak worth pulling out that vintage bottle of wine to celebrate.

Serves 4	Hands on: 30 minutes	Total: 1 hour, 30 minutes

☐ Four 6- to 8-ounce rib eye cap steaks, tied with butcher's twine around the perimeter of the cut into a filet-like shape

☐ Kosher salt

1 About an hour prior to cooking, remove the steaks from the refrigerator and season all sides of the steaks liberally with kosher salt. Place the steaks on a wire rack set inside a rimmed baking sheet and allow the steaks to dry brine for 1 hour. Just prior to grilling, pat the steaks completely dry with a paper towel.

2 Open the bottom vent of a charcoal grill completely. Light a charcoal chimney starter filled with charcoal. When the coals are covered with gray ash, pour them onto the bottom grate of the grill, and then push to one side of the grill. Adjust the vents as needed to maintain an internal temperature of 500° to 550°F. Coat the top grate with oil; place on the grill. (If using a gas grill, preheat to high [500° to 550°F] on one side.)

3 Place the steaks over direct heat and grill for 2 minutes, undisturbed. Rotate the steaks approximately 30 degrees, picking them up and putting them back down on a different portion of the grate to ensure a new sear, and cook for an additional 1½ minutes. Rotate the steaks a final 30 degrees and cook for 1½ minutes more. Next, transfer the steaks to the indirect side of the grill and continue to cook an additional 3 to 5 minutes, until the internal temperature reads 130°F for medium rare. Immediately transfer the steaks off the grill onto a plate and tent with aluminum foil to rest for 10 minutes.

4 Remove the foil tent, season the steaks with additional kosher salt to taste, and serve.

REVERSE-SEARED COULOTTE STEAKS

A somewhat harder-to-find cut in grocery stores, coulotte steaks are a butcher favorite, known for being relatively affordable, tender, and full of flavor. Sometimes known as sirloin strip or caps, it's probably better known in Brazil and South America, where it's called the picanha cut. The coulotte steak is situated at the top of the sirloin, and I often will ask my butcher to give me the whole rump, either with the fat cap left on or sliced into thick-cut (at least 2-inch) steaks. In my experience, the thicker the cut, the better to take advantage of the reverse-sear method of cooking. Though it's not necessary, I like to place the steaks into an overnight marinade to tack on more flavor. If you are not familiar with the reverse sear, take everything you know about cooking a steak (searing it on both sides over direct heat, followed by indirect heat until it reaches your desired temperature), and do it all backward. That's right—it's all about slowly cooking the steak over indirect heat to an internal temperature that's 5° to 7°F shy of your final desired serving temperature. After that, get the fire hot, and place the steaks right over the heat to let the beautiful Maillard reaction of "brown food is good food" do its thing. Unlike the traditional technique of allowing a steak to rest, you can serve a reverse-seared steak immediately.

Serves 4	Hands on: 1 hour 15 minutes	Total: 13 hours to 25 hours, depending on marinade time

- ☐ ½ cup extra-virgin olive oil
- ☐ ¼ cup red wine vinegar
- ☐ 2 cloves garlic, finely minced
- ☐ 1 tablespoon kosher salt

- ☐ ½ tablespoon fresh-cracked black pepper
- ☐ 1 teaspoon ground cinnamon
- ☐ 1 teaspoon dried oregano

- ☐ 4 coulotte or sirloin cap steaks, 2 inches thick with fat cap trimmed to ¼- to ½-inch thick

1 In a large ziplock bag, combine the oil, vinegar, garlic, salt, pepper, cinnamon, and oregano and add the steaks. Place the sealed bag into the refrigerator to marinate overnight, or up to 24 hours, turning once.

2 Open the bottom vent of a charcoal grill completely. Light a charcoal chimney starter filled with charcoal. When the coals are covered with gray ash, pour them onto the bottom grate of the grill, and then push to one side of the grill. Adjust the vents, nearly closing them as needed to maintain an internal temperature of 225°F. Coat the top grate with oil; place on the grill. (If using a gas grill, preheat to low [225°F] on one side.)

3 Remove the steaks from the marinade, shaking off any excess, and discard the marinade. Add the steaks to the grill over indirect heat. Cook

the steaks, keeping the lid partially closed and checking the steaks' internal temperature in several areas with a thermometer every 10 minutes, until the steaks reach 110° to 115°F, 20 to 25 minutes. When the steaks reach 100°F, it is important to monitor the internal temperature every few minutes.

4 Remove the lid and take the steaks off the grill. Increase the heat to high on one side if using gas, or add more lit coals to one side of the grill from a chimney if using charcoal, to create a high heat (500°F or more) direct zone close to the cooking surface.

5 If possible, rotate the "cold grates" (from the indirect zone) over the direct heat. (Using cold grates will prevent grill marks from conductive heating and provides a more even, uniformly browned exterior.) Add the steaks over direct

heat. Sear the steaks for 1 minute, then rotate the grates and flip the steaks. Continue in this manner for 1 minute per side, until the steaks reach an internal temperature of 130°F for medium rare. Remove the steaks from the grill. Serve immediately.

HANGER STEAK "NEW VIDE"

My wife and I are always entertaining, which means I'm the one doing the cooking! Part of being a great entertainer means actually spending time with your guests, not being stuck in the kitchen or at the grill. Truth be told, I created this "new vide" method because I wanted to have dinner ready to go, without having to work when my guests arrived. Instead of the reverse-sear or sous vide methods (low and slow, then seared), I do the exact opposite (and you can do this with nearly everything you like to grill). The goal is to cook the steak as hot and as fast as possible to a temperature that's 7° to 10°F under the final temp you desire. Stealing a page out of my pitmaster playbook, I then quickly wrap the food in heavy-duty foil and rest it for at least an hour (while my guests hang out). What you will get is a perfect, edge-to-edge temperature without the hassle. While I often like to serve my steaks family style—at or slightly above room temperature and sliced to serve—you can quickly resear these steaks after they rest, if serving a hot steak is required. Just sear for a minute or so on each side. I love using the hanger steak, a true butcher's cut, prized for its tenderness and flavor. While I plan to write a whole book on this topic, if you are wrapping more than two steaks in foil, each one of those steaks will provide extra heat energy, thus you'll need to pull them a degree or two earlier than the 10°F because that extra energy will cook the steaks more during the rest period.

Serves 4	Hands on: 25 minutes	Total: 3 hours, 30 minutes

- ☐ Two 1½-pound hanger steaks
- ☐ Kosher salt
- ☐ Fleur de sel, to finish

1 About an hour prior to cooking, remove the steaks from the refrigerator and season all sides of the steaks liberally with kosher salt. Place the steaks on a wire rack set inside a rimmed baking sheet and allow the steaks to dry brine for 1 hour. Just prior to grilling, pat the steaks completely dry with a paper towel.

2 Open the bottom vent of a charcoal grill completely. Light a charcoal chimney starter filled with charcoal. When the coals are covered with gray ash, pour them onto the bottom grate of the grill, and then push to one side of the grill. Adjust the vents as needed to maintain an internal temperature of 500° to 550°F. Coat the top grate with oil; place on the grill. (If using a gas grill, preheat to high [500° to 550°F] on one side.)

3 Sear the steaks over direct heat, as hot as possible, turning every 1½ minutes to ensure an even sear on both sides. Keep a close watch on the internal temperature of the steak, closing the grill as necessary to control the fire. When the internal temperature of the steaks reaches 120°F (for medium rare), immediately remove the steaks from the grill and wrap them tightly in heavy-duty aluminum foil. Allow the steaks to rest in the foil for 1 hour. The resting process will cause the internal temperature of the steaks to rise approximately 10°F.

4 To serve, remove the steaks from the foil and cut against the grain into slices. Season with fleur de sel. Serve.

LIVER 'N' ONIONS

A comfort cut, tender calf's liver served well seared and medium with tangy caramelized onion is an affordable, hearty meal that is worthy as a weeknight favorite. If you've never tried liver and onions, I recommend sourcing young calf's liver, as it will be tender and less metallic in flavor. The key here is frankly technique: You need to ensure that the pan is hot to get a nice sear on the thinly sliced liver portions and create the best opportunity for the Maillard reaction, that deep, browned crust. Paired up with the onion, this is a protein-forward meal that can be rounded out with a starch and vegetable of your choosing. I'm totally fine serving these as is, with no extra pan sauces or drippings, but if desired, you can add a tablespoon or so of flour into the drippings after removing the cooked liver and onion, and deglaze with about a half cup of wine or beef stock, reducing by half over low heat to create a quick pan sauce to serve. Sauce or no sauce, this will quickly become a favorite.

Serves 4	Hands on: 30 minutes	Total: 30 minutes

- ☐ 1 pound calf's liver, thinly sliced
- ☐ 1 teaspoon kosher salt
- ☐ ½ teaspoon fresh-cracked black pepper

- ☐ ½ teaspoon garlic powder
- ☐ 2 tablespoons extra-virgin olive oil
- ☐ 1 medium Vidalia onion, very thinly sliced

- ☐ 1 teaspoon finely chopped fresh parsley

1 Arrange the slices of liver on a wire rack set inside a rimmed baking sheet. Pat the slices dry and season on both sides with the salt, pepper, and garlic powder.

2 Meanwhile, heat a cast-iron skillet over medium heat and add the oil. Next, add the onion and cook, stirring regularly, until the onion is softened and browned, 8 to 10 minutes.

3 Remove the onion from the skillet, increase the heat to medium high, and add the liver slices, working in batches and being careful not to overcrowd. Sear the liver slices until browned for 2 to 3 minutes per side. To finish, add the onion back into the pan and heat through, 4 to 5 minutes. Garnish with the parsley. Serve.

LONDON BROIL

As the author of *The South's Best Butts*, I certainly know a thing or two when it comes to misnomers. You see, the pork butt has nothing to do with the hindquarter, and much more to do with the front shoulder. The same goes for a London broil, as it doesn't originate from our British friends. Instead the name is more related to preparation of the dish than the cut. Traditionally, before flank steak became cool and expensive, butchers would sell the cut in heavy marinades and call it London broil. But as time has gone on, you will typically see a cheaper cut, like top round or coulotte, as the cut of choice for this dish. After giving the meat a lengthy marinade, I like to take it straight to the grill, searing it off as hot as possible and resting to temperature. Sliced super thin and across the grain, this flavorful steak is delicious in its own right, or served sandwiched between some bread. A crowd-pleaser and affordable, this can be a good cut for serving a humble steak dinner to a hungry group. Leftovers in my house are usually fried off in the morning with some eggs—a perfect cure for too much red wine from the night before.

Serves 4 to 6	Hands on: 35 minutes	Total: 5 to 25 hours

- ☐ One 3- to 4-pound top round steak or London broil
- ☐ ½ cup extra-virgin olive oil
- ☐ 3 tablespoons red wine vinegar

- ☐ 2 tablespoons dijon mustard
- ☐ 1 tablespoon Worcestershire sauce
- ☐ 3 cloves garlic, minced

- ☐ 1 tablespoon kosher salt, plus more as needed
- ☐ ½ tablespoon fresh-cracked black pepper
- ☐ 1 tablespoon dried parsley

1 At least 4 hours prior to cooking, or up to 24 hours, combine the steak, olive oil, vinegar, mustard, Worcestershire, garlic, salt, pepper, and parsley in a ziplock bag, tossing to combine. Allow the steak to marinate in the refrigerator—the longer the better—turning the bag over a few times during the process.

2 Open the bottom vent of a charcoal grill completely. Light a charcoal chimney starter filled with charcoal. When the coals are covered with gray ash, pour them onto the bottom grate of the grill, and then push to one side of the grill. Adjust the vents as needed to maintain an internal temperature of 500° to 550°F. Coat the top grate with oil; place on the grill. (If using a gas grill, preheat to high [500° to 550°F] on one side.)

3 Remove the steak from the marinade, shaking off any excess, discarding the marinade. Place the steak over direct heat and grill, undisturbed, for 3 minutes. Rotate the steak 45 degrees and cook for an additional 2 minutes. Rotate the steak another 45 degrees and cook for 2 minutes more. Flip the steak and cook an additional 3 to 5 minutes, until the internal temperature reaches 128° to 130°F for medium rare. Immediately transfer the steak off the grill and into aluminum foil and wrap tightly. Allow the steak to rest at least 20 minutes.

4 Carefully unwrap the steak (saving the juices) and place on a cutting board. Cut the steak thinly and across the grain, then transfer the sliced steak to a serving platter. Brush or drizzle the juices from the foil over the steak. Lightly season the sliced steak with additional salt, if desired. Serve.

THE BEEF HAMMER

A relatively new and trendy cut in the world of barbecue, the beef shin, or shank, as it's more commonly known, is primed for the mainstream. Made popular on social media by our German friends, the hammer cut is marbled, beefy, and tender. For our Italian-loving friends, this same shank cut is what makes up the crosscut osso buco, where the hammer is left whole. Many butchers who specialize in this cut will french the bone portion, giving it its hammer-like shape. When this whole cut is smoked low and slow, then braised in shallow drippings, it yields a tender and delicious flavor akin to your favorite beef ribs or brisket—usually coming in at a quarter of the cost. With time and temperature, the intimidating cut will gently give way until it completely falls off the bone, yielding its beefy, juicy flavor.

You can serve the pulled meat on its own or accompanied with some sliced onion and pickles, or pile it up between two slices of bread for a meaty sandwich. My mouth is watering already.

Serves 4–6	Hands on: 1 hour	Total: 9 hours

- ☐ One 5- to 6-pound beef hammer cut (or one 6- to 7-pound whole shank, frenched, 1½ to 2 inches wide at narrow bone portion)
- ☐ 3 tablespoons kosher salt
- ☐ 2 tablespoons fresh-cracked black pepper
- ☐ One 12-ounce bottle dark amber beer
- ☐ 1 cup beef stock
- ☐ 1 bay leaf
- ☐ Sliced Vidalia onion, to serve
- ☐ Sliced dill pickles, to serve
- ☐ Sliced bread, to serve (optional)

1 Open the bottom vent of a charcoal grill completely. Pour a large pile of charcoal onto the bottom grate on one side of the grill. Light a charcoal chimney starter filled halfway with additional charcoal. When the coals are covered with gray ash, pour them onto the pile of existing charcoal. Adjust the vents, nearly closing them, as needed to maintain an internal temperature of 200° to 225°F. Coat the top grate with oil; place on the grill. (If using a gas grill or smoker, preheat to low [200° to 225°F] on one side.)

2 Secure the meat with butcher's twine, tying a secure knot portion at the bottom, and tightly spiraling and wrapping the cut with twine, approximately 1 inch between each wrap, and knot again at the top portion to secure. Season all sides of the meat with an even distribution of salt and pepper.

3 Place the meat on the grill over indirect heat, cover, and smoke for 3 to 4 hours, until a thermometer inserted into the thickest part of the meat registers 160°F.

4 In an aluminum tin (or casserole dish) large enough to fit a roasting rack, add the beer, stock, and bay leaf. Place a wire roasting rack over the braising liquid and rest the meat on top of the rack. Tightly wrap the entire dish with aluminum foil and place it on the grill over indirect heat to slowly braise for an additional 3 to 4 hours, until the internal temperature reaches approximately 205°F. Note: The thermometer should be able to penetrate any portion of the meat without resistance.

5 Remove the meat from the grill, uncover, and place on a cutting board to rest for 20 minutes. Using your hand, carefully pull the bone from the meat. Use two forks to gently pull the meat into generous portions. Serve immediately with onion, pickles, and bread, as desired.

BRAISED OXTAILS OVER YELLOW RICE

For centuries Caribbean, Spanish, and Hispanic cultures have celebrated this cut of tail meat that comes from cattle, primarily steers. I say that because "oxtail" can be a misnomer, i.e., this is not something usually sourced from an ox, for those wondering. I can't argue with those who love this cut. With a bit of moisture and a low and slow technique, you can delve out this tender, fall-off-the-bone savory dish in a half day's cooking time, with incredible gourmet results. Nowadays you will find the skinned and butchered tails cut into sections, perfect for this recipe so that the cooked portions will lie in a silky gravy served atop hearty, saffron-laced rice. This is a weekend go-to dinner that will have the house smelling like heaven as it comes together. Pair this with a deep, rich red, like a cabernet, or a spicy, young beaujolais, depending on your mood.

Serves 4	Hands on: 1 hour	Total: 5 hours

- ☐ 3 to 4 pounds oxtails, cut into 1- to 1½-inch sections
- ☐ 1½ tablespoons kosher salt
- ☐ 1 tablespoon fresh-cracked black pepper
- ☐ 1 cup all-purpose flour
- ☐ ¼ cup extra-virgin olive oil

- ☐ 1 Vidalia onion, roughly chopped
- ☐ 2 carrots, roughly chopped
- ☐ 2 tablespoons tomato paste
- ☐ 3 cloves garlic, minced
- ☐ ½ teaspoon crushed red pepper
- ☐ 1 cup dry red wine

- ☐ One 10.5-ounce can beef consommé soup
- ☐ 2 bay leaves
- ☐ 2 sprigs fresh rosemary
- ☐ 1 cup frozen green peas
- ☐ 1 pound packaged yellow rice, prepared according to instructions

1 Allow the oxtails to sit at room temperature at least 30 minutes and up to 1 hour prior to cooking. Using paper towels, pat the oxtails dry, and season evenly on both sides with the salt and black pepper. Place the flour in a shallow bowl. Dredge the oxtails, coating all sides evenly with the flour and shaking off any excess.

2 Place a large dutch oven over medium-high heat and add the oil. Working in batches and being careful not to overcrowd, add the oxtails to the pot and brown them for 5 to 6 minutes per side, until they've developed a dark crust on each side. Transfer the seared oxtails to a wire rack set inside a rimmed baking sheet. Repeat until all the oxtails have been evenly seared.

3 Next, add the onion and carrots to the dutch oven and cook, stirring often, until the carrots are tender and the onion is translucent, 5 to 7 minutes. Add the tomato paste, using a wooden spoon to stir, and cook for 2 minutes. Add the garlic and red pepper, stir, and cook for 1 minute. Deglaze the pot by adding the wine, followed by the consommé, using a wooden spoon to scrape up any of the browned bits from the bottom. Fill the empty can of consommé 1½ times with water and add that to the pot too. Add the oxtails back into the pot along with bay leaves and rosemary and bring the mixture to a slow simmer. Reduce the heat to low, cover, and braise the oxtails until they pull apart easily from the bone when poked with a fork, about 3 hours.

4 Remove the cover, remove and discard the bay leaves and rosemary, add the peas, and stir to incorporate. Continue to cook the oxtails, uncovered, until the gravy is slightly reduced and thickened, 15 to 20 minutes.

5 Serve 4 to 6 oxtail sections over the hot yellow cooked rice, spooning the gravy over the dish as desired.

CAST-IRON MEAT-LOVER'S PIZZA

I'll probably never tire of waxing poetic about my love for cooking with cast iron. The truth is, I'll be able to bequeath a slew of cast-iron skillets, pots, and pans after I pass on—along with recipes galore. While always beloved in the South, cast-iron cooking is now celebrated worldwide, and its use continues to evolve, from traditional fried chicken to new favorites, including pizza. The super-even conductivity of a cast-iron skillet makes it the perfect chance to skip delivery and make pizza night at home. I've laid out a straightforward dough recipe that you can tackle, or you can save yourself some time by picking up a store-bought dough to make life a bit easier. Whatever your route, the technique of preheating the skillet prior to adding your ingredients and toppings will turn out a crispy, chewy crust that stands up well—especially in this meat-lover's version where I procure whatever meats I can find from my local butcher shop.

Serves 4	Hands on: 1 hour	Total: 1 hour

DOUGH
- ☐ 1½ teaspoons sugar
- ☐ 1¼ cups warm water
- ☐ 3 cups bread flour
- ☐ 1 packet active dry yeast
- ☐ 1 pinch kosher salt
- ☐ 1½ teaspoons extra-virgin olive oil

PIZZA
- ☐ 1 cup pizza sauce
- ☐ 4 cups shredded mozzarella cheese
- ☐ ¼ cup finely grated parmesan cheese
- ☐ 1 tablespoon dried oregano
- ☐ ¼ cup cooked and crumbled Italian sausage
- ☐ ¼ cup cooked and crumbled ground beef
- ☐ 3 slices cooked bacon, torn into small pieces
- ☐ 2 slices ham, cut into bite-sized pieces
- ☐ ¼ cup thinly sliced spicy capicola, or soppressata

1 In a small bowl, combine the sugar with the warm water and stir until the sugar is dissolved. In a large bowl or the bowl of a stand mixer, place 1½ cups of the flour, the yeast, and salt. Stream in the sugar water and olive oil. Using a spoon, or in a stand mixer fitted with the dough hook, mix the dough for 3 to 4 minutes, adding the remaining 1½ cups of flour as the ingredients come together. The mixture will be sticky.

2 Turn out the dough onto a floured surface and, using your hands, knead the dough for 5 to 7 minutes, turning it onto itself several times. Place the dough into a large oiled bowl and set aside in a warm place to rise for 10 to 15 minutes.

3 Remove the dough from the bowl, punch it, and divide the dough in half. Set aside one half

for the pizza. Tightly wrap the second half of dough in plastic wrap and keep refrigerated for up to 2 days. Alternatively, the excess dough can be frozen for up to 6 months.

4 Preheat the oven to 450°F. Place a 15-inch cast-iron skillet into the oven for 7 to 10 minutes to preheat.

5 Use a rolling pin or your hands to work the pizza dough into a round that's 15 inches across and ⅓ inch thick.

6 Carefully remove the skillet from the oven and fit the dough into the pan. Spoon and spread the sauce over the surface of the dough and top with the mozzarella, parmesan, and oregano. Evenly distribute the sausage, ground beef, bacon, ham, and capicola.

7 Very carefully place the pizza back into the oven and cook until the edges are brown and the cheese is melted, 8 to 10 minutes. Remove the pizza from the oven, cut into slices, and serve.

BRAISED SHORT RIBS OVER PAPPARDELLE

If you are in the mood for comfort food, this is your go-to dish. Short ribs are a gelatinous, lip-smacking, meaty protein that with some time and love lend their essence to this rich, tomato-based sauce. The method of braising these, low and slow, is foolproof and turns out tender, fall-off-the-bone chunks of meat every time. In my family, this is another classic dish that's perfect to serve up on a weekend evening, as it will perfume your house all day long. I like to serve it over thick strands of pappardelle pasta, as the tender pasta and meat combine harmoniously with the slow-cooked sauce. Since this recipe calls for an entire bottle of wine, go ahead and use a good bottle. I prefer a nice spicy and fruity Côtes-du-Rhône, but use whatever red varietal you would casually drink or serve friends. Of course, be sure to buy a few extra bottles to enjoy with this meal!

Serves 4	Hands on: 1 hour	Total: 5 hours

- ☐ 3 pounds short ribs
- ☐ Kosher salt
- ☐ Fresh-cracked black pepper
- ☐ ¼ cup extra-virgin olive oil
- ☐ 1 medium Vidalia onion, finely diced
- ☐ 2 carrots, finely diced
- ☐ 2 cloves garlic, minced

- ☐ 1 tablespoon dried oregano
- ☐ ½ teaspoon crushed red pepper
- ☐ One 6-ounce can tomato paste
- ☐ One 750-milliliter bottle red wine
- ☐ 2 cups beef stock

- ☐ One 28-ounce can whole San Marzano tomatoes
- ☐ 1 pound uncooked pappardelle pasta
- ☐ ½ cup Parmigiano-Reggiano cheese, plus more to serve
- ☐ ¼ cup chopped fresh parsley

1 Heat a large dutch oven over medium heat. Meanwhile, pat the short ribs dry using a paper towel, and season the ribs very liberally on all sides with salt and black pepper. Add 2 tablespoons of the oil to the dutch oven. Add the ribs, working in batches as necessary to not overcrowd the pan, and sear the ribs for 2 to 3 minutes on all sides, transferring the seared ribs to a rimmed baking sheet to rest.

2 When all of the ribs have been seared, add the remaining 2 tablespoons of oil to the pot. Add the onion and carrots and cook, stirring on occasion, until the onion is translucent and the carrots are just tender, about 10 minutes. Add the garlic, followed by the oregano and red pepper and cook, stirring, for 30 seconds. Use a spoon to push the vegetable mixture to the perimeter of the dutch oven, creating an open

well in the center of the pot. Next, add the tomato paste into the center and cook the paste, stirring on occasion, until the paste loosens and is warmed through, 2 minutes. Use a spoon to fold the vegetable mixture into the cooked paste.

3 Add the wine, and deglaze the dutch oven, using a wooden spoon to scrape up the browned bits from the bottom of the pot. Add the beef stock, followed by the entire can of tomatoes. Use the spoon to gently crush or break up the tomatoes. Add the ribs and their juices to the dutch oven, nestling the ribs into the sauce mixture to ensure they are all, or nearly all, submerged. Allow the mixture to come to a slow simmer, cover, and reduce the heat to low. Simmer for 20 minutes.

4 Meanwhile, preheat the oven to 350°F. Carefully transfer the dutch oven to the preheated oven and cook, undisturbed, for 2 hours. Remove the lid from the dutch oven and continue to braise the ribs for an additional hour. The sauce should reduce (and thicken) by about an inch or so when you look at the side of the dutch oven. Remove the pot from the oven, and place back on the stove top.

5 Meanwhile, bring a large pot of salted water to a boil, and cook the pappardelle pasta al dente according to the package instructions.

6 Use tongs to hold the bone portion of the short ribs and a fork to pull and shred the meat off the bones and into the sauce. Discard the bones. Continue until no bones remain, then stir the sauce and meat mixture until combined, keeping the sauce warm on low heat as needed.

7 Drain the pasta, and transfer the cooked hot pasta to the dutch oven with the sauce. Toss the mixture well, until the sauce and meat have coated the pasta. Add the cheese, and toss in the pasta until just melted. Transfer the pasta to a serving platter. Sprinkle the pasta with additional cheese as desired and garnish with parsley. Serve.

BEEF BOURGUIGNON

I know what you are probably thinking . . . aren't there thousands of recipes out there for this classic dish? Yes, there are. That said, I'm here to talk about the main ingredient—after all, where's the beef? Many larger markets, and even smaller shops, will sell prebutchered stew meat by the pound, which is the perfect cut for this recipe and many others. But I have a secret for you. That stew meat is simply rump or chuck roast cut into cube form for convenience. You can often save yourself thirty to forty percent by cutting it up yourself.

I've laid out a classic yet simple method for creating this wonderful dish at home. If you are not a fan of mashed potatoes, you can go with buttered egg noodles, a cauliflower purée, risotto, grits, or even a hearty quinoa to serve as the base of this delicious classic dish.

Serves 4	Hands on: 35 minutes	Total: 3 hours 30 minutes

- ☐ 3 pounds beef stew meat, cut into 1½- to 2-inch cubes
- ☐ 2 tablespoons kosher salt
- ☐ 1 tablespoon fresh-cracked black pepper
- ☐ ½ cup all-purpose flour
- ☐ 3 tablespoons vegetable oil, plus more as needed

- ☐ 3 cloves garlic, minced
- ☐ 1 shallot, minced
- ☐ One 750-milliliter bottle burgundy wine
- ☐ One 10.5-ounce can beef consommé soup
- ☐ 1 cup water
- ☐ 1 bay leaf

- ☐ 1 cup frozen pearl onions
- ☐ 3 carrots, ends removed and cut into 1-inch chunks
- ☐ Mashed potatoes, to serve
- ☐ Finely minced fresh parsley, as garnish

1 Preheat the oven to 300°F. Spread out the meat into a single layer and season evenly with the salt and pepper. Using your hands, toss the meat to evenly coat in the seasonings. Next, sprinkle the flour over the meat, and again toss to coat until all sides of the meat are lightly dusted with flour.

2 Heat a 6-quart dutch oven over medium-high heat and add the vegetable oil. Working in batches, sauté the meat on all sides, allowing each side to brown for 2 to 3 minutes to develop a nice, dark sear. Remove the meat to a plate while you repeat with the remaining batches, about three batches in total, adding more vegetable oil as needed.

3 Add the garlic and shallot to the empty pot and sauté for 1½ minutes, pushing the ingredients around in the drippings to develop flavor. Add the wine to deglaze the pot and use a wooden spoon to scrape up the browned bits from the bottom. Next, add the consommé, water, and bay leaf. Transfer the meat and any juices back to the pot and bring to a slow simmer. Cover and place in the oven for 1½ hours.

4 Meanwhile, place the frozen pearl onions on a baking sheet and bake for 30 minutes, to slightly caramelize and brown.

5 After the meat has been cooking for 1½ hours, remove from the oven and add the onions and carrots. Stir to immerse the ingredients in the liquid, cover, and return to the oven for 30 more minutes.

6 Remove the cover from the dutch oven and continue to bake, allowing the mixture to reduce and thicken for an additional 1 hour.

7 Remove the pot from the oven and rest for 10 minutes, discarding the bay leaf. Serve the dish with a base of mashed potatoes, followed by a generous ladle of the beef mixture. Garnish with parsley.

MISSISSIPPI BEEF with CREAMY GRITS

The origins of this regional classic might be hard to exactly track down, but if you've ever tasted this tangy, juicy style of pot roast, you instantaneously know it was cooked with love. Perhaps we truly owe those in Mississippi for this luscious creation, but instead of hunting down its creator, I say we all eat. While most folks will cook this dish in a slow cooker for eight to ten hours, I prefer to utilize a dutch oven, typically cutting the cooking time in half with better results. I liken that to the strong sear on the chuck roast and cooking everything in one single pot. Sure, there are some processed ingredients, but at the same time, it's an effortless dish that always pleases. You could serve this with some mashed potatoes, buttered pasta, or rice, but I prefer the creamy grits over anything else. This is a weekend meal that's also impressive enough to entertain with. Leftovers go nicely on some toasted bread, topped with melted cheese, for a hearty sandwich. Two for the price of one, folks!

Serves 6	Hands on: 45 minutes	Total: 5 to 6 hours

MISSISSIPPI BEEF
- One 4- to 5-pound chuck roast
- 1 tablespoon kosher salt
- ½ tablespoon fresh-cracked black pepper
- ½ tablespoon garlic powder
- 4 tablespoons unsalted butter
- 2 cups beef stock

- 1 cup red wine
- One 1-ounce package ranch dressing mix
- 12 jarred pepperoncini peppers
- Thinly sliced fresh chives, as garnish

GRITS
- 1 cup stone-ground grits

- 2 cups water
- 2 cups whole milk
- 1 tablespoon kosher salt
- ⅓ cup heavy cream
- 4 tablespoons unsalted butter

- Sliced fresh chives, as garnish

1 Preheat the oven to 325°F. Heat a dutch oven over medium-high heat. Meanwhile, season the chuck roast evenly on all sides with the salt, pepper, and garlic powder. Add the butter to the dutch oven and cook until foamy, about 1 minute. Add the roast to the dutch oven and sear on all sides, 3 to 4 minutes per side, until very well browned. Add the stock and wine and bring to a slow simmer. With the mixture simmering, stir in the ranch dressing mix. Top the roast with the pepperoncini, cover the dutch oven, and place it into the preheated oven. Bake for 4 to 5 hours, until the meat is pull-apart tender. Remove from the oven, keep covered, and allow to rest for 30 minutes.

2 Meanwhile, prepare the grits. Rinse the grits vigorously under cold running water in a large bowl, removing any chaff that floats to the top.

Drain. In a large heavy-bottomed saucepan, bring the water and milk to a slow boil over medium heat. While stirring the liquid, add the grits in a steady stream and stir constantly while you bring the mixture back to a slow simmer. Reduce the heat to low, cover, and cook the grits, stirring every 10 to 15 minutes, until they are just tender to the bite, about 1 hour.

3 Remove the grits from the heat and stir in the salt, cream, and butter until combined. Cover and keep warm until ready to serve.

4 Remove the lid from the dutch oven and use two forks to gently pull apart the meat, soaking it in its juices. Ladle a generous portion of grits onto the bottom of a shallow bowl and top with the pulled meat, peppers, and drippings. Garnish with sliced chives. Serve.

THE HEMINGWAY BURGER

Back in 2009, a trove of Ernest Hemingway's personal documents became digitized and made their way into the John F. Kennedy Presidential Library and Museum in Boston, Massachusetts. Most of the documents came from the time Hemingway spent in Cuba, where he produced classics like *For Whom the Bell Tolls* and *The Old Man and the Sea*. One of the docs—handwritten, typed, stained, and tattered—included detailed instructions for "Papa's Favorite Hamburger." In 2013 *The Paris Review* caught wind of it and made this burger go viral. If Hemingway's detail and dedication to his writing is any precedent, the precise instructions he uses to prepare this burger are in perfect alignment with his literary perfection.

I will go so far to tell you that this is one of the best burgers I've ever put together, with a few of my own spins, of course. Today, one of the original ingredients—Spice Islands Mei Yen Powder—is out of production, but I sub in salt, sugar, and soy (you can also add a pinch of MSG if you have it on hand). For the meat, getting the freshest grind that's been lightly packed is key. This is served as is (don't mess with perfection), but if you must, you can add your favorite condiments and toppings.

Serves 4	Hands on: 45 minutes	Total: 45 minutes

- ☐ 1 pound 80/20 coarse-ground beef
- ☐ 2 cloves garlic, minced
- ☐ 2 scallions, finely chopped
- ☐ 1 heaping teaspoon rubbed sage, preferably Spice Islands brand

- ☐ ½ teaspoon Spice Islands Beau Monde Seasoning
- ☐ ½ teaspoon kosher salt
- ☐ ½ teaspoon sugar
- ☐ 2 heaping teaspoons India relish, or dill pickle relish
- ☐ 2 tablespoons petite capers, drained

- ☐ 1 teaspoon soy sauce
- ☐ 1 large egg, beaten in a cup with a fork
- ☐ ⅓ cup dry red wine
- ☐ 1 tablespoon vegetable oil
- ☐ 4 toasted buns

1 Break up the ground beef with a fork and scatter the garlic, scallions, sage, Beau Monde Seasoning, salt, and sugar over it, then mix them into the meat with the fork or your fingers.

2 Let the bowl of meat sit out of the refrigerator for 10 to 15 minutes. Next, add the relish, capers, soy sauce, egg, and wine, and let the meat sit for an additional 10 to 15 minutes.

3 Form 4 patties, about an inch thick each. The patties should be soft in texture but firm.

4 Heat a large cast-iron skillet over medium-high heat and add the oil. Before the oil begins to smoke, add the patties to the pan and turn down the heat to medium. Cook the patties, undisturbed, for 4 minutes. Remove the pan from the burner, and return the heat back to high. Flip the burgers and place the pan back over the heat. Cook for 1 minute, reduce the heat to medium again, and cook the burgers another 3 minutes, undisturbed. Serve the burgers on the toasted buns.

DOUBLE-CHEESE SMASHBURGERS

The phenomenon and technique of smashing burgers on a griddle might be more popular due to viral videos and marketing, but the result of chomping down on ground meat that's essentially been fried and seared in its own fat is not something new. After all, we've been known to deep-fry anything if it will taste good! The key to a great smashburger is just that—smash the heck out of it so that it cooks in an even layer. A smashburger is a well-done burger, so don't worry about internal temps as much as allowing the burger to fry itself until the edges are crispy and browned. Frankly, even if you get a few holes in the meat, you are all good, as the fat will work itself into every nook and cranny to create an almost crispy, salty crunch that's out of this world.

If you don't have a griddle, no worries. Your best friend will be a cast-iron skillet. You can cook these inside on the stove top, but my preferred method is to put that skillet right on the grill, no oil, since I want the meat to almost stick to the surface and the burgers to pick up a bit of that seasoned grill taste, especially if I'm using charcoal. I recommend using a really sturdy metal spatula that has a sharper edge, since you will be scraping the patties off the skillet.

When cooked correctly, these burgers will be done in just a few minutes, so if necessary, work in batches to ensure the pan remains super hot—the meat needs to almost fry, not steam. The thinly sliced onion serves a dual purpose: to add flavor, but also to keep your spatula from sticking to the meat when you go in for the big smash. A quick flip to the other side will gently cook the onion while you add the cheese on top to just slightly melt.

Serves 2	Hands on: 15 minutes	Total: 15 minutes

- 12 ounces 80/20 ground beef, divided into four 3-ounce balls
- 1 cup very thinly sliced Vidalia onion
- 1 teaspoon kosher salt

- 1 teaspoon fresh-cracked black pepper
- 4 slices American cheese
- 2 seeded hamburger buns, warmed or toasted

- Thin-sliced dill pickle chips, to serve (optional)
- Yellow mustard, to serve (optional)
- Mayonnaise, to serve (optional)

1 Open the bottom vent of a charcoal grill completely. Light a charcoal chimney starter filled with charcoal. When the coals are covered with gray ash, pour them onto the bottom grate of the grill, and then push to one side of the grill. Adjust the vents as needed to maintain an internal temperature of 400° to 450°F. (If using a gas grill, preheat to medium high [400° to 450°F] on one side.)

2 Place a large cast-iron skillet over direct heat and allow it to preheat for 5 minutes, or until it begins to just smoke. Working in batches, add 2 of the balls with a good bit of distance between them, and evenly distribute a quarter of the onion over each ball. Using a stiff metal spatula, smash the burgers into the skillet. Season the patties evenly with salt and pepper, and allow the patties to cook, undisturbed, for 2 to 2½ minutes, or until the edges are crispy and browned.

3 Scrape and flip the patties over, making sure to get all of the browned edges off the pan. Top each patty with one slice of cheese, and grill for 1 to 1½ minutes, until the cheese is melted.

4 Remove the patties and stack on top of each other on a bun and top with pickles and condiments as desired.

5 Prior to repeating the process for the remaining 2 patties, use some folded paper towels to wipe out the skillet until dry, ensuring the skillet is preheated dry for 1 minute. Repeat the process for the remaining patties.

VENISON SPAGHETTI / PHOTO ON PAGE 257

It's no secret that wild game is making a well-deserved comeback. Venison, a common staple found in freezers of hunters throughout the world, is one of the most reliable sources of harvestable protein, which offers an array of options beyond the sportsman favorite of burgers and backstrap. Truth be told, you can follow this simple weeknight-friendly spaghetti recipe using a substitution of ground beef, lamb, or turkey—or less usual meats like ground bison, elk, or ostrich. Whatever your choice, I love the tangy and salty flavors of this quick sauce, as they permeate throughout every bite when tangled and twisted into the hearty pasta. This is a dish I commonly serve in late fall and throughout the winter. After all, the freezer is often stocked with a fresh bounty of goodness based on the hunting rules and regs wherever you live. If you can't source this either on your own or through coercing your outdoor friends, try your local butcher or a reliable online retailer so you can take advantage of this delectable comfort dish.

Serves 4	Hands on: 20 minutes	Total: 55 minutes

- ☐ 2 tablespoons extra-virgin olive oil
- ☐ 1 medium Vidalia onion, finely diced
- ☐ 1 medium green bell pepper, finely diced
- ☐ 3 cloves garlic, sliced very thin
- ☐ 1 teaspoon kosher salt
- ☐ 1 teaspoon fresh-cracked black pepper

- ☐ 1 teaspoon dried oregano
- ☐ ½ teaspoon crushed red pepper
- ☐ 1 pound ground venison
- ☐ ½ cup red wine
- ☐ One 14.5-ounce can diced tomatoes
- ☐ One 15-ounce can tomato sauce
- ☐ ¼ cup sliced green olives
- ☐ 1 teaspoon soy sauce

- ☐ 1 teaspoon Worcestershire sauce
- ☐ 1 bay leaf
- ☐ 12 ounces thin dry spaghetti
- ☐ Finely grated Parmigiano-Reggiano cheese, to serve
- ☐ Finely chopped fresh parsley, as garnish

1 Heat a dutch oven over medium heat and add the oil. Next, add the onion and bell pepper and cook 6 to 8 minutes, until the onion is tender and slightly beginning to brown. Add the garlic, followed by the salt, black pepper, oregano, and red pepper and stir for 1 minute, being careful to not burn the garlic.

2 Push the vegetable mixture to one side and add the venison so it makes direct contact with the bottom of the pot. Sear the venison for 3 to 4 minutes, undisturbed. Using a spatula or a large spoon, flip the seared venison onto the uncooked side and sear an additional 2 to 3 minutes. After searing, use the spoon to break apart the venison until it is crumbled and cooked through.

3 Deglaze the pot by adding the red wine, using a wooden spoon to scrape up any browned portions from the bottom. Add the tomatoes, tomato sauce, olives, soy sauce, Worcestershire sauce, and bay leaf, and bring to a simmer over medium heat. When the mixture begins to simmer, cover, reduce the heat to medium low, and cook for 15 minutes. Remove the cover and cook for an additional 15 minutes to slightly reduce and thicken the sauce. Remove from the heat, discard the bay leaf, and keep covered until ready to serve.

4 Cook the pasta al dente according to package instructions. Divide the drained pasta among shallow bowls and top each with a generous ladle or two of the sauce. Sprinkle with cheese and garnish with parsley. Serve.

LAMBURGER HELPER / PHOTO ON PAGE 256

I've never hidden my hefty penchant for all things nostalgic, including those busy sports and school nights when a box of Hamburger Helper came to the rescue. Though I might still sneak that box into the house once a year, I've also realized that I can make a better version without the "help." Take this simple recipe, for example. It's one of my favorite one-skillet dinners and it always aims to please. For this version, I like to pick up some fresh ground lamb—it adds a rich and hearty flavor that blends perfectly with the creamy pasta. While this comes together as a quick thirty-minute meal, like most pasta dishes, it always tastes even better the second day as a hot lunch. Pair it up with a crisp green salad to round out the rest of the meal.

Serves 4	Hands on: 30 minutes	Total: 30 minutes

- ☐ 2 tablespoons unsalted butter
- ☐ ½ Vidalia onion, diced
- ☐ 2 cloves garlic, minced
- ☐ 1 teaspoon kosher salt, divided
- ☐ 1½ pounds ground lamb

- ☐ 2 tablespoons all-purpose flour
- ☐ 1 cup red wine
- ☐ 1 cup beef stock
- ☐ 1 teaspoon Worcestershire sauce
- ☐ 4 ounces cream cheese, cut into fourths

- ☐ ¾ cup sour cream
- ☐ 12 ounces cavatappi pasta, cooked al dente, lightly buttered, and kept warm
- ☐ 1 teaspoon crushed red pepper
- ☐ 1 tablespoon thinly sliced fresh chives

1 Heat a large stainless-steel skillet over medium heat and add the butter. When the butter begins to foam, add the onion and cook until tender and translucent, 4 to 6 minutes. Add the garlic, stir for 30 seconds, being careful not to burn, and season with ½ teaspoon of the salt.

2 Increase the heat to medium high and add the ground lamb, using a wooden spoon to press the lamb into the butter and onion mixture to sear. Allow the meat to cook, undisturbed, for 3 minutes. Using the spoon, flip the seared lamb over and continue to cook, undisturbed, for another 3 minutes. Season with the remaining salt and reduce the heat to medium and use the spoon to break the seared lamb into smaller pieces.

3 Add the flour, stir into the meat mixture to evenly incorporate, and cook for 1½ minutes. Add the wine to deglaze the skillet, using the wooden spoon to scrape up any of the browned bits from the bottom. Add the beef stock and Worcestershire and allow the mixture to come to a slow simmer. Reduce the heat to medium low and simmer the liquid slowly, until reduced by one-quarter, 6 to 8 minutes.

4 Fold the cream cheese into the mixture. Mix until the cream cheese is thoroughly incorporated, remove from heat, then fold and mix in the sour cream. Add the pasta and stir until well blended.

5 Serve the pasta in a large bowl, sprinkled with the red pepper and chives.

LAMBURGER
HELPER
(PAGE 255)

VENISON
SPAGHETTI
(PAGE 254)

BEEF, PINEAPPLE, and RED ONION KEBABS

Savory and sweet combos are not typically part of my cooking repertoire, but it's pretty darn hard to turn down something this delicious. You can save a few bucks by using a top-sirloin cut instead of a more expensive rib eye or filet, as the marinade does a great job of making the beef super tender when cooked just to temperature over a hot grill. I prefer to keep the pineapple and onion in their pure forms, as both have enough natural sugar to caramelize nicely, while also maintaining a firm texture and beautiful color. Whether you skewer these for smaller, appetizer-sized portions or for large mains, this is a standout dish for entertaining that will always impress.

Serves 4	Hands on: 45 minutes	Total: 13 to 25 hours

- ☐ 2½ pounds top sirloin fillets, cut into 1½ x 1½-inch cubes
- ☐ ½ cup vegetable oil
- ☐ ¼ cup soy sauce
- ☐ ¼ cup pineapple juice
- ☐ 1 teaspoon crushed red pepper

- ☐ 2 cloves garlic, minced
- ☐ 1 teaspoon kosher salt
- ☐ 1 dozen metal skewers, or wooden skewers (soaked 30 minutes in water)

- ☐ 2 cups fresh pineapple, cut into 1½-inch cubes
- ☐ ½ large red onion, cut into 1½-inch cubes

1 Combine the sirloin, oil, soy sauce, pineapple juice, red pepper, garlic, and salt in a large ziplock bag and place in the refrigerator overnight, or up to 24 hours.

2 Open the bottom vent of a charcoal grill completely. Light a charcoal chimney starter filled with charcoal. When the coals are covered with gray ash, pour them onto the bottom grate of the grill. Adjust the vents as needed to maintain an internal temperature of 400° to 450°F. Coat the top grate with oil; place on the grill. (If using a gas grill, preheat to medium high [400° to 450°F].)

3 Remove the beef from the marinade, shaking off any excess and discarding the marinade. Skewer the kebabs, ensuring an even distribution of beef, pineapple, and red onion, and being careful not to pack too tightly.

4 Grill the kebabs for about 3 minutes per side, for a total of 12 minutes, or until the internal temperature of the beef reaches 135°F. Remove from the heat and serve.

SUNDAY ROAST

Now that I'm officially a grown-up, one of my favorite family traditions is a proper Sunday supper. As a father and a husband, I use the meal as a chance to connect with my family after a long week, as well as fuel to start a new adventure. I'm a big believer in family meals—the discipline not only yields delicious food but also time to honor and savor the blessing of community. For this Sunday roast, I prefer to use the leaner rump roast as opposed to a chuck roast, which is fattier and more often referred to as pot roast. After church, I will stud the roast with garlic, sear it off in a dutch oven, and place it in the oven to "perfume" the house throughout the afternoon. Frankly, there are few things in this world more comforting than this smell. I finish the roast with a simple gravy enhanced with, yes, a store-bought concoction (don't hate!), usually serving it alongside a big ole pile of mashed potatoes and green beans. A glass or three of red wine usually finds its way into the mix as well. This dish is why I cook. It's one of my favorite meals and experiences.

Serves 4 to 6	Hands on: 45 minutes	Total: 6 hours

- ☐ One 4-pound rump roast
- ☐ 6 cloves garlic, peeled
- ☐ 1½ tablespoons kosher salt
- ☐ 1 tablespoon fresh-cracked black pepper
- ☐ 2 tablespoons vegetable oil
- ☐ 1 Vidalia onion, cut into eighths
- ☐ 1½ cups red wine
- ☐ 2 sprigs fresh thyme
- ☐ 4 carrots, ends removed and cut into 1½-inch pieces
- ☐ One 10.5-ounce can cream of mushroom soup

1 Preheat the oven to 275°F. Meanwhile, using a sharp paring knife, cut six 1½-inch slits into the roast, dispersing the cuts as broadly as possible to ensure an even distribution. Place a garlic clove into the bottom of each slit. Season the roast liberally on all sides with the salt and pepper.

2 Heat a dutch oven over medium-high heat and add the oil. When the oil just begins to smoke, sear the roast on all 6 sides, until deeply browned and caramelized, 3 to 4 minutes per side. Note: A hood vent or an open window will help reduce smoke. Once the roast is browned, use tongs to lift and remove it from the pot.

3 Evenly spread the onion across the bottom of the dutch oven. Add the wine to deglaze, using a wooden spoon to stir the onion and wine mixture and scrape up any of the browned bits from the bottom. Add the roast back to the pot, followed by the thyme. Cover the dutch oven and bake for 3 hours. Add the carrots to the pot, and bake for another 2 hours.

4 Place the dutch oven on the stove top. Remove the roast and carrots to a platter and tent with foil. Set the pot over medium-high heat and reduce the drippings and onion mixture by half, about 12 minutes. Once the mixture is reduced, fold in the soup. Bring the mixture back to a simmer, whisking to ensure the soup is evenly incorporated. Turn off the heat, remove and discard thyme sprigs, and allow the gravy to set for 3 to 5 minutes prior to serving. Slice the roast and serve with the carrots and gravy.

GRILLED PORK TENDERLOINS GOCHUJANG BBQ SAUCE

If you ask me, pork tenderloins are one of the most underrated cuts of meat, especially when it comes to entertaining. Typically at most grocers, you will find two tenderloins to each pack, requiring you to spend a few minutes to strip off the silver skin for a little bit of at-home prep. Your local butcher has most likely already done this work for you, delivering a tender, forgiving cut that cooks up quickly with plenty of flavor. To play up the smoke and spice from the grill, I'm adding in one of my favorite Korean ingredients, gochujang (a fermented pepper paste), to serve as my base on an otherwise classic BBQ-style sauce. I like to cook these tenderloins to just above medium rare, then slice them thin after a bit of a rest, and serve them on a platter on their own or alongside an array of fresh salads or grilled vegetables.

Serves 4	Hands on: 35 minutes	Total: 1 hour 45 minutes

TENDERLOINS
- ☐ 2 pork tenderloins, 2½ to 3 pounds in total, silver skin removed
- ☐ ¼ cup vegetable oil
- ☐ 2 tablespoons soy sauce
- ☐ 3 cloves garlic, minced

- ☐ 1 tablespoon kosher salt
- ☐ ½ tablespoon fresh-cracked black pepper

GOCHUJANG BBQ SAUCE
- ☐ 1½ cups apple cider vinegar
- ☐ 6 tablespoons gochujang

- ☐ 2 tablespoons ketchup
- ☐ 2 tablespoons honey
- ☐ 1 tablespoon soy sauce
- ☐ ½ teaspoon garlic powder
- ☐ ¼ teaspoon kosher salt
- ☐ ¼ teaspoon fresh-cracked black pepper

1 About an hour before cooking, marinate the pork. Combine the pork, oil, soy sauce, garlic, salt, and pepper on a rimmed baking sheet or in a ziplock bag, tossing to combine. Allow the tenderloins to marinate at room temerature, either tossing on the pan or shaking the bag halfway through the process.

2 Open the bottom vent of a charcoal grill completely. Light a charcoal chimney starter filled with charcoal. When the coals are covered with gray ash, pour them onto the bottom grate of the grill, and then push to one side of the grill. Adjust the vents as needed to maintain an internal temperature of 400° to 450°F. Coat the top grate with oil; place on the grill. (If using a gas grill, preheat to medium high [400° to 450°F] on one side.)

3 Meanwhile, make the sauce. In a large mason jar, combine the vinegar, gochujang, ketchup, honey, soy sauce, garlic powder, salt, and pepper. Shake the jar until the ingredients are evenly incorporated and set the sauce aside until ready to serve.

4 Grill the tenderloins over direct heat, 4 to 5 minutes per side, for a total of approximately 20 minutes, until the internal temperature reaches 135°F. Remove the tenderloins from the grill, wrap in foil, and rest for 15 minutes.

5 Slice the tenderloins on the bias into ½-inch-thick slices. Serve with the sauce on the side.

SHALLOW-FRIED PORK CHOPS

I'm definitely one of those folks who craves a thick-cut, meaty pork chop. Heck, I will often opt for a thick-cut pork chop over a steak. But every now and then, I find goodness in a thinly cut chop, fried in just a bit of oil in a hot cast-iron pan. These little guys pack plenty of crispy flavor, and the good news is it's totally appropriate to eat several of these. Truth is, you can't have just one! The method of soaking the chops in soy sauce then dredging in flour is an old, classic family recipe. The soy adds plenty of salinity to mimic a quick brine, and the light coating of flour crisps up nicely in the oil for a crunchy, savory bite. I like to serve these with some rice to help round out a full meal.

Serves 4	Hands on: 30 minutes	Total: 1 hour

- ☐ 8 thinly sliced bone-in pork chops
- ☐ 1 cup light soy sauce, plus more to serve

- ☐ 1 teaspoon kosher salt
- ☐ 1½ teaspoons fresh-cracked black pepper
- ☐ Vegetable oil, for frying

- ☐ 2 cups all-purpose flour
- ☐ 1 tablespoon garlic powder
- ☐ White rice, to serve
- ☐ ½ cup sliced scallions

1 About 30 minutes prior to cooking, place the chops on a rimmed baking sheet and cover with the soy sauce. Allow the chops to sit in the sauce, turning over once, for 30 minutes. Remove the chops from the soy sauce, discard the sauce, shake off the excess, and season both sides evenly with the salt and pepper.

2 Heat a 14-inch cast-iron skillet over medium-high heat. Add oil until it reaches ¼ inch up the side of the skillet. Reduce the heat to medium, targeting an oil temperature around 350°F.

3 Place the flour in a shallow dish, season with garlic powder, and stir until mixed. Dredge the pork chops in the flour, ensuring an even coating on both sides. Shake off the excess flour. Working in batches so as not to overcrowd, add 2 or 3 pork chops to the skillet. Shallow-fry the chops for 4 to 5 minutes per side, or until golden, and transfer to a wire rack set inside a rimmed baking sheet to drain the excess oil. (The chops can be kept warm in an oven heated to 200°F.) Repeat with the remaining chops.

4 Serve the chops over hot rice, sprinkled with the scallions and finished with a few dashes of soy sauce.

PORK SCHNITZEL

A weeknight family-friendly main, these tender, thin chops cook up crispy and crunchy. To make my life easy, I usually source boneless pork chops from my butcher. You can request that they pound them thin for this recipe, or do it yourself for more fun. After that, it's a simple dredge in flour, eggs, and panko breadcrumbs. The thin chops will panfry up quickly, ensuring the outside breadcrumbs and edges are super crunchy, while the meat is still meltingly tender. To round out a whole meal, I like to serve these over buttered noodles or rice, along with a green salad. If pork is not your go-to, you can follow the same method with thin-sliced chicken or turkey breasts.

Serves 4	Hands on: 35 minutes	Total: 35 minutes

- ☐ 2 pounds boneless pork chops
- ☐ 1 cup all-purpose flour
- ☐ 1 teaspoon kosher salt
- ☐ 1 teaspoon fresh-cracked black pepper

- ☐ 1 teaspoon garlic powder
- ☐ 1 teaspoon smoked paprika
- ☐ 3 eggs
- ☐ 2 cups panko breadcrumbs
- ☐ ½ cup olive oil, plus more as needed

- ☐ ¼ cup finely chopped fresh parsley
- ☐ 2 lemons, sliced into wedges

1 Place plastic wrap over a large counter or cutting surface. Lay the chops on top of the plastic, and cover the chops with an additional layer of plastic wrap. Using a mallet, or a rolling pin or heavy skillet, pound the chops until they are consistently about ⅛ inch in thickness throughout.

2 Combine the flour, salt, pepper, garlic powder, and paprika on a plate and ensure the seasonings are blended into the flour. Whisk the eggs in a large shallow bowl, and place the panko breadcrumbs on another separate plate.

3 Heat a very large cast-iron skillet over medium heat and add the oil. Working quickly, dredge a chop on both sides in the flour mixture, followed by a dip in the eggs, and finally an even coat on both sides in the breadcrumbs. Repeat with as many chops as will fit in the skillet at once. Place the chops in the cast-iron skillet and panfry until golden brown, 3 to 4 minutes per side, being careful not to burn. Remove the cooked chops to a wire rack set inside a rimmed baking sheet. (The chops can be kept warm in a 200°F oven, if desired.) Repeat with the remaining chops, adding more oil to the pan as needed.

4 When all of the chops are cooked, sprinkle them with the parsley and serve with the wedges of lemon.

BRAISED SPICE-RUBBED LAMB SHANKS OVER COUSCOUS

This is one of my favorite dishes for entertaining. Meaty lamb shanks flavored in a Moroccan-inspired spice rub become effortlessly tender and rich in flavor. The nice thing about this dish is that you can prep it to finish prior to your guests' arrival and then slowly reheat the lamb and sauce while the couscous comes together in just a few minutes. Your kitchen—heck, your whole house—will smell rich and warm, ensuring an inviting atmosphere for an entertaining evening. If the dish itself weren't deliciously impressive enough, the sight of the vibrant couscous with hearty lamb shanks studded with bright pops of pomegranate and herbs will make you swoon. While each person can certainly take command of their own shank, you can stretch this dish to serve a few extras by gently pulling the meat off of the shanks and allowing folks to share in the experience. This dish is best served with a spicy syrah or Côtes-du-Rhône.

Serves 4 to 6	Hands on: 1 hour	Total: 4 hours

- ☐ 1 tablespoon kosher salt, plus more as needed
- ☐ ½ tablespoon fresh-cracked black pepper, plus more as needed
- ☐ ½ tablespoon ground cumin
- ☐ 1 teaspoon ground cinnamon
- ☐ ½ teaspoon ground allspice
- ☐ Four 1- to 1¼-pound lamb shanks

- ☐ ¼ cup extra-virgin olive oil
- ☐ 1 large Vidalia onion, thinly sliced
- ☐ 2 carrots, finely diced
- ☐ 3 cloves garlic, minced
- ☐ 1 bay leaf
- ☐ 2 cups red wine
- ☐ One 28-ounce can whole San Marzano tomatoes, crushed by hand with juices reserved

- ☐ 2 cups water
- ☐ ¼ cup dried cranberries
- ☐ 1 tablespoon unsalted butter
- ☐ One 10-ounce box couscous
- ☐ 1 tablespoon finely minced fresh mint
- ☐ 2 tablespoons chopped fresh parsley
- ☐ ¼ cup pomegranate arils

1 Preheat the oven to 350°F. Combine the salt, pepper, cumin, cinnamon, and allspice in a small bowl and stir to combine. Using your hands, sprinkle and rub the spice mixture evenly onto each lamb shank, ensuring a liberal distribution. Reserve any remaining spice rub.

2 Heat a large dutch oven over medium-high heat and add 2 tablespoons of the olive oil. Add the lamb shanks, working 2 at a time if needed to prevent overcrowding the pot, and brown on all sides, 10 to 12 minutes total. Transfer to a rimmed baking sheet. Repeat with the remaining shanks.

3 Add the remaining 2 tablespoons of olive oil, followed by the onion and carrots, and cook the mixture for 6 to 8 minutes, or until the onion is translucent and soft. Add the garlic, bay leaf, and any remaining spice rub and cook for an additional 2 minutes. Deglaze the dutch oven by adding the wine, using a wooden spoon to scrape up any of the browned bits from the bottom. Allow the wine to come to a steady simmer and cook for 10 minutes to reduce and thicken. Add the crushed tomatoes and their juices and stir to incorporate. Taste the mixture and add additional salt and pepper, if necessary.

4 Nestle the lamb shanks into the vegetable mixture and cover the dutch oven. Place the pot into the oven and braise about 2½ hours. The meat should be just falling off the bone.

5 Carefully transfer the lamb shanks to a clean rimmed baking sheet and tent with foil. Remove the bay leaf and discard. Place the dutch oven over medium heat and bring the sauce to a simmer to reduce for 10 minutes, skimming the fat off of the top surface with a spoon. Turn off the heat, add the lamb back to the dutch oven, and cover. Note: If serving a few hours later, you can gently warm the dish over low heat prior to serving.

6 Meanwhile, in a separate saucepan add the water, cranberries, and butter. Bring the mixture to a boil over high heat, stir in the couscous, and cover the pan. Turn off the heat and allow it to rest for 5 minutes. Fluff the couscous lightly with a fork and transfer it to a large serving platter or individual serving bowls. Garnish with the mint.

7 Place the lamb shanks on top of the couscous and spoon the sauce and vegetable mixture over them. Sprinkle with the chopped parsley and pomegranate arils. Serve.

PIT BEEF SANDWICHES

Perhaps this sandwich is Baltimore's answer to barbecue, or perhaps it needs no description of any kind other than delectable. What I love most about this creation rarely found outside of Maryland (something that needs to change) is the fact that technique trumps all. Typically the top round, a leaner and more affordable cut, is used in this recipe. It's charred over a hot charcoal fire until it's cooked just about rare. Unlike a roast beef that uses a fattier cut with long and slow cooking times in order to produce tenderness, this top round requires cooking quickly and to rare, then slicing it against the grain as thinly as possible, turning this humble cut into an all-star. This can be a great cookout and crowd-pleaser too. You can use the thinner cuts or end cuts to serve to those who might wish for a medium or well doneness. When it is cooked properly, you will be rewarded with a tender, juicy sandwich that has elements of crispy char in every bite. The horseradish sauce and piquant onion add just enough heat and spice to complement the smoky meat.

Serves 8	Hands on: 1 hour	Total: 5½ hours to 3 days

PIT BEEF
- ☐ 1½ tablespoons kosher salt
- ☐ 1 tablespoon fresh-cracked black pepper
- ☐ 1 tablespoon garlic powder
- ☐ 1 tablespoon dried oregano
- ☐ 1 teaspoon onion powder
- ☐ 1 teaspoon smoked paprika
- ☐ 2 to 3 pounds top round

HORSERADISH SAUCE
- ☐ ½ cup sour cream
- ☐ ½ cup mayonnaise, preferably Duke's brand
- ☐ ½ cup prepared horseradish
- ☐ 1 teaspoon dijon mustard
- ☐ ½ teaspoon kosher salt
- ☐ ½ teaspoon fresh-cracked black pepper

SANDWICHES
- ☐ 8 kaiser rolls, warmed
- ☐ 1 cup very thinly sliced yellow onion
- ☐ 1 cup thinly sliced tomatoes (optional)
- ☐ 2 cups thinly shredded iceberg lettuce (optional)

1 At least 4 hours prior to cooking, or up to 3 days prior, combine the salt, pepper, garlic powder, oregano, onion powder, and paprika in a jar and mix. Rub the spice mixture all over the beef, working it into the meat using your hands. Cover the meat with plastic wrap and place it in the refrigerator to marinate for a few hours, or up to 3 days, turning the meat daily.

2 Next, make the horseradish sauce. Combine the ingredients in a small bowl, cover, and keep in the refrigerator for up to 3 days.

3 Open the bottom vent of a charcoal grill completely. Light a charcoal chimney starter filled with charcoal. When the coals are covered with gray ash, pour them onto the bottom grate of the grill, and then push to one side of the grill. Adjust the vents as needed to maintain an internal temperature of 400° to 450°F. Coat the top grate with oil; place on the grill. (If using a gas grill, preheat to medium high [400° to 450°F] on one side.)

4 Add the beef to the grill over direct heat and cook, tossing regularly to char the meat without burning, until the internal temperature reaches 120°F, 30 to 40 minutes, depending on the size of the cut. Remove the meat from the grill and rest for 15 minutes.

5 To assemble the sandwiches, slice the meat against the grain on a meat slicer, or as thin as possible using a sharp knife. The end pieces or flatter portions of the beef can be reserved for those who prefer their beef cooked to medium. Pile the beef high on the warm rolls, drizzle with the horseradish sauce, and top with the onion. If desired, add tomatoes and lettuce too. Serve.

LOOSE MEAT "CHEESESTEAK" SANDWICHES

A loose meat, or tavern, sandwich is adored in parts of the Midwest, most specifically the state of Iowa and its origin city of Sioux City. While you can find these in local taverns or the statewide Made-Rite chains, perhaps most of the recognition and notoriety came from the 1990s hit sitcom *Roseanne*, where their local Lanford Lunch Box diner served these up as a specialty of delight. Wherever the credit is due is less on my radar—the fact is this sandwich is delicious. A loose meat sandwich is more hamburger than sloppy joe: Cooked ground beef and onion are piled high on a bun, often accompanied with traditional burger toppings like pickles, ketchup, mustard, and cheese. While that's all fine and great, I'm here to confuse the process even more with my version—leaning a bit more sloppy joe with the tomato paste, and also a bit Philly cheesesteak, or perhaps even pizza steak. Moral of the story, there are endless ways to use up that ground beef from your butcher. Not only is this a quick and hearty, delicious sandwich, it's fun to eat. Enjoy stuffing your mouth while using your hands to pick up the crumbled beef and gooey cheese that falls to the plate. This is the late-night sandwich of your dreams.

Serves 4	Hands on: 30 minutes	Total: 30 minutes

- ☐ 2 tablespoons unsalted butter
- ☐ 1 pound 80/20 ground beef
- ☐ 1 teaspoon kosher salt
- ☐ ½ teaspoon fresh-cracked black pepper

- ☐ ½ teaspoon garlic powder
- ☐ 1 cup very thinly sliced onion
- ☐ 1 cup very thinly sliced green bell pepper
- ☐ 1 teaspoon tomato paste

- ☐ ½ cup dark amber beer
- ☐ 8 slices white American cheese
- ☐ 4 soft sandwich rolls, such as Amoroso brand, toasted and split

1 Melt the butter over medium-high heat in a large cast-iron skillet. Add the beef, season with the salt, black pepper, and garlic powder, and brown, breaking up the beef into small pieces or crumbles, 4 to 5 minutes.

2 Reduce the heat to medium, add the onion and bell pepper and sauté until tender, 5 to 7 minutes, stirring occasionally. Add the tomato paste and stir into the beef and pepper mixture for 1 minute. Next, add the beer and

deglaze the skillet, using a wooden spoon to scrape up any of the browned bits from the bottom. Allow the mixture to simmer and reduce for 5 minutes. Turn off the heat and allow the mixture to rest and thicken for 3 to 5 minutes.

3 Place 2 slices of cheese into the split of each of the rolls. Generously fill the rolls with the loose meat mixture. Serve immediately.

PAN "SEARED" DUCK BREASTS

The secret among chefs is that a duck breast is one of the easiest things to perfect at home. The truth is, with minimal ingredients and essentially a fail-proof "searing" technique, you can enjoy this delicious offering with the same, or perhaps more, satisfaction than a steak night.

The fail-proof technique used by chefs is actually the opposite of what we traditionally think of when it comes to searing. Use a cold pan and allow the direct contact of the scored skin with the medium-low heat to gently melt the fat as it begins to work its magic, making the skin super crispy and rendered while leaving the meat a perfect medium rare. You simply set it and forget it once the breast is bubbling and hissing at a consistent cadence. If it's smoking and popping, you've got the pan too hot. If there's no melt, then there's no magic, and you need to increase the heat a little. The quick pan sauce comes together with my preferred orange pairing, but any citrus will do. Be sure to reserve that duck fat. It's liquid gold for roasting potatoes or other vegetables.

Procuring duck breasts from your butcher might require a quick heads-up, depending on their normal schedule and stocking, but doing so will be well rewarded when it comes time to eat. Duck breasts are shrouded by a thick layer of fatty skin that when cooked properly will become the most crispy, fatty, flavorful taste and texture in the world.

Serves 4	Hands on: 35 minutes	Total: 35 minutes

- ☐ 4 duck breasts, about 6 ounces each
- ☐ 1 tablespoon kosher salt, plus more as needed

- ☐ ½ tablespoon fresh-cracked black pepper, plus more as needed
- ☐ ½ cup white wine
- ☐ 1 cup chicken stock

- ☐ 2 tablespoons orange marmalade
- ☐ 4 tablespoons unsalted butter
- ☐ 1 tablespoon thinly sliced fresh chives

1 Using a knife, score the duck breasts with a crosshatch pattern, being careful to not cut into the meat. Pat the scored breasts very dry with a paper towel, and season both sides of the breasts evenly with the salt and pepper.

2 Place the breasts, skin sides down, into a large skillet. The breasts should be close together but with spacing between. Work in batches if the pan is overcrowded. Place the pan over medium-low heat. Allow the breasts to cook, gently rendering the fat with little to no sounds for the first 3 to 4 minutes. After 5 or so minutes, the fat should begin to gently hiss and bubble. If it is popping and smoking, reduce the heat. Continue to cook the breasts for an additional 8 minutes, draining out the excess fat, if necessary, into a dish during the

cooking process. Flip the breasts flesh side down and cook 1 to 2 minutes, or until the internal temperature reaches 125° to 130°F. The skin should be rendered and golden brown.

3 Transfer the breasts, skin sides up, to a wire rack set inside a rimmed baking sheet. Meanwhile, drain all of the excess fat from the pan into the dish and save for another use. Increase the heat to medium high. Deglaze the pan by adding the wine, using a wooden spoon to scrape up any of the browned bits from the bottom. Let the wine reduce by half, about 2 minutes, then add the stock and bring to a boil. Cook again until the liquid is reduced by half, 3 to 5 minutes. Turn off the heat and swirl in the marmalade until it is evenly

dispersed and incorporated into the stock mixture. Add the butter and swirl until melted and thickened. A pinch of salt or pepper can be added to adjust the flavor.

4 Slice the duck breasts through the skin and fan out on a serving plate. Drizzle the sliced duck breasts with the pan sauce and sprinkle with the chives. Serve.

SPATCHCOCKED SMOKED CHICKEN

During the beginning of the pandemic, finding food became a relatively tough gig given all the shortages throughout the country. While limiting my outings, I was often able to find whole chickens at the store, which was a quick and easy pickup for a weekly family meal. Frankly I prefer purchasing whole chickens, as it's one of the easier things you can butcher at home, while saving a few bucks per pound by doing so. That said, cooking a whole chicken, especially on a grill or smoker, challenges most folks, mainly because the breast meat ends up dry and overcooked while you're trying to ensure the leg and thigh are cooked to the proper temperature. That can really be solved by spatchcocking (removing the backbone from the chicken to allow it to lie flat), which ensures an even cook time throughout the bird. This method holds up whether the chicken is grilled quickly or, as in this method, smoked low and slow to produce that fall-off-the-bone tenderness that everyone enjoys. The dry rub recipe goes especially well on this bird, but it can be used for ribs, pork shoulders, and chops.

Serves 4	Hands on: 30 minutes	Total: 3 hours

- ☐ One 4- to 5-pound whole chicken
- ☐ ¼ cup extra-virgin olive oil
- ☐ 4 tablespoons unsalted butter, softened

DRY RUB
- ☐ ¼ cup packed light brown sugar
- ☐ 2 teaspoons kosher salt
- ☐ 2 teaspoons fresh-cracked black pepper
- ☐ 2 teaspoons smoked paprika

- ☐ 2 teaspoons garlic powder
- ☐ ½ teaspoon mustard powder
- ☐ ½ teaspoon chili powder
- ☐ ½ teaspoon ground allspice
- ☐ ½ teaspoon cayenne pepper

1 Open the bottom vent of a charcoal grill completely. Pour a large pile of charcoal onto the bottom grate on one side of the grill. Light a charcoal chimney starter filled halfway with additional charcoal. When the coals are covered with gray ash, pour them onto the pile of existing charcoal. Adjust the vents, nearly closing them, as needed to maintain an internal temperature of 250° to 275°F. Coat the top grate with oil; place on the grill. (If using a gas grill or smoker, preheat to medium low [250° to 275°F] on one side.)

2 Place the chicken, breast side down, on a cutting board. Using poultry shears, cut along both sides of the backbone and remove the backbone. (Discard or reserve for stock.) Turn the chicken, breast side up, and open the underside of the chicken like a book. Using the heel of your hand, press firmly against the breastbone until it cracks.

3 Prepare the dry rub. In a small bowl, combine the brown sugar, salt, pepper, paprika, garlic powder, mustard powder, chili powder, allspice, and cayenne. Use a fork to mix the ingredients until evenly combined.

4 Using your hands, coat the entire chicken in all areas and on all sides with the olive oil. Next, place the 2 tablespoons butter underneath the skin of both breasts. Liberally sprinkle the dry rub over the chicken, rubbing the spice mixture into every crevice of the chicken to ensure an even distribution.

5 Place the chicken, skin side up, on the grill over indirect heat and smoke the chicken for approximately 2½ hours, or until a thermometer inserted into the thickest part of the breast registers 160° to 165°F, and the thigh reads 165°F. Remove the chicken from the grill and rest 10 minutes. Serve.

CHICKEN PAPRIKASH

This tangy and meaty dish that screams comfort food brilliantly makes the most of chicken leg quarters. This particular cut often can be sourced at your local butcher shop rather cheaply, and the combination of the dark thigh and leg meat, along with the flavorful skin, creates a satisfying foundation to an array of recipes. The key here is to always use good-quality, fresh paprika—nothing more than a few months old, as it becomes bitter in flavor. I prefer to sear the chicken quarters on the stove top, getting a good texture on the skin prior to building the rest of the dish and finishing the chicken in the oven until it's effortlessly tender. This is one of those meals you can cook all the way through the day before, cool to room temp, chill overnight, and reheat gently the next day to serve. Frankly I think it's better this way. The dish works as a casual family meal or gussied up for entertaining a large crowd without breaking the budget. While this dish is cooked as a one-pot meal, it goes incredibly well with another pot of buttered noodles or hot cooked white rice.

Serves 6 to 8	Hands on: 45 minutes	Total: 1 hour 30 minutes to 2 hours

- ☐ 8 to 10 chicken leg quarters, rinsed and patted dry
- ☐ 1 tablespoon kosher salt
- ☐ ½ tablespoon fresh-cracked black pepper
- ☐ 1 tablespoon vegetable oil
- ☐ 4 tablespoons unsalted butter
- ☐ 1 medium Vidalia onion, thinly sliced

- ☐ 4 cloves garlic, minced
- ☐ 3½ tablespoons smoked paprika
- ☐ 3 tablespoons all-purpose flour
- ☐ ½ cup dry white wine
- ☐ One 14.5-ounce can whole San Marzano tomatoes, crushed by hand

- ☐ 1 cup chicken stock
- ☐ 1 pound uncooked wide egg noodles
- ☐ 1 cup sour cream
- ☐ ½ cup chopped fresh parsley

1 Preheat the oven to 425°F. Next, heat a large dutch oven or skillet over medium heat. Meanwhile, evenly season the chicken leg quarters on both sides with the salt and pepper. Add the oil and 2 tablespoons of the butter to the pan. When the butter and oil mixture begins to foam, add half of the chicken quarters, skin sides down, to the pot and cook until the skin is rendered and crispy, 6 to 8 minutes. Flip the chicken and cook on the other side for an additional 5 minutes, then transfer the seared chicken to a rimmed baking sheet. Repeat the searing process with the remaining chicken and transfer to the baking sheet to rest.

2 Leave about 2 tablespoons of oil in the pot and drain off the rest. Add the onion and use a wooden spoon to stir it and break up any bits from the bottom of the pot. Cook for 4 to 6 minutes, until the onion is just translucent. Add the garlic, stir, and cook for 2 minutes. Next, sprinkle in both the paprika and flour and stir to coat evenly in the onion mixture, about 3 minutes.

3 Deglaze the pot by pouring in the wine and again scraping up any bits from the bottom. Add the tomatoes and stock, stir, and bring to a slow simmer, about 5 minutes. Gently transfer the chicken quarters, skin sides up, into the sauce and place the pot into the heated oven, uncovered. Bake for 30 to 35 minutes, until bubbly and the sauce has slightly reduced.

4 Meanwhile, cook the egg noodles according to the package instructions for al dente. Drain the noodles and toss with the remaining 2 tablespoons of butter.

5 Working quickly, plate the buttered noodles into shallow bowls and top with portions of the chicken. Quickly swirl the sour cream into the sauce in the pot until well combined. Ladle the sauce mixture over the plated chicken and noodles, sprinkle with the parsley, and serve.

SMOKED CHICKEN
LOLLIPOPS
(PAGE 282)

FRIED CHICKEN
WINGS (PAGE 283)

CHICKEN WINGS WITH
HOUSE BLUE CHEESE
(PAGE 284)

SMOKED CHICKEN LOLLIPOPS / PHOTO ON PAGE 280

Sometimes food is just as cool to look at as it is to eat. Such is the case with this chicken leg recipe that utilizes a simple technique of cutting around the leg to reveal the bone. It gives it that "lollipop" look, while also making it easy for you and your friends to get a sturdy hold of this meaty masterpiece. The darker meat stands up well to the low and slow cook time, ensuring the chicken will be bite-off-the-bone tender and juicy. You can purchase accessory racks to suspend these over the grate, but you don't technically need any fancy equipment to pull these off, as the recipe calls for cooking the meat over indirect heat throughout the process.

I prefer to sauce these in my favorite barbecue sauce, just in the last 10 minutes of cooking so the sauce doesn't burn. You could also baste these in a buffalo-style sauce, or whatever you prefer. Don't skip out on placing a small bit of foil around the exposed bone; otherwise it will burn during the grilling.

Serves 4	Hands on: 20 minutes	Total: 3 hours

- ☐ 12 chicken drumsticks
- ☐ 2 tablespoons vegetable oil
- ☐ 1½ tablespoons Creole seasoning
- ☐ 1 cup barbecue sauce (optional)

1 Open the bottom vent of a charcoal grill completely. Pour a large pile of charcoal onto the bottom grate on one side of the grill. Light a charcoal chimney starter filled halfway with additional charcoal. When the coals are covered with gray ash, pour them onto the pile of existing charcoal. Adjust the vents, nearly closing them, as needed to maintain an internal temperature of 200° to 225°F. Coat the top grate with oil; place on the grill. (If using a gas grill or smoker, preheat to low [200° to 225°F] on one side.)

2 Place the chicken legs on a sturdy, clean surface. With a leg lying on its side, use a paring knife to carefully cut entirely around the bone, about 1½ inches from the bottom of the leg. Using your hands or pliers, pull the cut meat away from the bone. Continue with the remaining leg pieces.

3 Drizzle the frenched legs with the vegetable oil and season with the Creole seasoning. Place a small piece of foil over each exposed bone portion to prevent from burning.

4 Place the legs on the grill over indirect heat and cook for 1½ to 2 hours, turning on occasion, until the internal temperature reaches 165°F. In the last 10 minutes of cooking, baste the meat portions with barbecue sauce, if desired. Serve.

FRIED CHICKEN WINGS / PHOTO ON PAGE 280

Sometimes it is what it is, and my craving for fried chicken can't be stopped until I have it. But at least with chicken wings, I can stop after a wing or three into the process without caving into the whole bird. The truth is most folks are used to eating fried wings buffalo style, or in restaurants where they skip breading altogether and toss in a sauce of sorts to add flavor after the cooking process. In my method, I suppose I meet somewhere in the middle by applying a light coat of flour on the wings, allowing them to quickly fry in oil until they are golden brown, crispy, and delicious. Frankly I don't see a need to add anything else to these wings besides some salt, but if you want a dipping sauce, be my guest. These are certainly worthy as an all-star appetizer or starter, but more often than not, I will serve a half dozen of these with some steamed rice and vegetables for a simple and delicious dinner.

Serves 4	Hands on: 30 minutes	Total: 45 minutes

WINGS
- ☐ 2 pounds chicken wings, separated into wingettes and drumettes and patted dry

- ☐ 1 tablespoon kosher salt, plus more to serve
- ☐ ½ tablespoon fresh-cracked black pepper
- ☐ ½ tablespoon garlic powder
- ☐ Vegetable oil, for frying

DREDGE
- ☐ 1½ cups all-purpose flour
- ☐ ¼ cup corn starch
- ☐ 1 tablespoon kosher salt
- ☐ ½ teaspoon cayenne pepper

1 Arrange the wings on a baking sheet and season both sides evenly with the salt, black pepper, and garlic powder.

2 Fill a dutch oven with oil until it measures 4 inches from the bottom of the pot and place it over medium-high heat until it reaches 350°F. Reduce the temperature as necessary to maintain 350°F.

3 In a mixing bowl, combine the flour, corn starch, salt, and cayenne pepper and stir until evenly incorporated. Dredge the seasoned wings in the flour mixture, ensuring each wing is evenly coated.

4 Working with 4 or 6 pieces at a time, add the wings to the dutch oven and fry, turning on occasion, until the wings are golden brown and crispy, about 8 minutes. Transfer the cooked wings to a wire rack set inside a rimmed baking sheet. Repeat with the remaining wings.

5 Season the wings with additional salt to taste. Serve.

CHICKEN WINGS with HOUSE BLUE CHEESE / PHOTO ON PAGE 281

I make it no secret that I'm a connoisseur of chicken wings. In fact, nearly every book I've ever written has a few variants of recipes to pay homage to the handheld treats. Whether it's for a game-day treat or a Sunday lunch, I just can't get enough of the smoky, tender perfection from a perfectly grilled wing. While your local butcher might already prepare these for you, oftentimes you will find the wingette and drumette sold as one. Have no fear: A sharp knife will allow you to separate them. Simply spread the two apart, and you will find a joint where they meet. Some pressure from your knife will tell you if you are in the right spot, as it will simply separate the two easily. If you are on the bone, stop, reassess, and try again. This can be a learning process, but a fruitful one, as it just means you are cooking more deliciousness! I also like to remove the tip from the wingette, as it doesn't have much to offer and it's the first thing to burn up over the hot fire. Though I'm known for a few recipes with this cut, there is one thing I've not given away, until now. My creamy house blue cheese. It's a staple with wings, a big crudités platter, or a wedge salad. This, my friends, is a secret family recipe that I'm happy to share.

Serves 4	Hands on: 1 hour	Total: 1 hour

HOUSE BLUE CHEESE
- ☐ 1 clove garlic, peeled
- ☐ 1 teaspoon Worcestershire sauce
- ☐ 1 teaspoon lemon juice
- ☐ ½ teaspoon hot sauce
- ☐ ½ teaspoon kosher salt
- ☐ ½ teaspoon fresh-cracked black pepper
- ☐ ½ cup sour cream

- ☐ ½ cup mayonnaise, preferably Duke's brand
- ☐ ½ cup whipped cream cheese
- ☐ 1 cup crumbled blue cheese

WINGS
- ☐ 2 pounds chicken wings, separated into wingettes

and drumettes and patted dry
- ☐ 3 tablespoons vegetable oil
- ☐ 4½ teaspoons kosher salt
- ☐ 1 tablespoon fresh-cracked black pepper
- ☐ 1 tablespoon garlic powder
- ☐ Assorted sliced carrots, celery, and bell peppers, to serve

1 Make the dressing by combining the garlic, Worcestershire sauce, lemon juice, hot sauce, salt, and black pepper in a blender. Pulse until the garlic is broken down. Next, add the sour cream, mayonnaise, cream cheese, and ½ cup of the blue cheese, and pulse until the mixture is smooth and incorporated. Transfer to a bowl and fold in the remaining ½ cup of blue cheese. Cover and keep chilled until ready to serve. You can make this in advance and keep, covered, in the refrigerator for up to 5 days.

2 Open the bottom vent of a charcoal grill completely. Light a charcoal chimney starter filled with charcoal. When the coals are covered with gray ash, pour them onto the bottom grate of the grill, and then push to one side of the grill. Adjust the vents as needed to maintain an internal temperature of 400° to 450°F. Coat the top grate with oil; place on the grill. (If using a gas grill, preheat to medium high [400° to 450°F] on one side.)

3 Place the wings in a large bowl and add the oil, salt, black pepper, and garlic powder. Toss the wings with the seasoning until evenly coated.

4 Place the wings on the grill over direct heat. Cover and grill until charred, about 8 minutes, turning once, halfway through the cook time.

5 Move the wings to indirect heat. Cover and grill until a thermometer inserted in the thickest portion of the wings registers 160°F, about 10 minutes. Transfer the wings to a serving platter and serve with the house blue cheese and vegetables.

PORK BLADE STEAKS ⓦⓘⓣⓗ CORN RELISH

/ PHOTO ON PAGE 218

Sometimes you just don't have the time to cook a whole butt. Confused? I'm talking about the pork butt, which is where this steak cut is derived, which actually has nothing to do with the butt of a pig. It's entirely from the shoulder. While all of us love the deliciously tender, melt-in-your-mouth pulled pork you get from slowly smoking a whole ten- to twelve-pound butt, the truth of the matter is that the preparation takes a lot of time and patience. So for another route, when I'm craving that meaty fix on a weeknight, I opt for these hearty pork blade steaks, which are sliced thick from the shoulder and cook up in just a few hours. While you can slather these in BBQ sauce, I prefer to serve them rather simply, letting the smoke and the tender meat shine. A dollop or two of the pickled corn relish, however, does add a nice cool contrast and just the right amount of sweetness to make this an impressive main.

Serves 4	Hands on: 45 minutes	Total: 3 hours

BLADE STEAKS
- ☐ Four 1½-inch-thick pork blade (or butt) steaks
- ☐ 1 tablespoon extra-virgin olive oil
- ☐ 4½ teaspoons kosher salt
- ☐ 1½ teaspoons fresh-cracked black pepper
- ☐ 1½ teaspoons garlic powder

RELISH
- ☐ 1 cup apple cider vinegar
- ☐ 2 tablespoons sugar
- ☐ 1 teaspoon kosher salt
- ☐ 2 cups fresh corn kernels cut from the cob
- ☐ ½ jalapeño, finely minced
- ☐ 1 clove garlic, minced
- ☐ ¼ cup finely chopped cucumber
- ☐ 1 plum tomato, seeds removed and finely diced
- ☐ ½ cup thinly sliced scallions
- ☐ 1 tablespoon chopped fresh cilantro

1 Open the bottom vent of a charcoal grill completely. Light a charcoal chimney starter filled with charcoal. When the coals are covered with gray ash, pour them onto the bottom grate of the grill, and then push to one side of the grill. Adjust the vents as needed to maintain an internal temperature of 350°F. Coat the top grate with oil; place on the grill. (If using a gas grill, preheat to medium [350°F] on one side.)

2 Meanwhile, lightly coat the pork steaks in the olive oil and season both sides of the steaks evenly with the salt, pepper, and garlic powder. Place the steaks on the grill over direct heat, cover, and grill for 30 minutes, flipping halfway through the time.

3 While the pork cooks, prepare the relish by combining the vinegar, sugar, and salt in a small saucepan over medium-high heat. Bring the mixture to a boil, reduce the heat to medium, and simmer for about 15 minutes, until the mixture is reduced by half. Remove the pan from the heat and let it sit for 15 minutes. In a serving bowl, combine the corn, jalapeño, garlic, cucumber, tomato, scallions, and cilantro. Add the vinegar mixture and toss to coat. Serve immediately, or cover and place in the refrigerator until ready for use, up to 1 day.

4 Transfer each steak onto a large piece of aluminum foil, and tightly wrap the steaks in the foil. Place the steaks over indirect heat, cover, and grill for 1½ hours, or until tender and the internal temperature registers 200°F. Remove the steaks from the foil and serve, topped with the relish.

SMOKED GREEK PORK BUTT

As the author of *The South's Best Butts*, I certainly know there are a thousand different ways to cook a pork butt, which is how this recipe came about in the first place. The pork butt is one of the most forgiving, delicious cuts of meat, which will always feed and please a crowd. I came up with this version one summer afternoon, when I wanted to have a Mediterranean focus for the main, as I planned to serve it alongside some orzo pasta and a big ole Greek salad. The seasoning and technique used here was a huge hit, and it's become one of my favorite ways to cook my butt! I could say that over and over, but hope you like it too!

Serves 6 to 8	Hands on: 1 hour 30 minutes	Total: 11 hours

- ☐ One 8- to 12-pound pork butt
- ☐ 10 cloves garlic, peeled
- ☐ ¼ cup extra-virgin olive oil
- ☐ 3 tablespoons kosher salt

- ☐ 4½ teaspoons fresh-cracked black pepper
- ☐ 1 tablespoon dried oregano
- ☐ 1½ teaspoons crushed red pepper

- ☐ 1 Vidalia onion, cut into eighths
- ☐ 1 bay leaf
- ☐ 1 lemon, cut in half
- ☐ 2 cups red wine
- ☐ Toasted pita bread, to serve

1 Rinse the pork butt under cold running water and pat dry using paper towels. Using a sharp paring knife, score the fat layer in alternate diagonal cuts, cutting the fat just to the meat. Use the knife to make ten 1½- to 2-inch incisions into the butt, spacing the incisions evenly across the entire butt, and fill each incision with a clove of garlic.

2 Coat the pork butt in the olive oil. In a small mixing bowl, combine the salt, black pepper, oregano, and red pepper until evenly mixed. Using your hands, rub the seasoning mixture into the meat, ensuring it gets into every nook and crevice.

3 Open the bottom vent of a charcoal grill completely. Pour a large pile of charcoal onto the bottom grate on one side of the grill. Light a charcoal chimney starter filled halfway with additional charcoal. When the coals are covered with gray ash, pour them onto the pile of existing charcoal. Adjust the vents, nearly closing them, as needed to maintain an internal temperature of 200° to 225°F. Coat the top grate with oil; place on the grill. (If using a gas grill or smoker, preheat to low [200° to 225°F] on one side.)

4 Place the pork butt on the grill over direct heat and cook for 15 minutes per side, omitting the fat cap, for a total of 5 sides. Move the pork butt to the indirect heat, fat cap up, cover, and smoke for 5 hours.

5 In a dutch oven, layer the onion, bay leaf, and lemons in the bottom. Pour in the red wine. Transfer the pork butt to the dutch oven. Cover, place the pot over indirect heat, cover the grill, and continue to cook for an additional 3 to 4 hours, or until the internal temperature reaches 200°F.

6 Remove the cover of the pot and allow the meat to cool for 30 to 45 minutes. To serve, remove the fat cap and discard the lemon and bay leaf. Pull and discard the shoulder bone. Using your hands or two large forks, pull and shred the meat into the sauce. Serve with toasted pita bread. ▶▶

T-BONE PORK STEAKS ⬤ CAPER SALSA

Everybody is familiar with the beefy T-bone steak, but did you know you can get that same cut from the pig? Bet your butt you can, and the payoff can be just as impressive! Similar in structure to its beef cousin, the pork T-bone features a strip loin on one side of the bone, with a tenderloin on the other. The strip portion is denser, packed with plenty of meaty flavor, while the tenderloin is super tender and flavorful. The loin and tenderloin sections tend to have slight variances in how they are cooked, so the key to perfecting this cut, in my opinion, is to grill the steak hot and fast over direct heat while using convection heat (by closing the lid) around the steak to ensure that it cooks evenly and quickly. Contrary to old-school opinion, these are best served at a medium temperature. I like to buy thick chops, about 1½ inches thick, and ask my butcher to preserve as much of the tenderloin as possible for a well-rounded steak. The briny, garlicky caper salsa adds just the right bite to balance out these cookout favorites.

Serves 4	Hands on: 30 minutes	Total: 3 to 7 hours

PORK STEAKS
- ☐ 4 bone-in T-bone pork steaks (10 to 12 ounces each)
- ☐ ½ cup light soy sauce
- ☐ ½ tablespoon kosher salt
- ☐ ½ tablespoon fresh-cracked black pepper
- ☐ ½ tablespoon garlic powder

- ☐ ¾ teaspoon crushed red pepper

CAPER SALSA
- ☐ 2 tablespoons capers, drained and minced
- ☐ 1 tablespoon minced shallot
- ☐ 1 clove garlic, minced

- ☐ ½ cup chopped fresh flat-leaf parsley
- ☐ 1 scallion, finely minced
- ☐ 1 tablespoon red wine vinegar
- ☐ ¼ cup extra-virgin olive oil
- ☐ ¼ teaspoon kosher salt
- ☐ ¼ teaspoon fresh-cracked black pepper

1 At least 2 hours prior to cooking, or up to 6 hours, combine the pork steaks and soy sauce in a ziplock bag, seal the bag, and toss the chops in the sauce to evenly coat. Place the bag in the refrigerator for at least 1½ hours, or up to 5½ hours, removing the bag to set at room temperature 30 minutes prior to cooking.

2 Drain off the excess soy sauce, discard, and season the steaks evenly with the salt, black pepper, garlic powder, and red pepper.

3 Open the bottom vent of a charcoal grill completely. Light a charcoal chimney starter filled with charcoal. When the coals are covered with gray ash, pour them onto the bottom grate of the grill, and then push to one side of the grill. Adjust the vents as needed to maintain an internal temperature of 500° to

550°F. Coat the top grate with oil; place on the grill. (If using a gas grill, preheat to high [500° to 550°F] on one side.)

4 Place the pork steaks on the grill over direct heat, cover, and cook for 6 to 8 minutes per side, turning often to ensure an even sear. Remove the steaks from the grill when the internal temperature reaches 140°F. Transfer the steaks to a plate to rest for 5 minutes.

5 Meanwhile, in a small bowl, combine the capers, shallot, garlic, parsley, scallion, vinegar, oil, salt, and black pepper. The salsa can be made up to 4 hours in advance and kept at room temperature.

6 Serve the pork steaks with a generous dollop of caper salsa.

GUANCIALE CARBONARA

A classic carbonara pasta is built on simplicity—just a few quality ingredients to bring together one of the most satisfying comfort dishes in the world. For best results, I prefer to use guanciale over bacon or pancetta. Guanciale comes from the jowl of the pig. It's salted and dried and has similar flavors to both bacon and pancetta. However, it typically has more fat content, which is the key to getting that glossy, lip-smacking finish that coats the cooked pasta and helps bind the cheese. I recommend always having a hunk of this stuff in your fridge. I use it all the time as my secret ingredient to ramp up not only pastas but cooked greens, soups, and stews. This dish comes together fairly quickly, and the technique of combining the egg into the hot pasta needs to happen à la minute, so while the ingredient list is paltry, it's important to have your ingredients prepped to execute and enjoy.

Serves 2	Hands on: 20 minutes	Total: 30 minutes

- ☐ 1 tablespoon kosher salt
- ☐ 12 ounces uncooked linguine pasta

- ☐ 6 ounces guanciale, skin removed and cut into ¼-inch dice
- ☐ 1 clove garlic, minced
- ☐ 2 eggs, beaten

- ☐ 1 cup finely grated Pecorino Romano cheese
- ☐ 1 teaspoon fresh-cracked black pepper, plus more as needed

1 Fill a large stainless-steel pot three-quarters of the way with water and place over high heat. When the water comes to a rolling boil, add the salt and pasta, and cook for approximately 9 minutes, or al dente according to package instructions.

2 Meanwhile, add the guanciale to a dutch oven, and place over medium heat. Allow the guanciale to cook and slowly render, stirring on occasion, for 5 minutes. Continue to cook the guanciale, stirring as needed, until browned and crispy, another 4 to 6 minutes. Add the garlic, stir, and cook for 1 minute, being careful not to let it burn. Turn off the heat.

3 In a small bowl, combine the eggs, ½ cup of the cheese, and the pepper, and stir until incorporated.

4 Using tongs, immediately transfer the cooked pasta to the dutch oven, allowing some of the pasta water to make its way into the pot to help stop the cooking, as well as to loosen the sauce. Toss the pasta with the cooked guanciale and garlic several times to emulsify the fat with the starchy pasta water. While tossing, stream in the egg mixture, continuing to toss the pasta and ingredients together until a creamy sauce is formed. If necessary, add in some additional pasta water in tablespoon increments to reach the desired texture.

5 Plate the pasta onto a large serving platter, sprinkle with the remaining ½ cup of cheese, and season with additional pepper, if desired. Serve.

GRILLED CABBAGE "STEAKS"

It has become quite trendy over the past decade to carve out vegetables such as cauliflower or mushrooms into "steaks" for preparation. I tend to be late to trends, though I do like the idea of creatively implementing more and more vegetables into delicious, accessible forms of preparation. Thus this recipe provides a great way to utilize one of my favorite, and largely underrated, ingredients: cabbage. Often sautéed with onions and peppers, or served raw in slaw or kimchi form, the sturdy nature of this vegetable combined with its ability to taste great in cooked or raw form makes this a perfect candidate for the grill. It's important to remove the tough core. I'll usually take a paring knife to slice away the tough portion that doesn't make the cut, butchering the cabbage vertically so it holds its shape on the grill. You can choose your "doneness" per se, but I often like for the outer surface areas to garner plenty of char, while still leaving some crunch in the center. The tangy feta and sliced scallions provide a good bit of bite and acidity to round out the smoky, meaty flavor.

Serves 4	Hands on: 35 minutes	Total: 35 minutes

- ☐ 1 large green savoy cabbage
- ☐ 2 tablespoons extra-virgin olive oil
- ☐ 3 teaspoons kosher salt
- ☐ 3 teaspoons fresh-cracked black pepper
- ☐ ½ teaspoon fennel seeds
- ☐ ½ cup crumbled feta
- ☐ ¼ cup thinly sliced scallions

1 Open the bottom vent of a charcoal grill completely. Light a charcoal chimney starter filled with charcoal. When the coals are covered with gray ash, pour them onto the bottom grate of the grill, and then push to one side of the grill. Adjust the vents as needed to maintain an internal temperature of 400° to 450°F. Coat the top grate with oil; place on the grill. (If using a gas grill, preheat to medium high [400° to 450°F] on one side.)

2 Meanwhile, use a paring knife to remove the stem and core of the cabbage, and discard. Set the cabbage on top of a cutting board and, using a sharp chef's knife, remove the outer edge by slicing ¼ inch into the cabbage, creating a flat surface. From there, continue to slice the cabbage in the same manner, making steaks that are about 1¼ inches thick. You should get 4 to 6 steaks, depending on the size of the cabbage.

3 Arrange the cabbage steaks on a baking sheet and drizzle with 1 tablespoon of the olive oil, 1½ teaspoons each of the salt and pepper, and ¼ teaspoon of the fennel seeds. Flip the cabbage steaks and repeat on the other side with the remaining 1 tablespoon of oil, 1½ teaspoons each of salt and pepper, and ¼ teaspoon of fennel seeds.

4 Add the cabbage steaks to the grill over direct heat and cook for 5 to 7 minutes per side, until charred and softened.

5 Remove from the grill, and top the steaks evenly with the feta and scallions. Serve.

SIMPLY SEARED SALMON

If you ask my wife, Callie, what she wants for dinner, six out of seven nights she'll ask me to make this dish. Truth is, there's not much to it. Buy the best, freshest salmon possible and treat it with a bit of love and technique and it's a dish that will give back to you for the rest of your life. Speaking of technique, I'm a big believer here that a well-seasoned cast-iron pan is your best friend. Whether using the stove top or the grill, you can gently cook this fish over medium heat, allowing the conductive properties of the cast-iron to work their magic. Pretty soon I imagine everyone in your family will be asking for this dish on a nightly repeat.

Serves 4	Hands on: 35 minutes	Total: 35 minutes

- ☐ Four 6- to 8-ounce salmon fillets, skin on
- ☐ 1 teaspoon garlic powder
- ☐ 1 teaspoon kosher salt

- ☐ ½ teaspoon fresh-cracked black pepper
- ☐ 2 tablespoons unsalted butter

- ☐ ½ lemon
- ☐ Chopped fresh parsley, as garnish

1 Pat the salmon fillets dry using a paper towel, and season evenly with the garlic powder, salt, and pepper.

2 Heat a large cast-iron skillet over medium heat and add the butter. When the butter begins to foam, add the salmon fillets, flesh sides down, and sear, undisturbed, for 5 minutes. Using a spatula, carefully flip the salmon fillets to skin sides down and continue to cook until medium, about 140°F, or another 4 minutes. Using a towel to protect your hand, tilt the skillet to capture the butter and drippings and use a spoon to baste the fish during the process.

3 Finish by evenly squeezing some of the fresh lemon over each fillet and garnishing with parsley. Serve.

COCONUT CURRY SALMON / PHOTO ON PAGE 176

This is my go-to dish on cold, rainy evenings when I'm craving delicious Thai-style flavors and a warm comforting meal without busting my beltline. While this dish tastes like it took hours to prepare, the honest truth is it can be whipped up in under thirty minutes, making it a weeknight-friendly family meal. You can throw an array of different veggies into the curry, from diced squash and zucchini to a handful of fresh spinach—it's a good way to sneak in some extra goodness that gets enveloped by the sauce. I prefer to sear the salmon separately, rather than poach it in the sauce, as I like the seared texture. That said, if you are really in a pinch, you can put together the curry, add the uncooked salmon to the dish, cover, and cook for about ten minutes, until medium. I like to serve this over fragrant basmati rice, so it soaks up all the sauce, but if you want to lighten the load, you can sub in brown rice, quinoa, or cauliflower rice.

Serves 4	Hands on: 30 minutes	Total: 30 minutes

COCONUT CURRY

- ☐ 4 tablespoons unsalted butter
- ☐ 1 cup thinly sliced Vidalia onion
- ☐ 1 cup thinly sliced yellow bell pepper
- ☐ 1 cup thinly sliced red bell pepper
- ☐ 3 cloves garlic, minced
- ☐ 1-inch piece fresh ginger, peeled and finely minced
- ☐ 2 tablespoons red curry paste
- ☐ 1 tablespoon honey

- ☐ Two 13.5-ounce cans coconut milk
- ☐ 3 tablespoons light soy sauce, plus more as needed
- ☐ 1 tablespoon sriracha
- ☐ 1 tablespoon grated lime zest
- ☐ 3 tablespoons lime juice, plus more as needed

SALMON

- ☐ Four 6- to 8-ounce salmon fillets, skin removed
- ☐ 1 teaspoon garlic powder
- ☐ 1 teaspoon kosher salt

- ☐ ½ teaspoon fresh-cracked black pepper
- ☐ 2 tablespoons unsalted butter

TO SERVE

- ☐ 6 cups hot cooked basmati rice
- ☐ ¼ cup chopped fresh cilantro
- ☐ ¼ cup thinly sliced scallions
- ☐ 1 ripe avocado, peeled, pitted, and chopped into ½-inch chunks
- ☐ Lime wedges

1 For the coconut curry, heat a dutch oven over medium heat and add the butter. When the butter is melted, add the onion and bell peppers and cook, stirring often, for 3 to 4 minutes, or until just tender. Next, add the garlic and ginger and cook, stirring, for 1 minute. Add the curry paste and honey, stir, and cook for 2 minutes to toast the paste. Next, add the coconut milk, stir the mixture well, and allow it to come to a slow simmer. Add the soy sauce, sriracha, lime zest, and lime juice, and taste for seasoning, adding a bit more soy if more salt is needed, or more lime to balance out the salt flavor. Simmer the curry slowly for 15 to 20 minutes, until it's slightly thickened and reduced by one-third.

2 Meanwhile, pat the salmon fillets dry using a paper towel and season evenly with the garlic powder, salt, and black pepper.

3 Heat a large skillet over medium heat and add the butter. When the butter begins to foam, add the salmon fillets with the side the skin was on facing up. Allow to sear, undisturbed, for 5 minutes. Using a spatula, carefully flip the salmon fillets and continue to cook until medium, about 140°F, or another 2 to 3 minutes. Using a towel to protect your hand, tilt the skillet to capture the butter and drippings and use a spoon to baste the fish during the process.

4 To serve, divide the rice among four shallow bowls. Place the salmon fillets on top of the rice, and ladle a cup or so of the coconut curry over the salmon. Divide the cilantro, scallions, and avocado among the bowls. Place the lime wedges on the side and serve.

GRILLED COBIA STEAKS

A sport fish beloved just as much for its fight as it is for its steak-like texture, a line-caught cobia is one of the many pleasures one can take in while fishing offshore. I have many a fond memory of spending a few fishing charters with my father in the Gulf of Mexico as we sourced red snapper, Spanish mackerel, or if we were lucky, cobia, these almost prehistoric-like creatures. If you are not close to a local purveyor who might sell this particular fish, quality and readily available swordfish or mahi-mahi steaks can easily be substituted. I prefer to impart a very basic marinade on these fillets, as the high heat from the grill does the rest of the work for you rather quickly. Serve over a bed of rice or grains, with some lemon wedges to garnish.

Serves 4	Hands on: 20 minutes	Total: 45 minutes

- ☐ Four 8- to 10-ounce cobia steaks, about 1½ inches thick, skin removed
- ☐ 4 tablespoons unsalted butter, melted

- ☐ 1 teaspoon dried oregano
- ☐ ½ tablespoon Creole seasoning
- ☐ 2 tablespoons lemon juice
- ☐ Hot cooked rice, to serve

- ☐ 1 lemon, cut into wedges, as garnish

1 Open the bottom vent of a charcoal grill completely. Light a charcoal chimney starter filled with charcoal. When the coals are covered with gray ash, pour them onto the bottom grate of the grill, and then push to one side of the grill. Adjust the vents as needed to maintain an internal temperature of 400° to 450°F. Coat the top grate with oil; place on the grill. (If using a gas grill, preheat to medium high [400° to 450°F] on one side.)

2 Meanwhile, place the steaks in a single layer on a rimmed baking sheet. In a small bowl, combine the butter, oregano, Creole seasoning, and lemon juice and pour over the fillets. Allow the fish to sit in the marinade, turning on occasion, for 30 minutes at room temperature.

3 Remove the steaks from the marinade, reserving the marinade, and place on the grill. Cook over direct heat for 4 to 6 minutes, until charred. Flip the fillets and carefully brush with the remaining marinade, cooking for an additional 4 to 5 minutes on the remaining side, or until internal temperature reaches 140°F.

4 Remove the fillets from the grill and serve atop the cooked rice with the lemon wedges.

USC
Basketb.
MARCH 4: TBA.
CSU Women
Basketba.
Season over
C of C
Ba

FRIED CATFISH NUGGETS (with) FISH CAMP SLAW

I couldn't call myself a Southern gentleman without paying homage to one of our favorite foods—fried catfish. The "catfish trail," as it's known in the South, spreads throughout the Delta, from Arkansas through Mississippi and Louisiana, eventually finding its way to the Gulf. A meaty, mild fish, catfish can be prepared in many ways, but my preferred is cornmeal battered and crispy fried. My father grew up in a small town in Enterprise, Mississippi, which still boasts Long's Fish Camp, one of the oldest and best restaurants in the region. I always think of childhood visits to this special place whenever I cook up this recipe, especially when I'm tearing into the unique coleslaw that must accompany each crunchy bite. While you can find whole fish or fillets, don't overlook the butcher-cut nuggets. Typically cut from the abdominal muscle or trimmings, the nuggets are meaty and tender, cook up quickly, and are usually half the cost of fillets.

Serves 4	Hands on: 35 minutes	Total: 1 hour 30 minutes

SLAW
- ☐ 1 head green savoy cabbage, core removed and cut into quarters
- ☐ ¼ medium Vidalia onion, finely minced
- ☐ ¼ cup minced dill pickles
- ☐ 1½ cups mayonnaise, preferably Duke's brand
- ☐ 1 tablespoon red wine vinegar
- ☐ 1 teaspoon kosher salt
- ☐ 1 teaspoon fresh-cracked black pepper

CATFISH NUGGETS
- ☐ 1 pound catfish nuggets or fillets, cut into 2- to 3-inch pieces
- ☐ 1 lemon, juiced
- ☐ 2 tablespoons Creole seasoning
- ☐ ½ cup yellow cornmeal
- ☐ ½ cup cornstarch
- ☐ ½ cup all-purpose flour
- ☐ Vegetable oil, for frying

1 Prepare the slaw by placing a box grater on a large cutting board. Grate the cabbage and transfer it to a serving bowl. Add all the slaw ingredients, and mix until well combined. Place the slaw in the refrigerator to chill at least 1 hour, or up to overnight.

2 Pat the catfish dry to remove any excess water and arrange the nuggets on a baking sheet. Drizzle the nuggets with the lemon juice and season both sides of the nuggets with 1 tablespoon of the Creole seasoning.

3 In a shallow bowl, combine the remaining 1 tablespoon of Creole seasoning, the cornmeal, cornstarch, and flour. Use a fork to mix the ingredients until evenly combined. Dredge the nuggets in the cornmeal mixture until evenly coated and place the battered nuggets on a dry surface.

4 Fill a large dutch oven with vegetable oil until it measures approximately 2 inches from the bottom of the pot. Heat the oil over medium-high heat until it reaches 350°F.

5 Working in batches and being careful not to overcrowd, fry the nuggets in the oil for 2 to 3 minutes, turning every 45 seconds or so, until golden brown. Transfer the cooked nuggets to a large paper towel–lined plate. Continue until all pieces have been cooked. Note: The fried catfish nuggets can be kept warm in a 200°F oven. Serve the catfish nuggets with the slaw.

ROASTED SHRIMP PASTA SALAD

Sometimes an oven can do magic tricks that no other cooking appliance or technique can beat. Take, for instance, baking off crispy flat bacon. I'm a big cast-iron skillet fan, but the roasting technique is a clear winner for perfect bacon every time (see page 324). I like to employ that same technique here for roasting beautiful, plump shrimp to perfection. This method ensures each shrimp is cooked exactly the same, making each delicious bite of this creamy, hearty pasta salad consistent and beloved. Since the recipe calls for cutting the shrimp in thirds, it's important to pick up some larger, fresh shrimp from your favorite purveyor. Leaving the tails on adds more flavor, but it also helps to protect the tail while cooking, which ensures it's a consistent, sweet bite like the rest of the shrimp.

Serves 4 to 6	Hands on: 45 minutes	Total: 5 hours

SHRIMP
- ☐ 1½ pounds extra-large shrimp, peeled and deveined, with tails on
- ☐ 2 tablespoons extra-virgin olive oil
- ☐ ½ teaspoon kosher salt
- ☐ ½ teaspoon fresh-cracked black pepper

PASTA SALAD
- ☐ ¼ medium Vidalia onion, very finely diced
- ☐ 1 stalk celery, very finely diced
- ☐ 12 ounces tricolor rotini pasta, cooked al dente, rinsed, and at room temperature
- ☐ ¼ cup sliced green olives
- ☐ 1¼ cups mayonnaise, preferably Duke's brand, plus more as needed
- ☐ ½ teaspoon kosher salt, plus more as needed
- ☐ ½ teaspoon fresh-cracked black pepper, plus more as needed

1 Preheat the oven to 400°F. Arrange the shrimp in a single layer on a rimmed baking sheet, drizzle with the olive oil and season with the salt and pepper. Using your hands or tongs, toss the shrimp to coat evenly, and rearrange again into a single layer. Roast the shrimp in the oven until pink and firm, 8 to 10 minutes.

2 Remove the shrimp to a separate, clean baking sheet or large platter in a single layer to gently cool. When the shrimp have cooled, remove the tails and chop each shrimp into thirds.

3 In a serving bowl, place the onion, celery, pasta, olives, mayonnaise, salt, and pepper. Add the shrimp and gently toss the ingredients together until well combined, adjusting the seasoning as necessary. Place the bowl in the refrigerator to completely chill, 3 to 4 hours. Additional mayonnaise, in tablespoon increments, can be added and mixed in prior to serving if a creamier texture is desired.

FARFALLE "MEAT SALAD"

Back in 2004 my band OverflO had the opportunity to record an EP with the legendary John Keane from Athens, Georgia. John has made a tremendous mark on music throughout his long career, bringing artists like R.E.M., Indigo Girls, Widespread Panic, and countless others to prominence. While we were recording, I couldn't help but notice a small wooden engraved sign that sat on the control board. It simply read Meat Salad. While we were all a bit intimidated by the master himself, one day I finally had the courage to ask John what in the world was up with that sign. John explained that it came from an old country buffet, describing the dish literally.

While this dish is more of an Italian-inspired pasta salad, made from an array of your favorite charcuterie, I couldn't help but pay a bit of homage to some old memories. This is a great picnic favorite since it doesn't have any mayo base to the dressing—and also a good late-night snack!

Serves 4 to 6	Hands on: 20 minutes	Total: 3 hours

- ☐ 6 ounces hard salami, diced into ¼-inch cubes
- ☐ 6 ounces pepperoni, diced into ¼-inch cubes
- ☐ 6 ounces soppressata, diced into ¼-inch cubes
- ☐ 1 pound farfalle pasta, cooked al dente, rinsed, and cooled

- ☐ 2 stalks celery, very finely diced
- ☐ 1 small carrot, very finely diced
- ☐ ¼ cup pitted kalamata olives, finely chopped
- ☐ ¼ cup pitted green olives, finely chopped
- ☐ 1 clove garlic, minced

- ☐ ½ cup extra-virgin olive oil
- ☐ ¼ cup red wine vinegar
- ☐ 1 teaspoon kosher salt, plus more as needed
- ☐ 1 teaspoon dried oregano
- ☐ ½ teaspoon fresh-cracked black pepper, plus more as needed

In a large serving bowl, combine the salami, pepperoni, soppressata, pasta, celery, carrot, olives, garlic, oil, vinegar, salt, oregano, and pepper. Using tongs, toss to combine the ingredients until evenly incorporated, adjusting the seasoning to taste. Place the bowl in the refrigerator to chill at least 2 hours prior to serving and up to overnight. Serve.

SAUSAGE 🅐🅝🅓 TOMATO RISOTTO

In this dish, a vibrant variation on the comforting creaminess of risotto, I like to add nuggets of locally sourced sausages and canned tomatoes to add some heft and acidity. While you can source an array of different sausages, my go-to here is a classic hot Italian-style sausage, since it plays nicely with the tomatoes and fresh basil. This creamy, hearty rice-forward dish is a change of pace for pasta and pizza lovers who crave similar flavors. The canned tomatoes add a nice bit of brightness and acidity to balance the flavors. If you wish to skip on the meat, no worries—this dish is great with or without the sausage. If you wish, you may also sub the traditional pork Italian sausage with chicken or turkey varieties.

Serves 4	Hands on: 55 minutes	Total: 55 minutes

- ☐ 4 cups chicken stock, plus more as needed
- ☐ One 28-ounce can petite diced tomatoes
- ☐ 1 tablespoon extra-virgin olive oil
- ☐ 1 pound hot Italian sausages

- ☐ 1 Vidalia onion, finely diced
- ☐ 1 teaspoon kosher salt
- ☐ 1 teaspoon fresh-cracked black pepper
- ☐ 1 teaspoon dried oregano
- ☐ 2 cloves garlic, finely minced
- ☐ 2 cups arborio rice

- ☐ ¾ cup dry white wine
- ☐ 4 tablespoons unsalted butter, plus more as needed
- ☐ 1 cup grated Parmigiano-Reggiano cheese
- ☐ 4 to 6 basil leaves, torn by hand, as garnish

1 In a medium saucepan, combine the stock and entire contents of the canned tomatoes. Warm the mixture over medium-low heat.

2 Meanwhile, heat a dutch oven over medium heat and add the oil. Remove the sausages from their casings and add to the dutch oven. Brown and sear the sausages, using a wooden spoon to break them into bite-sized portions. After the sausages are cooked through, about 8 minutes, use a slotted spoon to transfer them to a plate.

3 Next, add the onion, salt, pepper, and oregano to the dutch oven and cook for 4 to 6 minutes, until the onion is tender. Add the garlic, stir, and cook for 1 minute. Next, add the rice, and stir the rice into the onion and drippings, ensuring each of the grains are coated. Continue stirring and toasting the rice for 1 to 1½ minutes, or until just slightly golden. Deglaze the pot by adding the wine, using a wooden spoon to scrape up any of the browned bits from the bottom.

4 When the wine is nearly all reduced, about 3 minutes, begin ladling in the stock and tomato mixture 1 cup at a time. Stirring constantly, allow the rice to absorb nearly all of the liquid before adding more. Continue to ladle in the stock mixture and stir constantly, until the rice is al dente, firm to the bite, about 25 minutes.

5 When the rice reaches the desired texture, add sausage back into the rice and stir in the butter and the cheese until incorporated. Garnish with the torn basil leaves. Serve.

NOTE: The final consistency of the risotto should be fluid. It should spread on a plate or in a bowl and not lay stiff. If the risotto is too dry, add additional stock and butter in tablespoon increments to reach the desired consistency.

STUFFED BELL PEPPERS

A classic and hearty recipe that packs a well-balanced meal of lean protein, starch, and vegetables into every bite. There are hundreds of twists and combinations on what you can stuff into these peppers, but my take really shines with a bit of smoky, fragrant curry powder. While I often pursue the route of using green bell peppers, you can get away with whatever color you like. Using the slightly sweeter yellow and red varieties creates a nice splash of color and a change of pace. Typically the peppers will cook themselves tender while in the oven, but if you find that your peppers are a bit stiffer or less flexible when squeezed, they are likely out of season and will benefit from being dunked in boiling water for a minute or two prior to putting this recipe together.

Serves 4	Hands on: 25 minutes	Total: 1 hour 30 minutes

- ☐ 8 bell peppers, any color
- ☐ 2 pounds 80/20 ground beef
- ☐ ½ Vidalia onion, finely minced
- ☐ 3 cloves garlic, finely minced

- ☐ 2 teaspoons kosher salt
- ☐ 1 teaspoon fresh-cracked black pepper
- ☐ 1 teaspoon dried oregano
- ☐ 1 teaspoon curry powder

- ☐ 2 cups cooked rice
- ☐ Two 15-ounce cans tomato sauce
- ☐ ¼ cup chopped fresh parsley

1 Preheat the oven to 350°F. Place the bell peppers on their sides, and using a sharp knife, cut a thin slice about ¼ inch below the crowns of the peppers to remove the tops. Reserve the tops for another use. Using your hands or a spoon, remove the ribs, membranes, and seeds from the peppers and discard. Set the peppers aside.

2 In a large skillet over medium-high heat, add the ground beef and cook, stirring on occasion, until the beef begins to brown and the fat begins to render, 5 minutes. Add the onion and continue to cook until the onion is softened, 4 to 6 minutes. Next, add the garlic, stir for 1 minute, then season with the salt, black pepper, oregano, and curry powder. Stir the seasonings into the meat mixture to ensure everything is incorporated and cook for 4 to 5 minutes.

3 Next, add the rice and one can of the tomato sauce, stir, and bring to a slow simmer. Simmer for 3 to 4 minutes to ensure the mixture is warmed and evenly combined. Turn off the heat and allow the stuffing to sit for 5 minutes.

4 Using a large spoon, stuff the bell peppers with the rice and meat mixture, filling each pepper to about ¼ inch from the top. Place the peppers side by side in a deep glass baking dish. Pour the remaining can of tomato sauce over the tops.

5 Tightly wrap foil over the dish and bake for 15 to 20 minutes, until the peppers are just softened. Remove the foil and continue to bake an additional 10 to 15 minutes, until the peppers are easily pierced by a sharp knife. Remove the peppers from the oven, sprinkle with the chopped parsley, and serve.

PRINCESS RICE

A good-quality, house-ground beef is probably one of the more common items you will find at any great butcher shop. When steaks and other items are all cut in-house, leftover trimmings and fat are combined in blends to ensure nothing goes to waste. That said, many times we find ourselves in the cyclical ground beef rut of hamburgers, tacos, chili, and spaghetti. I always keep a pound or two of ground beef in the freezer, which comes in handy for a quick, filling weeknight meal, even when cooking the beef from frozen, which is often the case when I've forgotten to thaw it!

This recipe came about as a happy accident. Both of my girls are in love with our family's traditional-style Lebanese grape leaves stuffed with meat and rice. But stuffing and rolling all of those grape leaves takes time, something I don't normally have on a busy weeknight. So instead, I created this simplified version to deliver the same flavor and goodness without all of the work. My girls first dubbed it grape-leaf rice, but I noticed they cleaned their plates a bit more when I started calling it princess rice. Round this out with a Greek salad containing hunky chunks of feta and olives and you've got a healthy weeknight meal in no time.

Serves 4	Hands on: 25 minutes	Total: 1 hour

- ☐ 1 tablespoon unsalted butter
- ☐ 1 pound frozen 80/20 ground beef, or fresh ground beef
- ☐ 1 teaspoon kosher salt
- ☐ 1 teaspoon fresh-cracked black pepper

- ☐ 1 teaspoon ground cinnamon
- ☐ ½ teaspoon ground allspice
- ☐ ¼ teaspoon crushed red pepper
- ☐ 3 cloves garlic, minced

- ☐ 1½ cups basmati rice
- ☐ 3 cups chicken stock
- ☐ 1 lemon, juiced
- ☐ ¼ cup finely chopped fresh parsley
- ☐ ¼ cup toasted pine nuts

1 Heat a large stainless-steel skillet over medium-high heat. Add the butter and cook until it foams, about 30 seconds. Next, add the block of beef and allow to sear for a few minutes. Flip the block over and, using a wooden spoon, scrape the cooked portions of beef off of the block to reveal the frozen interior. Continue flipping, searing, and scraping in this method until all of the meat is browned and cooked through, 12 to 15 minutes. Note: If using fresh ground beef, simply brown the beef in the skillet, breaking up and stirring the beef on occasion, for 6 to 8 minutes.

2 Add the salt, black pepper, cinnamon, allspice, red pepper, and garlic to the beef and stir to incorporate. Next, add the rice, and toast the rice for 4 to 5 minutes, stirring in the beef mixture to coat the rice in the drippings. Add the stock and lemon juice, stir to incorporate, and allow the mixture to come to a medium simmer. Cover the skillet, reduce the heat to low, and gently cook the rice for 20 minutes. Turn off the heat, keeping the skillet covered, and set aside for 10 minutes.

3 Remove the cover and fluff the rice with a fork. Transfer the rice to a serving platter and sprinkle with the parsley and pine nuts. Serve.

CATCHALL PAELLA

A classic dish of Spain, paella is a comforting weeknight-friendly dish that I enjoy serving throughout the year. Perhaps what I love most about this dish is its versatility—from sausage to meats to seafood to even vegetables, you can really layer in whatever you have on hand because the saffron-infused rice adds love to whatever you throw in the pan. Speaking of pans, you do not need a specific paella pan to cook this dish—a skillet will always do the trick. Let's not underemphasize the fact that this is truly a one-pot dish, leaving you little to clean. I've perfected this recipe while cooking it year after year at Cavendish Beach Music Festival in Prince Edward Island, Canada. Up there, a butcher by the name of Marty Taylor will create local sausages of delight for me to use in my concoctions each year. With tens of thousands of festival-goers in attendance, we usually cook up a version of this dish in a ten-foot-diameter pan over a live fire while drinking as many Molson Canadians as possible. That, my friends, is a day well spent.

Serves 4–6	Hands on: 35 minutes	Total: 1 hour

- 1 pound cured chorizo sausages, casings removed and sliced into ½-inch-thick rounds
- 2 tablespoons Spanish extra-virgin olive oil
- 1 pound boneless, skinless chicken thighs
- 1 teaspoon smoked paprika
- ½ tablespoon kosher salt
- 1 teaspoon fresh-cracked black pepper

- 1 medium Vidalia onion, finely diced
- ½ green bell pepper, finely diced
- 1 carrot, finely diced
- 3 roma tomatoes, seeds and ribs removed and finely diced
- ¼ cup sliced green Spanish olives
- 4 cloves garlic, minced
- 1 bay leaf
- 1 generous pinch saffron threads

- ½ cup white wine
- 2 cups paella rice, or medium-grained white rice
- 5 cups good-quality chicken stock, plus more as needed
- 1 pound large shrimp, peeled and deveined, with tails on
- ½ cup frozen peas, at room temperature
- ¼ cup finely chopped fresh parsley
- Sliced lemons, as garnish

1 Heat a large skillet or paella pan over medium heat and add the sausages. Cook the sausages, stirring on occasion, until slightly browned and the fat has rendered, 4 minutes. Using a slotted spoon, remove the sausages to a paper towel–lined plate.

2 Add the oil, and then the chicken thighs. Season the thighs with the paprika, salt, and black pepper and panfry the chicken on both sides for 4 minutes, for a total of 8 minutes. Using tongs, transfer the chicken to the same plate as the sausages.

3 Next, add the onion, bell pepper, carrot, tomatoes, and olives. Cook the vegetable medley for 4 to 6 minutes, until the onion is slightly tender and translucent. Add the garlic, bay leaf, and saffron and stir into the vegetable mixture. Deglaze the skillet by adding the wine, using a wooden spoon to scrape up any of the browned bits from the bottom.

4 Add the rice and stir in the mixture to coat the grains. Slowly pour in the stock, stir to combine, and allow the mixture to come to a slow boil without stirring again. Add the reserved sausage and chicken into the rice mixture. When the mixture reaches a boil, reduce the heat to low, and cook, covered, for 15 minutes.

5 Nestle the shrimp into the rice mixture and sprinkle the peas over the top. Continue to cook the rice, uncovered, for 5 minutes. At this point the rice should be tender and most of the liquid absorbed. If the rice is not tender, you may add an additional ¼ cup of stock to continue cooking.

6 Remove the pan from the heat, cover, and rest for 10 minutes. Remove and discard the bay leaf. Sprinkle the dish with the parsley and garnish with sliced lemons. Serve.

DIRTY RICE

I always take great pleasure when uttering the name of this dish to guests or family, usually serving up a dad joke to follow, that you'll have to take a bath after eating it. Silly, I know. Jokes aside, this hearty one-stop meal of protein, veggies, and carbs is a traditional favorite served throughout Cajun country. While some folks might be familiar with a "safe" version (usually with ground beef), the true essence of this dish involves other, less familiar butcher cuts, including chicken livers, gizzards, ground pork, and bacon. The array of additional spices and simmered stock helps provide that signature "dirty" look, but rest assured, there ain't nothing dirty about this flavor. This dish can serve as the centerpiece of a meal rounded out with some hot French bread and a simple green salad. Otherwise, it can also take the back seat, as a comforting side to broiled shrimp and seafood. Get dirty and have some fun.

Serves 4–6	Hands on: 50 minutes	Total: 90 minutes

- ☐ 4 tablespoons unsalted butter
- ☐ ½ pound chicken livers, minced
- ☐ 4 cups chicken stock
- ☐ 1 cup dark amber beer, such as Abita Amber
- ☐ 1 pound chicken gizzards
- ☐ ½ pound ground pork
- ☐ ½ pound thick-cut bacon, chopped

- ☐ 2 stalks celery, finely chopped
- ☐ ½ medium Vidalia onion, finely chopped
- ☐ ½ large green bell pepper, finely chopped
- ☐ 2 bay leaves
- ☐ 3 cloves garlic, peeled
- ☐ ½ tablespoon kosher salt
- ☐ 1 teaspoon fresh-cracked black pepper

- ☐ 1 teaspoon paprika
- ☐ 1 teaspoon dried oregano
- ☐ ½ teaspoon cayenne pepper
- ☐ 1 tablespoon Louisiana-style hot sauce
- ☐ 2 cups converted rice, such as Uncle Ben's
- ☐ ½ cup thinly sliced scallions

1 Heat a large dutch oven over medium heat and add 2 tablespoons of the butter. When the butter begins to foam, add the chicken livers and cook, stirring on occasion, for 2 to 3 minutes, until just firm. Using a slotted spoon, transfer the livers to a paper towel–lined plate.

2 Next, add the stock, beer, and chicken gizzards to the pot, increase the heat to medium high, and bring the mixture to a slow boil. Once the mixture reaches a boil, reduce the heat to low and simmer the gizzards for 30 minutes. Using a slotted spoon, remove the gizzards to a plate, allow to cool, and chop finely. Transfer the stock to a mixing bowl and set aside.

3 Add the remaining 2 tablespoons of butter to the dutch oven over medium heat. When the butter begins to foam, add the ground pork

and the bacon. Cook the meat, stirring on occasion, for 5 to 7 minutes, until well browned. Next, add the celery, onion, bell pepper, bay leaves, garlic, salt, black pepper, paprika, oregano, cayenne pepper, and hot sauce and cook the vegetables until just tender, about 6 minutes.

4 Add the rice, stirring to coat the grains, followed by the reserved chicken livers and gizzards. Add the reserved stock and increase the heat to medium high and bring the mixture to a slow boil. When the mixture reaches a boil, cover and reduce the heat to low. Cook for 20 minutes, undisturbed.

5 Remove the dutch oven from the heat, uncover, and remove and discard the bay leaf. Use a fork to fluff the rice. Sprinkle with the scallions. Serve.

ALTERNATIVE CUTS

ODDS AND ENDS, BASICS, DRINKS AND DESSERTS

Perhaps the greatest part of knowing your local butcher is having access to all of the scraps, trimmings, and other items that you can put to good use on their own or incorporate as a base to future recipes. Here we explore some of the uses of raw materials, as well as some alternative ideas, including drinks and desserts, that will help you make the most from your shopping efforts and round out your meals.

BACON
BOULEVARDIER
(PAGE 326)

**BACON
BLOODY MARY
(PAGE 327)**

MAKING STOCK AT HOME

Homemade stocks are a labor of love, but they will give back to you throughout the year when you need to amp up flavor in homemade soups, risottos, pastas, greens, and other dishes. Typically I will spend an entire day pulling out leftover frozen bones and carcasses from prior meals to add to what I have on hand, and cook up a few versions of stock. On average, I have three or four "stock days" per year, usually on slower weekends when a football game is in the background and I'm enjoying a cold beer. Or three. Of course, I always have a stock day on or around the New Year, after the holidays, when I've worked my way through a few whole chickens as well as beef rib roasts and other leftovers. From there, I will make more batches of stock as I have time, freezing the rest to use in monthly cycles. They're especially useful for gumbo season, in the fall. The good news is that your local butcher likely has leftover bones and pieces that you can pick up at nearly any time of the week. If you don't have a stash laying around your fridge or freezer, holler at your Butcher on the Block and get to work.

There are a few key rules for making great stock at home.

1   Use a pot bigger than you think you need, preferably taller than wide. The last thing you want to do is pile in your bones and pieces with aromatics and realize as you are filling the pot with water that you need a larger pot. I prefer a twelve-quart pot, heavy bottomed, and stainless steel.

2   Collagen is your friend. Connective tissues and whole bones will produce rich, lip-smacking stock that's deep in flavor and rich in color. For chicken stock, especially, be sure to ask or reserve the feet, wings, and leg bones to add to the pot.

3   Skim constantly, adding more water to make sure your bones and aromatics are completely submerged.

4   Do not keep the mixture boiling. Otherwise, you will disintegrate the aromatics and also disburse the fat throughout, making it hard to skim. Once the stock comes to a simmer, regulate the heat so that it's very slowly simmering. A few bubbles rising to the top is a good indicator that you're in the magic zone.

5   Strain the stock. I can't emphasize how important it is to have a clean, strained stock for immediate or future use.

6   Make it your own. Choosing aromatics beyond the standards will help your stock stand apart. Be aware, though: Adding too much of a certain item or adding new flavors can create stocks that are not as general for use. Sometimes I prefer sticking to the tried-and-true standards for the stock, and then I can amp up the stock for each individual recipe, based on what I'm preparing.

7   Freeze the stock in an array of different quantities, from using ice cube trays for smaller recipes to up to two quarts (or any premeasured portion), to make future cooking simple and efficient.

8   Solidified fat can be reserved and/or frozen and used in place of butter or oil.

On the following pages are two foundational recipes for the most commonly used stocks in an at-home kitchen. Note that there can be several varieties as well as methods to produce different variations, including the use of a slow cooker or pressure cooker to achieve similar results with varying time formats. The Chicken Stock recipe can serve as a suitable starting point for other similar stocks, such as turkey or game birds. Fish carcasses and shellfish can be substituted for the chicken for a fish or seafood stock, but reduce the simmering time by roughly half. Vegetable stock can be made using either recipe (roasting or not roasting the vegetables based on preference), reducing the water content as desired along with the simmering time. Finally, the beef stock recipe can be amended for other meats, including game, such as venison, elk, and bison.

CHICKEN STOCK

Makes 5–6 quarts	Hands on: 2 hours	Total: 10 hours

- ☐ 2 bay leaves
- ☐ 1 bunch fresh parsley
- ☐ 8 to 10 sprigs fresh thyme
- ☐ 4 to 5 pounds chicken carcasses and bones, including feet, legs, and wings
- ☐ 3 carrots, cut into 1-inch portions
- ☐ 3 stalks celery, cut into 1-inch portions
- ☐ 1 large Vidalia onion, peeled and cut into quarters
- ☐ 3 cloves garlic, peeled
- ☐ 10 whole peppercorns

1 Stack together the bay leaves on top of the parsley and thyme sprigs. Using butcher's twine, wrap the twine tightly around the herb mixture several times to secure, and tie a knot to hold the bouquet garni together. Place the bouquet followed by the chicken, carrots, celery, onion, garlic, and peppercorns into a large, 12-quart stockpot and cover with water, about 2 gallons. Be sure that all of the ingredients are completely submerged in the water.

2 Over medium-high heat, bring the mixture to a slow simmer, about 15 minutes. Just as bubbles begin to make their way to the surface, reduce the heat to medium low to maintain a gentle simmer. Maintain this temperature throughout the process, using a spoon or a mesh skimmer to remove the scum from the top of the stock every 30 minutes for the first few hours of cooking. For the following 6 to 8 hours, continue skimming the surface of the stock, adding water as necessary to ensure all of the ingredients remain submerged in liquid.

3 After 6 to 8 hours, remove the stockpot from the heat. Very carefully, working in batches as necessary, strain the stock through a fine-mesh strainer into a heatproof bowl or pot. Discard the solids. Nestle the bowl or pot into a large ice bath to chill the stock (a large sink or bathtub provides a good base), then place in the refrigerator overnight. Remove the stock from the refrigerator and remove the solidified fat from the surface. Use the stock immediately, or keep, covered, in the fridge for up to 5 days or in the freezer for up to 6 months.

BEEF STOCK

Makes 5–6 quarts	Hands on: 2 hours 30 minutes	Total: 12 hours

- ☐ 1 bunch fresh parsley
- ☐ 8 to 10 sprigs fresh thyme
- ☐ 4 to 5 pounds beef bones, such as oxtails, necks, and quarters
- ☐ 3 carrots, cut into 1-inch portions
- ☐ 1 large Vidalia onion, peeled and cut into quarters
- ☐ 3 cloves garlic, peeled
- ☐ ¼ cup extra-virgin olive oil
- ☐ 10 whole peppercorns
- ☐ 2 cups red wine

1 Preheat the oven to 450°F. Stack together the parsley and thyme sprigs. Using butcher's twine, wrap the twine tightly around the herbs several times to secure, tying a knot to hold the bouquet garni together. Place the bones, carrots, onion, and garlic onto a large roasting pan, using two sheets if necessary to prevent overcrowding, and drizzle evenly with the olive oil. Roast the mixture, tossing and turning the bones halfway through, until well browned, about 50 minutes.

2 Transfer the bones and aromatics to a large, 12-quart stockpot. Add the bouquet garni and peppercorns and fill with approximately 2 gallons of water to completely submerge the ingredients.

3 Place the roasting pan over one or two burners. Heat the pan over medium-high heat for 4 to 5 minutes. Add the red wine to deglaze the pan, using a wooden spoon to scrape up any of the browned bits from the bottom. Transfer the wine mixture to the stockpot.

4 Place the stockpot over medium-high heat and bring the mixture to a slow simmer, about 15 minutes. Just as bubbles begin to make their way to the surface, reduce the heat to medium low to maintain a gentle simmer. Maintain this temperature throughout the process, using a spoon or a mesh skimmer to remove the scum from the top of the stock every 30 minutes for the first few hours of cooking. For the following 8 to 10 hours, continue skimming the surface of the stock, adding water as necessary to ensure all of the ingredients remain submerged in liquid.

5 After 8 to 10 hours, remove the stockpot from the heat. Very carefully, working in batches as necessary, strain the stock through a fine-mesh strainer into a heatproof bowl or pot. Discard the solids. Nestle the bowl or pot into a large ice bath to chill the stock (a large sink or bathtub provides a good base), then place in the refrigerator overnight. Remove the stock from the refrigerator and remove the solidified fat from the surface. Use the stock immediately, or keep, covered, in the fridge for up to 5 days or in the freezer for up to 3 months.

PERFECT ROASTED BACON ⓐ DRIPPINGS

As a Southerner, it's painful for me to admit that there is a better way to cook bacon other than frying it in a cast-iron skillet. While said method is great, roasting bacon on a baking sheet in the oven is a superior cooking method, producing perfectly crispy, uniformly cooked bacon without the mess each and every time. Also, since many butchers and purveyors now offer specialty cuts or seasonings, the gentle method of roasting everything evenly ensures that nothing is burned or goes to waste in the cooking process. I know, some things are hard to admit, but since I'm eating my pride here—you should give this a try. Better yet, the drippings yielded through this cooking technique make for easy-to-capture fat that can be used in my cast-iron skillet for frying eggs, cornbread, and other uses (enhancing booze, as on page 326) where a bit of bacon grease adds that undeniable flavor. Whether thick-cut or hotel-style (thin-sliced), all you need to do is simply adjust your cooking time to allow the bacon to reach your desired level of crispiness.

Serves 4	Hands on: 10 minutes	Total: 35 minutes

☐ 1 pound sliced bacon

1 Preheat the oven to 400°F. Place a sheet of parchment paper in a rimmed baking sheet, and fold up the ends and sides to capture the bacon drippings. Arrange the bacon in a single layer on the parchment without overlapping, using two baking sheets if necessary.

2 Place the bacon into the oven and roast until crispy, 15 to 20 minutes. Remove from the oven and transfer the bacon to a paper towel–lined plate. If you want to save the bacon drippings, place a single layer of cheesecloth over the mouth of a pint-sized mason jar and carefully pour the bacon drippings from the pan through the cheesecloth and into the mason jar. Cover the jar and store the bacon drippings at room temperature for immediate use, or up to 3 months in the refrigerator.

BACON-INFUSED SPIRITS

Honestly, you can infuse smoky bacon flavor into any one of your favorite spirits using this method, but my two favorites are bourbon and vodka, which will take the two classic cocktails that follow to the next level. The best practice is to use warm fat and room temperature spirits. If the fat is congealed, or the spirit is cold, the infusion is less effective. Of course, adding more bacon fat to less alcohol will increase the concentration of the flavor, and vice versa. You can play with your ratios accordingly until you hit the mark. I always buy good-quality spirits—no rotgut here. But since we're enhancing the spirit with the bacon flavor, I don't find it necessary to splurge on the most expensive spirits.

☐ Drippings from 8 to 10 strips bacon, baked in the method on

page 324, bacon reserved for another use

☐ One 750-milliliter bottle of bourbon or vodka

Combine the drippings and spirit in a large pitcher. Stir the mixture, cover with plastic wrap, and let it sit at room temperature for 24 hours. Next, place the pitcher into the freezer for at least 4 hours, or up to overnight. The fat will congeal, separating it from the spirit. Using a spoon, remove the congealed fat. To finish, pour the spirit through a fine-mesh strainer lined with cheesecloth to remove any particles. The infused spirit is best kept cold and stored in the freezer.

BACON BOULEVARDIER / PHOTO ON PAGE 318

Serves 1

☐ Ice
☐ 1½ ounces Bacon-Infused Bourbon (above)

☐ 1 ounce semisweet red vermouth
☐ 1 ounce Campari

☐ Orange peel, as garnish

Add a handful of ice to a shaker, then add the bourbon, vermouth, and Campari. Using a long spoon, stir the mixture rapidly for 1 minute. Strain the mixture into a glass, straight up or on the rocks, as desired. Garnish with orange peel. Serve.

BACON BLOODY MARY / PHOTO ON PAGE 319

/ PHOTO ON PAGE 319

Serves 1

- ☐ 4 ounces tomato juice
- ☐ 2 ounces Bacon-Infused Vodka (opposite)
- ☐ 1 teaspoon lime juice
- ☐ 1 teaspoon prepared horseradish
- ☐ ¼ teaspoon celery salt

- ☐ ¼ teaspoon fresh-cracked black pepper
- ☐ 2 dashes Tabasco hot sauce
- ☐ 2 dashes Worcestershire sauce

- ☐ Ice cubes, to fill glass ¾ full
- ☐ Cooked bacon, crumbled as garnish
- ☐ Lime wedge, as garnish
- ☐ Pickled okra, as garnish

Combine the tomato juice, vodka, lime juice, horseradish, celery salt, pepper, Tabasco, and Worcestershire in a shaker and shake a few times to combine. Strain the mixture into a glass filled with ice. Garnish with the bacon, lime wedge, and okra. Serve.

YORKSHIRE PUDDING

A dish born of necessity, this classic side makes use of beef tallow, with a simple batter that puffs to perfection when heated quickly. In the old days, this pudding was often served with gravy as a first course to a meal, because as the main course of meat cooked, it provided a sufficient pool of drippings and fat to be put to use in these savory treats. As versatile as a popover, today you can find these prepared as both savory and sweet. Sometimes they're stuffed with mashed potatoes and sausages, or with jam and topped with sugar. Tallow is like gold, and it can be used not only for cooking but also for making soaps, candles, and other products. This basic recipe serves as a base concept of the classic—put your own riff on it as you see fit.

Serves 6 to 8	Hands on: 35 minutes	Total: 1 hour

- ☐ 4 large eggs
- ☐ 1 cup all-purpose flour
- ☐ 1 cup whole milk
- ☐ ¾ teaspoon kosher salt
- ☐ 1 tablespoon water
- ☐ ½ cup beef tallow, rendered

1 Combine the eggs, flour, milk, salt, and water in a mixing bowl and mix vigorously until just combined. Do not overmix. Cover the bowl and place it in the refrigerator to rest at least 30 minutes, or overnight.

2 Preheat the oven to 425°F. Remove the batter from the refrigerator. Add two teaspoons or so of the beef tallow to each well of a 12-cup muffin tin. Place the muffin tin in the oven and cook until the fat begins to smoke, 8 to 10 minutes.

3 Remove the tin from the oven and place on a heatproof surface. Working quickly, evenly divide the batter among the wells, filling them one-half to three-quarters full. Place the tin back into the oven and bake until the puddings have nearly tripled in size and are crispy and browned, 15 to 18 minutes. Remove from the oven and serve immediately.

ALASKAN ICE CREAM
Akutaq

Believe it or not, desserts made with tallow or fat have served as a staple for Alaskan natives for thousands of years. Nowadays when it comes to making akutaq, most folks use vegetable shortening or fish fat in place of the tallow, but given the fact that tallow is so easily accessible, this sweet treat is a great and creative way to use it. The tallow needs to be rendered until it becomes a thin, stirrable liquid, but don't let the fat get too hot. You should be able to touch it by hand without being burned; think lukewarm water. After that, folding in some powdered sugar and ice water and using a bit of sweat equity to mix it all together with some fresh fruit will produce a protein-rich, creamy "ice cream" that's incredibly delicious.

Serves 4	Hands on: 30 minutes	Total: 1 hour 30 minutes

- ☐ 1 cup beef tallow, or Crisco
- ☐ 1 cup powdered sugar
- ☐ ½ cup ice water

- ☐ 3 cups fresh mixed berries (blueberries, blackberries, or strawberries, stems removed)

1 Place the tallow into a small stockpot over low heat. Heat the tallow slowly until it is in a liquid state, about 15 minutes. Remove the tallow from the heat and allow to cool, stirring on occasion, until it is just warm to the touch, about 10 minutes. Add the powdered sugar and fold in until completely combined.

2 Working quickly, pour in the water ¼ cup at a time and mix vigorously after each addition.

The tallow and water will congeal, while the mixing will produce a white, fluffy consistency. Fold in the mixed berries and stir until incorporated.

3 Place the mixture into the freezer for at least 1 hour to set. Divide the akutaq among bowls and serve immediately.

MAPLE BACON CUPCAKES

As they say, bacon makes everything better, even desserts. Gussying up a boxed cake mix and claiming it as my own is one of my guiltiest entertaining pleasures. To serve a real convincing "fake it till you make it" cake, add one more egg than the instructions call for, sub the oil for butter and then some, and do the same with milk for the water. Geez, I feel a lot better confessing. You can use your favorite cake mix for this recipe, but the crispy bacon and icing is so standout, I prefer to stick to the deliciously moist, classic, yellow cake. Since the bacon adds a crisp and savory note, whenever possible I add it just prior to serving to maintain its best presentation.

Serves 12	Hands on: 30 minutes	Total: 1 hour 30 minutes

CUPCAKES
- ☐ One 15.25-ounce box yellow cake mix
- ☐ 1 cup whole milk
- ☐ 1 cup (2 sticks) unsalted butter, melted
- ☐ 4 large eggs
- ☐ 1 teaspoon vanilla extract
- ☐ 3 tablespoons maple syrup

ICING
- ☐ 4 cups powdered sugar
- ☐ 1 cup (2 sticks) unsalted butter, softened
- ☐ 3 tablespoons maple syrup
- ☐ ¼ teaspoon cayenne pepper
- ☐ 1 pinch kosher salt
- ☐ 8 to 10 pieces center-cut bacon, cooked until crispy (page 324) and crumbled by hand

1 Preheat the oven to 350°F. In a mixing bowl, place the cake mix, milk, butter, eggs, vanilla, and syrup and whisk constantly with a hand mixer for 2 minutes until combined. Place paper liners into a 24-cup muffin tin and pour in the batter, filling each well about two-thirds full. Place the tin into the oven and bake for 15 to 20 minutes, or until a toothpick inserted into the center of the cupcakes pulls out clean. Remove the tin from the oven and allow the cupcakes to slightly cool in the tin, 5 minutes.

2 Meanwhile, make the icing. In a large bowl, combine the sugar and butter and beat vigorously until creamy using a hand mixer on high speed, about 2 minutes. Add the syrup, cayenne pepper, and salt and mix until just combined.

3 Frost the cupcakes generously and top with the crumbled bacon. Serve.

INDEX